£3
Rel
W46

Give a
Boy a Gun

Give a Boy a Gun

FROM KILLING TO PEACE-MAKING

Alistair Little
with Ruth Scott

DARTON · LONGMAN + TODD

First published in 2009 by
Darton, Longman and Todd Ltd
1 Spencer Court
140–142 Wandsworth High Street
London SW18 4JJ

ISBN: 978–0–232–52763–6

A catalogue record for this book is available from
the British Library.

Designed and produced by Sandie Boccacci
Set in 10.25/13.5pt Sabon
Printed and bound in Great Britain by
Athenaeum Press, Gateshead, Tyne & Wear

ALISTAIR:

For Amy

RUTH:

For all the survivors of violent conflict who,
often at great personal cost, seek to break the cycles
of revenge and to build peace

Acknowledgements

'Better to light a single candle than to curse the darkness.'

Chinese proverb

Emotionally, writing this book was much harder than I ever imagined it could be. The long hours spent with Ruth reflecting on my past, discussing my present and wondering about my future were exhausting. I want to extend a warm, sincere and deeply appreciative thank you to Ruth who had the courage, strength and dedication to want to undertake this journey with me, and her family – Chris, Tian and Freya – for their patience and support of Ruth and myself throughout the process.

To the few friends who knew I had made the decision to put pen to paper in an attempt to create a deeper understanding of conflict, and offered invaluable words of support and encouragement to help tell my story, thank you.

To my family, I would like to say that there are no words strong enough to convey how thankful I am to you for your constant love and support.

To my wife Louise, without your support this book would not have been written.

Alistair Little

It takes great courage to trust another person to help you tell your personal story of violent conflict, particularly when you've been responsible for some of that violence, as well as on the receiving end of it. It's been a challenge and a privilege to share this storytelling journey with Alistair. He is not only my colleague and most valued teacher in the field of conflict transformation, he is my friend.

My thanks also go to Louise, Alistair's wife, not only for her care of me on the many occasions she and Alistair have put me up in Belfast, but also for the support she gave us both in what hasn't always been an easy task.

Without the unfailing love, encouragement and patience of my husband, Chris, I might not have completed this book in one piece, particularly when my computer deleted 14 of the 16 chapters just as I was putting in the final references!

I'm blessed to have Jenny Brown as my agent. Her expertise has been invaluable to me. She and David Moloney at DLT have worked with Alistair and me with great sensitivity. I am deeply grateful to them both.

Ruth Scott

Foreword

by *His Royal Highness Prince El Hassan bin Talal, of Jordan*

It is much easier to condemn violence than to understand why it happens. With war and the threat of war casting its shadow over many parts of the world, understanding what motivates individuals and communities to take up arms against each other is an urgent task. Although the context and scale of conflict may vary considerably, the same human dynamics can be seen at work from one battleground to another. These dynamics are clearly illustrated in Alistair Little's compelling personal story. His insights have been hard won, coming as they do from his own experience of being both a victim *and* a perpetrator of violence. His story challenges clear-cut ideas about good and evil, why people resort to violence, why they renounce it and what it means to live with the legacy of conflict. His account is told with painful honesty and touching sensitivity. He conveys the complexity of human responses. He illustrates powerfully that when it comes to conflict, *everyone* bears some responsibility for its existence, including those who feel it has nothing to do with them at all. This is a courageous book and is essential reading for anyone who wants to understand the cycle of violence and how it can be broken to build peace.

Prologue

Many people talk of peace but few realise the cost of making it.
Alistair and Ruth in conversation

This isn't a book about Northern Ireland. Although my own particular experience is set in that context, it shares much in common with the stories of young men caught up in situations of conflict across the world. My purpose in sharing my story isn't to help you understand the conflict in Northern Ireland in greater depth, but to shed light on what turns an ordinary boy growing up in a loving family anywhere, into a man of violence, and then what helps him turn his back on bloodshed. There's an urgent need to understand these dynamics. Youth violence in the UK is reported today more than ever before. In civil and international conflicts across the continents, child soldiers are an ever-present reality. It's easy to distance ourselves from a person by calling them a terrorist, but terrorists aren't born. They're shaped by the circumstances in which they live. They share the same basic humanity as those who label them. Unless we understand why one person hits out and another holds back, we'll perpetuate the contexts and cycles that fuel terror. Unless we recognise the humanity in the one we have labelled as inhumane, we'll never address our own capacity for inhumanity. My own story shows how people are deluding themselves if they think their own lack of violent action, or indeed of any action, in a time of conflict exempts them from responsibility for the violence within their community and beyond.

I could write down what I've learnt in an academic format, but storytelling is central to my work in conflict transformation. I know the power of story to touch the heart as well as the mind. When it comes to healing traumatised individuals and communities, you have to be able to work at the level of the heart if you're to have any understanding of the pain people have endured. The right stories can penetrate the mental defences we sometimes erect to protect ourselves from uncomfortable reality. They can reflect back to us elements of our own experience without leaving us feeling exposed. They can help to create the right climate in which understanding can flourish.

My personal experience may be extreme, but there are common roots to the responses that shaped my story and those that are part of normal daily life for any human being. Friends, who grew up in England watching television reports of riots and bombings in Northern Ireland, comment on how chaotic and mad it all seemed. Looking back, that's how it seems to me as well, but at the time it was just 'normal' life. The extraordinary felt ordinary. I didn't know anything else. That's why I've tried to write my story without sensationalising it. The risk is that I won't convey the atmosphere of fear and madness that was present, but back then violence was a normal and justifiable way of life. Only now can I see how desensitised we became to it, and in such a way that we weren't aware of that happening.

Some of my present-day work brings me into discussions where I have a very real sense of what I can only describe as evil. In my youth similar conversations wouldn't have felt unusual in any way. Behaviour I no longer consider acceptable felt really good at the time. If I'm honest, there are still occasions when I long for something of that past. Then I get scared. I feel like I've travelled a long way, but in those moments I wonder if I'm still the same person who enjoyed the power and kudos that violence brought.

Mine is a still an unfolding story. I hope in reading it, you'll find it sheds light not only on your own experience, but on the stories of other people and situations close to you and far from home. The world has been condemning acts of atrocity for centuries, but condemnation doesn't change anything. Only understanding will help us to prevent such tragedies, or to work effectively with their aftermath.

Chapter 1

The first duty of love is to listen.

Paul Tillich

March 1972

The coffin stands on wooden supports in the street outside the terraced brick-and-pebbledash house that was the dead man's home. It's draped with a Union Jack. A beret and a pair of gloves lie on top of the flag. The body in the coffin is the father of my friend Peter. His dad, a part-time UDR (Ulster Defence Regiment) sergeant, was shot dead by the IRA (Irish Republican Army) in the house, where all the curtains are now closed. They broke in and gunned him down in front of his 11-year-old daughter. She was hit in the legs. Today she's in a wheelchair beside the coffin, wrapped in blankets against the cold, her dark curls defining her drawn face from the pale wrappings around her. She's screaming for her Daddy to come back. The sound of her pain will haunt me and fuel my hatred for her attackers for years to come.

The weather is bitterly cold and grey. It matches the mood of the crowd gathered around the coffin and down the street. Everyone is in black, apart from the soldiers. This is the first funeral I've ever attended. I'm 14 years old. I was afraid to come to my friend's house; afraid of what I might see. Would the coffin be open? As a child of the conflict in Northern Ireland, I've watched the news of many funerals on television, but it's not the same as experiencing death in the flesh on your own doorstep.

When we arrived, I pushed my way through the silent company of mourners and onlookers, slipping to the front between the older, taller men. We had a long wait before six UDR men went in and brought out the coffin. Once they'd set it on the stands, two sergeants arranged the flag, gloves and beret on top of it. Tears flooded out of me. I was embarrassed because I thought boys weren't supposed to show their feelings, but when I looked around I saw all the men were crying. They were saying that someone needed 'to do something about' what had happened, and I agreed. The IRA couldn't be allowed to get away with it.

13

A young piper from the 3rd Battalion of the UDR came out and began to play a lament. Finally, a platoon from the dead sergeant's regiment led off the cortege. It was the largest funeral our town had ever seen. Over 3000 people accompanied the coffin to the cemetery. Shops, offices and factories closed as a mark of respect. At the graveside, a bugler played 'The Last Post'. I wondered about the body being buried – how one moment it could be living, then dead the next. I wondered what it meant to be dead, and where was my friend's Dad now? I was scared seeing the coffin lowered into the gaping grave. I thought it could have been my Dad disappearing into the ground. The Alistair who left that cemetery at the end of the funeral was not the same Alistair who'd arrived to see the coffin being brought out earlier in the day. I returned home determined that if ever I got the chance for revenge, I would take it, and I would never let anything like this happen to my family. My anger and distress were immense.

Fast-forward 20 years through my life, and those same emotions threaten once more to get the better of me. I'm sitting outside the dining-room of a Centre for Peace and Reconciliation up in the hills of the Irish Republic. I've been invited here to talk to members of a Victims/Survivors Group. (Some people see themselves as survivors rather than victims because 'survivor' suggests you have more control over your life than 'victim'. 'Victim' ties you in some way to the 'perpetrator'.) On my arrival, I learn that they've decided I can't eat lunch with them. I'm a terrorist, guilty of murder, just like the men who shot dead or blew up members of their own families. Now that I'm here, they aren't sure they can be in the same room as me, let alone talk to me. I feel furious. Why the fuck did I come? What the hell's the matter with the organisers, whose lack of preparation and sensitivity has precipitated this state of affairs? Don't they know how vulnerable people are in my position and in the position of this group? I'm tempted to get back in my car and drive back to Belfast. What's the point of trying to live by a different pattern when no one seems to understand how difficult that is, and people treat me like I'm the scum of the earth, devoid of human feeling?

In another part of the centre, the group members discuss what to do. My presence has disturbed them far more than they'd expected. Can they be in the same space as me? Even if they can, they're not sure they feel able to speak to me. How will the organisers facilitate the encounter so they feel safe? Should they call the whole thing off?

Now, instead of sitting in what they call the 'hot seat' sharing my story, responding to questions and addressing the issues raised, I'm waiting for a verdict about what will happen without even being able to put my case. I feel out of control. Yet again what I can or cannot do is being determined by others, just like all those long years in prison. It is not a good place to be.

While the group carry on their discussions, I try to think through my own position. Right now I don't want to be here but I can't walk away. This is why I became involved in conflict transformation work. I know from personal experience the legacy of pain that conflict in the past and present leaves with us. I've listened to the stories of people I once thought of as the enemy, and been changed by them, just as they have been changed by mine. I see the possibility, in this process, of us slowly working towards some new understanding that doesn't involve the use of violence and the creation of yet more people who are victims or perpetrators or both. No one ever said that would be easy. Why should I expect it to be? Walk away now, and I might as well give up.

Finally, the group decide that they'll listen to my story, although some have stated their intention to keep silent when it comes to questions and discussion. I agree to go ahead with whatever happens. When I've shared my experience there is a silence, then the questions begin. Two hours later we're still talking. Everyone has become involved.

'Do you still suffer because of what you've done?' one woman eventually asks.

'Yes,' I say. 'The pain of my past and what I've done is with me every day.'

'Good,' she says.

A murmur of concern ripples around the group. Some people think her response is too harsh. We've moved a long way since first we sat down together, suspicious and fearful of what the afternoon might unfold.

'No, I'm serious,' the woman continues. 'Today I have faced my worst nightmare – a murderer from the same terrorist organisation that killed my husband. It helps me to know that he suffers every day, just as I do; that murder has traumatic consequences for the murderer as well as the family of his victim.'

Eventually, reluctantly, the proceedings are brought to a conclusion.

For the members of the Victims/Survivors Group, I arrived at the Centre as 'the enemy'. I leave it as a human being who, like my listeners, has a story to tell. They do not condone the actions of my past, but they understand a little more why an ordinary boy came to see violence as the only solution to the threat he experienced against his family, his community and his way of life, and they see that no matter how murderous a person's actions, change is possible. Longfellow once wrote: 'My enemy is the person whose story I have not heard.' Time and again in my life I have discovered this to be true.

Some months after my encounter with the Victims/Survivors Group, when tensions in the Province flare up once more and the lives of former combatants and ex-prisoners like me are in danger, the woman who found comfort in my ongoing emotional pain rings me up to check that I am all right. Such acts of care keep me going in the work of conflict transformation in which I've been involved for the last 15 years.

Chapter 2

*There are things which a man is afraid to tell even
to himself.*

Fyodor Dostoevsky

I've moved a long way from my 14-year-old self. He could never have
imagined how I live now, yet the resolutions I made at the funeral of
Peter's father confirmed my course into violent conflict and opened up the
way that would bring tragedy to many families, including my own,
leaving me with a legacy of guilt and darkness from which I think I shall
never be free.

I wonder still about the complexity of factors that have shaped my
path – why I chose the way of violence when others in my community did
not. Take Peter, for example. After his Dad's funeral he was a changed
person. We'd fought together on the riot lines since I was only 12 years
old. In the 1970s these were a nightly occurrence in my home town, with
Catholic and Protestant boys lining up against one another to hurl home-
made petrol-bombs, rocks, steel ball-bearings and anything else we could
lay our hands on that would serve well as a missile. Before his Dad was
shot dead, Peter didn't really stand out in the crowd that surged forward
and fell back as we attacked, retreated, re-armed and attacked again.
When he returned to the riot lines after the funeral, he, like me, was a
changed boy. He'd take risks that no one else was taking, running
forward alone, crying and screaming all the time as the fighting went on,
his anger and grief driving him to tear apart anything of the opposition
that came within his reach. It wasn't that such emotion was unfamiliar to
us. When the rioting started and the adrenalin was pumping, all of us
knew the feeling of blind rage and hatred that kicks in, cutting off
rational thought that in moments of crisis can sabotage instinctive survival responses. No, what disturbed and frightened us was the change in
Peter's behaviour. He wasn't the same person any more.

Eventually he drifted away from the rioting. I didn't meet him again
until some years later. After his father's funeral I became increasingly

involved in acts of violence against the IRA and against Catholics who I believed supported them. I joined the UVF (Ulster Volunteer Force), an organisation considered by many to be the most ruthless and violent of the Loyalist paramilitary groups. It became my life. At the age of 17 I went to the home of a Catholic I'd been told had been threatening a Protestant colleague at work, and shot him dead in an attack not unlike the one carried out against Peter's dad. A couple of weeks later I was caught in the vicinity of an armed Post Office raid. The gun used on that occasion was the same one used in the earlier fatal attack. I was tried and convicted on a number of counts, including murder, and sentenced to be detained indefinitely during the Secretary of State's pleasure. Because I was just a lad, I couldn't be given a mandatory life sentence like an adult found guilty of the same offence. I went to the Long Kesh compounds and then the 'H' Blocks, known generally as the Maze prison, not knowing when, if ever, I'd be released.

It was during my imprisonment that I met up again with Peter. He was a Prison Officer. Perhaps that's how he took his revenge for his father's death, working in a place that he knew he could leave every day, while men like those who'd murdered his dad were incarcerated there for years. Perhaps it was part of his own attempt to come to terms with his past without resorting to violence. Perhaps it was the only job going at the time he needed one. What causes one traumatised child to take up arms, and another, who on the face of it had far more reason to seek revenge, to walk away from the use of violence?

Strangely, it was prison that enabled me to begin exploring such questions. To all intents and purposes I'd lost my freedom. The structure of my days, what I ate and drank and what I could or couldn't do, was determined by others but, paradoxically, life in Long Kesh and the 'H' Blocks opened up my world precisely because in that confinement I finally had the time and space to think about my experience, to read and reflect instead of constantly reacting to events around me.

So where to start with my story? In prison one of the painful things I had to come to terms with was the terrible impact of my actions on my family. Many people assume that violent men are the product of broken or inadequate families. Some are, but it's far from the whole picture, particularly in places where conflict is communal rather than individual. Blaming the family can be a way of protecting ourselves from the real truth about what can propel a person into violence.

Now that the need arises, I find I'm reluctant to talk about my family. I've caused them so much pain already. I don't want them to suffer any more. Even in the present time, when the peace process in Northern Ireland has moved us a long way from the fear and violence of the latter half of the twentieth century, many people, with family members directly caught up in the fighting, remain fearful of the repercussions of that involvement. The fear is well founded. Many acts of violence remain unresolved. The perpetrators are still at large. Government-appointed bodies have been commissioned to re-open investigations. In areas where paramilitaries and ex-paramilitaries live, people are wary. Feuds still fester between paramilitary groups supposedly on the 'same side'. While the peace process may have turned many places in Northern Ireland into towns and cities like any other elsewhere in the UK, there are still inter-face areas in working-class neighbourhoods, where people from both communities live in close proximity to one another, and where suspicion and animosity continue. Such attitudes, instilled over many generations and caught up in a person's or community's sense of identity, do not evaporate when others with different experiences sign agreements and seek to put the violence of the past behind them. It's for this reason that I've changed the names of many people in my story, and not recounted experiences that could put the well-being of others at risk.

If I'm not sensitive about what I say, I could endanger my own safety and the safety of my family. I could distress them with information that they didn't previously know. As a paramilitary it was essential not to talk: the fewer people that knew what was going on, the better for all concerned. Keeping secrets was a way of ensuring my family was kept safe. Later, when I could tell them things, I didn't. Secrecy had become a habit, and why stir up pain from the past? Of course, that pain finds its way out regardless, and it's only now, as I talk more with my surviving family members, that I realise just how much they've had to carry. In the face of that, *not* talking becomes as much a protection for me, as I think it is for them.

But I want to be as truthful as possible in exploring what moved me to murder, and the long, painful journey through years in prison and re-integration in the outside world to eventually working internationally with the victims/survivors and perpetrators of political conflict. I want to be clear about the complexity of factors that determined my path for good and ill. Inevitably home is my point of departure.

Had I been born in any other part of the United Kingdom instead of Northern Ireland, my story would be no different from that of millions of men who are born, live and die, unknown to any but their immediate family and community connections. But I was born in Lurgan, Northern

Ireland. It's a small market town about 20 miles south-west of Belfast, situated in North Armagh, the first area out of Belfast to experience the terrifying results of sectarian conflict. It falls within what some commentators of those times called 'the Murder Triangle'. Lurgan, along with nearby Portadown, were considered by many to be as sectarian and extreme as the communities living along the Shankill and Falls Roads in Belfast. That knowledge only came to me later. During the first ten years of my life, Lurgan was simply my home town, just like anyone else's.

It was football that determined Northern Ireland as my place of birth. My Dad, Alexander, was a Scot who'd once played for Stirling Albion. My Mum had been born in Northern Ireland, in Londonderry (or Derry, depending on which side of the divide you're born). Before she was three years old her family moved to Glasgow. That's where she and Dad met and married. Shortly after they came together, Dad was given the opportunity to do a trial with Glenavon, an Irish League team in Lurgan. In the end he couldn't agree terms with the team, but he liked the area and in 1950 he and Mum moved to a village not far from Lurgan. These were decisions made years before I was born that would shape the whole of my history.

One of the myths about the Northern Ireland of that time is that all Protestants lived in fancy houses and only Catholics experienced hardship. In reality, working-class families from both communities knew poverty and deprivation. In the cottage Mum and Dad rented there was no electricity or running water. The latter had to be collected from a nearby pump and carried home. The toilet was outside. Without transport, Mum was stuck in the middle of nowhere. It was a far cry from the greater comforts and caring family she'd left behind in Scotland. In 1951, when she became pregnant in their first year of married life, it was natural that she'd return to Glasgow to give birth to my sister, Dorothy, with the support of her family around her. While she was away, Dad managed to get a house on the Mourneview Estate in Ardboe Drive, Lurgan, complete with electricity and running water, and the idea of settling permanently became more acceptable.

By the time I was born in February 1958, Dorothy had been joined by my two older brothers. We'd just moved to 2 Glebe Terrace on the Wakehurst Estate, a largely Catholic part of the town. Although there were inter-communal tensions across the Province, the violence that caused families living in religiously mixed areas to flee their homes to find safety among 'their own kind', had not yet flared up again. Mum had Catholic as well as Protestant friends. Sectarianism was certainly not encouraged at home. During my childhood, if any anti-Catholic comments were made by any of us, Mum would tell us off and speak of the Catholic friends she had made on the Wakehurst Estate. Later that estate became a flashpoint for violence between the two communities – what we commonly call today an interface area – but by that time we'd moved to a new home on the Protestant Mourneview Estate. Later more houses were added to this development. It became known locally as 'the Grey Estate' since all the brickwork was grey.

The year was 1962. I was four years old. With this change in location, the opportunities for me to meet and mix peacefully with Catholics ceased. My memory suggests that I didn't meet a Catholic again until I was 12 years old. This may not be an entirely accurate recollection. Which young child will check out the religious persuasion of everyone he meets wherever he goes? What is significant is that by the time I was 12, I'd become sufficiently conscious of the communal divisions that meeting a Catholic became an extraordinary enough experience to be remembered. By that age I had a really strong sense of the town belonging to me and to Protestants. It was our town. I think when I became conscious of that belief, I felt that I'd always known it.

At the age of four, when youngsters begin to get to know people beyond their own family circle either through school or out on the street, I was living in an environment where there were no outsiders, so to speak. Everyone was Protestant on our estate. The school I went to was Protestant. All my friends were Protestant.

My memories of life before I was 12 are few and far between. When I first came out of prison in my late twenties, I tried to wipe out the memories of my life before imprisonment. Not just the traumatic memories or the recollections of violence from which I then wanted to distance myself, but also the events normal to any child raised in a happy family. I threw away photos and the other memorabilia of childhood – school reports, certificates of achievement, notes from friends, news cuttings, I binned them all.

My earliest accessible memory is playing on the beach in Newcastle, a seaside town on the east coast of the Province. We'd drive there in Dad's big black Zephyr car. By that time he'd become a car mechanic. He went on to rent a garage and run his own business. I remember the car because working-class families rarely owned one in those days. To my mind it was the biggest on the street.

Apart from this one holiday memory, I struggle to recall any other specific experiences from early childhood, but while I can't remember particular events, my overall memory is of being loved and well provided for at home. I never felt I wanted or needed anything. Although it didn't seem like it at the time, looking back, I think Mum and Dad were quite easy on me. I was the youngest in the family and full of energy. I found it hard to sit still and was always out and about with my friends.

Mum tells me I was a bit of a handful who, whatever she suggested, would always want something different. As far as school went, she didn't see me as having any major problems until I started at Lurgan Technical College when I was 14. Of course, like any child, I had my ups and downs. Mum says that if I returned from primary school and lay flat on the carpet, she knew something was wrong. Although I was quite a private child as far as sharing my thoughts and feelings was concerned, she could usually draw out the problem from me. If I'd done wrong, then Mum always supported the school when they took me to task, though she didn't approve of the corporal punishment they used. When we were naughty at home, she preferred to withhold privileges like watching television, than to smack us.

Until July 1969 I went to King's Park Primary School. I was often sent to the Headmaster for being cheeky in class, but I wasn't the kind of boy to pick on others. I had a strong sense of justice. It took a lot to provoke me, although once provoked, I didn't hold back. I remember being bullied by a big lad I'll call Rob. I put up with his bullying for some time until one day I finally snapped, and hit him back. He fell on the floor. All the pent-up fury of being his victim for the previous few months poured out. I continued to kick him as he lay trying to protect himself on the floor. I was caught by the teacher and caned by the Headmaster, not because I'd been fighting, but because I'd 'kicked a man while he was down'. That was considered cowardly. I never mentioned that Rob had been bullying me for months. After that, Rob and I became quite friendly. Although I was punished, I learnt that fighting back stopped the bullying.

It would be easy, of course, to seek in my childhood, traits that would help account for the violent teenager I became, but none of the scrapes I remember from my primary school years strike me as any more signifi-cant than the fights and flare-ups that any boy anywhere experiences as they grow up. More than that, despite my contrary, independent tempera-ment, Mum remembers me as being a soft-natured boy. Of course, I tried to hide that. I grew up in a time and place where big boys didn't cry, and my heroes were fighters like John Wayne and the stars of the many black-and-white war films that were shown on television during the sixties.

Closer to home, I was steeped in the stories of the Protestant heroes

22

who were commemorated annually in the Province during the marching season. In the lead-up to that time there were always kids on the street practising their flutes and drums and building bonfires in preparation for the celebrations. The kerb-stones and lamp-posts in Protestant areas like ours were painted red, white and blue. Bunting and British and Unionist flags adorned the streets. The main road from Belfast to Lurgan passed under a great Orange Arch on the outskirts of the town. This was, and still is a substantial structure covered in the symbols and icons of the Orange Order. Such arches, in different forms, have been erected in Ireland since 1790. They celebrate the victory in 1690 of the Protestant army of William III over the Catholic army of James II at the Battle of the Boyne.

We imbibed Loyalist history with our mother's milk. The events of the marching season not only celebrated our victorious past, but shaped our sense of identity in the present. Nothing could beat the intense pride children felt if they were asked to hold the long cords and tassels hanging from the great Orange Order banners that led each Lodge in the annual parades.

Closer still to home – in fact, right in my own back yard – my Dad was one of my greatest heroes. He wasn't a member of the Orange Order, although we followed the local Orange Day parades and had our own particular favourite flute band. His background was in the British Forces.

When the Second World War broke out he'd lied about his age and enlisted into the Royal Auxiliary Fleet. He was 15 years old. On convoy duty, the ship on which he served was torpedoed. He was awarded five medals for his actions in the Baltic, Italy and Africa, including the British Service Medal. From the Royal Auxiliary Fleet he joined the Gordon Highlanders, eventually becoming a fitness instructor after the war, and going on to succeed as a professional footballer in Scotland.

I looked up to him on account of the medals, the stories that he told about his war-time experience, and the fact that he joined up when he was under age. His history in the armed services fitted well with the high regard in which the Unionist community held the British Forces. At a key point in our history we'd served in them with great courage and sacrifice. At the end of the nineteenth century and the beginning of the twentieth, the British governments of the day tried on three occasions to push Home Rule Bills through Parliament. The Unionist community was horrified by what it saw as a betrayal by its government. Sir Edward Carson, a Protestant barrister from Dublin and Unionist MP for Trinity College,

Dublin, spoke against the last of these three Bills. He mobilised tens of thousands of Loyalists to march to Belfast's City Hall, where he and his supporters signed a Covenant stating:

> Being convinced in our consciences that Home Rule would be disastrous to the material well-being of Ulster as well as the whole of Ireland, subversive of our civil and religious freedom, destructive of our citizenship, and perilous to the unity of the empire, we, whose names are underwritten, men of Ulster, loyal subjects of his gracious Majesty King George V, humbly relying on the God whom our fathers in days of stress and trial confidently trusted, do hereby pledge ourselves in solemn covenant throughout this our time of threatened calamity to stand by one another in defending for ourselves and our children our cherished position within the United Kingdom, and in using all means that may be found necessary to defeat the present conspiracy to set up a Home Rule parliament in Ireland.
>
> Public Records Office of Northern Ireland, Belfast

By 1913, Carson had formed a private army of some 100,000 men from those who had signed the Covenant. These men, the original UVF, were brought together to resist Home Rule but, with the outbreak of World War I, it was against the Germans that the UVF went to war, and many didn't return home.

The heroism of the UVF, who were part of the 36th Ulster Division at the Battle of the Somme, is legendary in Unionist circles. Every year for many years, groups have gone out to France on the anniversary of the Battle to honour the men who died there. Their action is marked on the gable-end murals in Loyalist strongholds like the Shankill Road in Belfast. In 1965, a group of Shankill Loyalists, fearing renewed activity by the IRA, and concerned by the reforming actions of our Prime Minister of the time, Terence O'Neill, formed a new paramilitary organisation that called itself the UVF, after the original army brought together by Carson. In the early 1970s being a member of that group became my life, but it wasn't what I'd originally planned.

I think it was because of my father, and the strong images of heroic UVF soldiers in the First World War that were always in the background of our communal identity, that from an early age I wanted to join the British Forces. Circumstances, some beyond my control, ultimately destroyed my dream of distinguishing myself in the British Army, and confirmed my place in the latter-day UVF that soon had units operating all over the Province.

Seeing the images of teenage boys hurling missiles across the riot lines and getting into scuffles with the police and army, it's hard to believe that many of us who became paramilitaries were regular members of Sunday School throughout childhood and had been brought up to respect authority. That was exactly my experience. Later, when the violence was at its height and members of the British Army were raiding our home and roughing me up, Mum questioned that belief in authority, but even then she didn't voice her change of perspective for fear of further negatively influencing my behaviour.

Faith played a large part in our family life. Until I was 13 years old I went to two Sunday Schools each week, attending both the Nazarene Church in Carnegie Street and St John's Baptist Church. By the age of 13 I'd outgrown Sunday School and joined the Boy's Brigade instead. I remember little of what went on in Sunday School except that it instilled in me the idea that God was to be feared. Some people find that picture disturbing, but years later, when I was in the Maze prison, this fear of God was an important factor in turning me away from violence.

At home, things like television and football were restricted on Sundays, the day of rest. On Saturdays shoes were polished and Sunday clothes were laid out and, as far as was possible, Mum would prepare the Sunday lunch so that come the Sabbath, she had little work to do.

Is there anything in what I have said so far that would mark me out, more than any other boy, for the violence I embraced later? The sensitivity Mum speaks of, the excess of energy needing to be channelled, the preparedness to fight back when bullied beyond endurance, the tendency to keep my own counsel – all these things are visible in my later decision-making and actions, but of themselves they aren't characteristics peculiar to violent men and women. Add to that a family where love was secure and discipline firm and fair, and it's impossible to conclude that my family of itself produced a violent son.

One of the tragic legacies of my decision to kill a man is the guilt my family has lived with ever since, wondering if they could have done more to prevent my path into extreme violence. Yet these things are far more complicated. All I know is that when I was arrested for murder and brought the world crashing down around their ears, my family stood by me, and continued to love and support me through the long years of prison and beyond, often at great cost to themselves.

I'm not saying my family was perfect. No family is, but you have to look beyond them to see why I became caught up in violent action. As I moved into my teenage years, Northern Ireland entered the bloodiest years of its existence since the partition of Ireland in 1921. At that time 26 of Ireland's 32 counties became Eire, and the rest became the Province, created for Unionists to counter the ongoing threat of Loyalist rebellion that had been interrupted, but not diminished by the Great War.

Unrest in the Province steadily increased through the 1960s, with violence flaring in the latter half of that decade, to the extent that in 1969 the British Army was sent in to restore order. The resurgence of violence coincided with my entry into adolescence. That timing is not insignificant.

I was 11 when the Army arrived in Lurgan. I'd just started at Lurgan Junior High where I remained until I was 14. One memory stands out from my time there. There was a fight in the playground during which another boy gave my friend a bloody nose. I was so frightened by the bleeding that I ran away home. Just a couple of years later I was in the UVF, no longer a Sunday School boy frightened by the sight of blood, but an aggressive, foul-mouthed (at least with my friends) teenager who belonged to a paramilitary organisation, and was out to cause as much physical harm as I could to those who threatened our way of life. That threat was very real to us. My experience of violence and dysfunction came not from my home life, but from the streets of my home town where violence was fuelled by civil conflict on an island where the inhabitants defined themselves not by what they shared in common, but by what set them apart.

Back in the sixteenth century, the Gaelic chieftains wouldn't submit peacefully to Elizabeth I's desire to have them under central Tudor control. She feared that Catholic Spain would use Ireland as a back door into England. The rebellion of the Chieftains was put down, and they fled to the continent. In the wake of that conflict, under Elizabeth's successor, James I, thousands of English and Scottish Protestants sailed across the Irish Sea to make new lives for themselves in what became known as the 'plantation'. They took over land from the Catholic inhabitants of the time, and established their own family dynasties and particular patterns of life. The sense of identity that Unionists and Republicans have today, whether that's as part of the United Kingdom or as part of the Irish Republic, goes back a long way. For reasons of history, religion, politics and social struggle, this identity has, until very recently, always been claimed at the expense of the other community.

The impact on a young boy of the tensions that resurfaced in the 1960s and exploded into the terrible violence of the conflict was brought home

26

to me by a picture that came to light when I was looking through back copies of the local paper – *The Lurgan Mail* – at the Newspaper Library in the centre of Belfast. I was doing some research for this book, trying to retrigger memories from my childhood, and to remind myself of what was going on in the town during those early years. My fingers were already grey with newsprint when I turned yet another page and suddenly saw my younger self staring out at me from a black-and-white photo taken when I was 13.

It shows the Glenfield Road seven-a-side football team, after we've received the Streets' Cup, having beaten Mourne Road 3–1 in the final. I'm standing on the right-hand side, only just in the picture. I'm the team coach. I'd forgotten all about that. This younger version of me is like a stranger. He's a slim youth wearing slightly-too-large jeans that are held up with belt and braces. His shirt-sleeves are rolled up above his elbows, and his arms are crossed. His pale, boyish face is almost lost where the editor has cut away the photo to fit the space and the white of the page begins, but an almost-skinhead-short patch of dark hair tops the serious expression of a 13-year-old who is trying to appear tough as well as proud, yet looks wary and vulnerable.

What hit me so profoundly when I saw that photo was that I'd forgotten there was a time when I was a teenager who did normal things like playing football. From the age of 11 onwards my life in Lurgan became dominated by inter-communal conflict. So what were the experiences, both individual and communal, that turned a football-loving boy into a killer?

Chapter 3

The sad truth is that most evil is done by people who never make up their minds to be either good or evil.

Hannah Arendt

Hate. It's an ugly word, and one that's figured very little in my story so far. Every child knows what it is to hate someone or something, however fleetingly, but I can't recall when I started hating Catholics – all Catholics, simply because they were Catholic. In the latter half of the 1960s I picked up the growing concern and fear of the adults in my world. When he was around, my Dad followed the news on the hour, every hour, and we kids had to be quiet while it was on. Stories of riots, shootings and, later, bombings across the Province were commonplace. Lurgan experienced all three. Playground talk increasingly revolved around who'd been shot, what had been bombed, and how we should respond. The Alistair who ran away in fear when his friend's nose was bloodied in a school fight, was also the Alistair who tagged along with his older brother, drawn to the excitement of the riot lines, and was soon caught up in hurling missiles, screaming abuse, and running on the heady mix of adrenaline and hate. Vulnerability and violence co-existing in one boy. Injury experienced by friends was far more hard-hitting, far more frightening, than hurting 'the enemy' who, in our minds, wasn't human like we were. Unconsciously, we latched on to any story that confirmed our perspective. We defined violent acts perpetrated by the IRA as unforgivable outrages, whereas we saw our own violence as entirely justified.

While I can't pinpoint when I first became conscious of hating Catholics, I remember certain tragic events that fuelled my hatred towards them.

On 9 March 1971 three off-duty Scottish soldiers were drinking in a bar in central Belfast. It's thought that during the evening they were invited to a party by some girls they'd met at the pub. They were picked up and driven into the hills above Belfast. On a stretch of lonely road the car stopped, apparently to let them out to relieve themselves. While they were standing in a line doing just that, they were all shot in the head. Two of the soldiers, brothers John and Joseph McCaig, were just 17 and 18 years old. The third, Dougald McCaughey, was 23.

The murders sent shock-waves around the Province. At a public level they were seen as a key point in the descent of Northern Ireland into full-scale conflict. While the funerals of the three young men were taking place in Scotland, about 20,000 people turned out in Belfast and Carrickfergus in County Antrim to attend rallies in sympathy, and there was a general outpouring of grief.

In Lurgan, factory workers, both Protestant and Catholic, took to the streets to lay a wreath for the soldiers at the War Memorial. Women wept openly. Two minutes' silence was observed, not just at the Memorial, but in factories and businesses across the town.

The murders brought the conflict particularly close to home for me, because the soldiers served in the same regiment as had my Dad. In my mind, it could have been him in their position. Dead. In a few years' time it could even be me, since I was already committed to following in my father's footsteps and joining the British Army. The atrocity hit at the heart of all that I held dear and challenged my perceptions about how people were supposed to behave. Women picking up men in order for others to murder them were known as 'honey traps'. I was appalled that girls should have been involved in luring the soldiers to their deaths. They were supposed to be carers like my Mum, not playing their part in acts of violence.

A few years later, when I was in prison, I read about the women used as honey traps by the Israeli secret service to bring about the deaths of those responsible for the murder of 11 members of the Israeli team at the Munich Olympics. Then, I felt only admiration for these women. My reaction, standing as it did in sharp contrast to my response to the girls with the soldiers in 1971, pulled me up short. It made me realise how differently we assess conflicts in which we're involved, than those we observe from a distance. The change in my perspective was also an indication of how brutalised I had been by the conflict in Northern Ireland, and my own part in that.

As a child I didn't understand the politics behind the descent of the Province into violence. My reactions weren't reasoned responses to the wider context. They were provoked by stories like the murder of the soldiers, that touched me deeply, and by the reality of violence on the streets where I lived.

Back copies of the *Lurgan Mail* from the 1960s suggest that for most of that decade Lurgan was like any other small market town in the UK. It's full of stories about community get-togethers, successful schools and school-children, sporting occasions, news from the local churches, key memorial events like the fiftieth anniversary of the Battle of the Somme, the usual births, marriages and deaths, and the kind of repeating front-page news that covers arguments about parking in the High Street and plans for the economic development of the town. Perhaps this isn't surprising. The paper generally reflected middle-class life rather than focusing on working-class experience, but it's also true that when communities feel under threat, the desire is to cling to the illusion of normality. In Lurgan this may have led to a denial of what was happening on the ground, and holding at a distance the tensions and violence escalating 'elsewhere' until these could be ignored no longer.

It wasn't until October 1970 that the front page of the *Lurgan Mail* finally admitted to 'TERRORISTS IN OUR MIDST'. Gang warfare, it reported, was rife and an arms dump had been found between Lurgan and Portadown. It said nothing that I didn't already know first-hand. I felt we were a community living under siege. By 1969 civil conflict in the Province had reached such levels that the British government sent in the troops to restore order. Shortly afterwards various regiments were garrisoned behind Lurgan Technical College, where I spent the last years of my school life.

Order was only restored temporarily. The 1970s witnessed some of the bloodiest and most brutal murders of the conflict. For families like my own, the segregation of Catholics and Protestants ceased to be simply an issue of living different lives; it became essential for safety.

When I went into the town I knew not to go beyond the public toilets, because I'd be entering Catholic 'territory', and if caught by the kids there, I'd get a real beating, just as they'd get if they strayed into our space. It was accepted that in Lurgan Park, one end was Catholic and the other, Protestant, and if you knew what was best for you, you stayed at the right end.

Parents discouraged their children from having boyfriends or girlfriends from the other community because they risked attack by members from either community who saw them as traitors. In Belfast young people had been murdered simply because they were dating someone from the other side.

Key people in the town and its churches might be involved in cross-community activity, but at a grass-roots level, Lurgan, along with

Portadown, lived up to its reputation of being one of the most segregated and sectarian towns in Northern Ireland. Not that I would have described myself in that way. All I experienced was the violence and the fear, the threat to our way of life, and the desire to defend it and to fight against those who wanted to destroy it.

In April 1970 a Republican march through Lurgan, led by a man carrying an Irish Tricolour, sparked a major flare-up of violence. In response Unionists flocked to the Orange parade that year. It was the largest ever held, but it didn't deter the IRA.

At the end of July the bombing in Lurgan began. In August troops were sent in to deal with trouble in two Catholic areas of the town, using tear gas for the first time. A Protestant family was forced from its home. Riots erupted again on the street where I was born.

The town centre now had concrete bollards protecting the main road, and check-points in strategic positions. People went about their business as usual, but the fear of being caught up in a bomb explosion was always there.

I started at Lurgan Junior High School in September 1969, within weeks of the Battle of the Bogside in Londonderry, the riots in Belfast, and the eruption of even greater violence in Lurgan. If I hadn't had an elder brother who joined his mates in the rioting, I would probably still have ended up fighting. All my friends were involved, or had family members on the riot lines. I wasn't a reluctant participant. As a restless lad who felt things deeply and had a strong sense of justice, fighting back against those whose existence I felt threatened by was the obvious way to go. For a boy approaching teenage years, it was daring and exciting. I wanted to prove myself to the older boys. I felt part of something.

That 'something' took a more formal shape following the murders of the three Scottish soldiers in 1971. In memory of them, young Loyalists on the Shankill Road set up 'Tartan' gangs, and these quickly grew in popularity. Boys of my age and older were keen to belong to the 'Tartans', often with their parents' approval. In Lurgan there were mothers who came to the Community Centre where the local Tartan Gang regularly met and practised marching, to complain because their child hadn't been accepted. Selection was a somewhat arbitrary process that depended upon who you knew, your physical size, and how brave you'd already proved yourself to be in the rioting. My Mum didn't approve, but one of my brothers was a member and I was known to the gang organisers. I'd shown I was prepared to fight. My place was assured.

Our purpose was to cause Catholics as much grief as possible, because we believed they supported the men responsible for the soldiers' deaths. We trimmed our knee-length jeans and denim jackets with tartan. We wore tartan scarves and belts, and twists of tartan around our wrists. The uniform was completed with 'bovver' boots like Doc Martens.

The Tartan Gangs provided boys willing not only to attack Catholics in riots, but also to collect anything that could be used for ammunition. Milk bottles were ideal for making petrol bombs. These were frequently stolen from doorsteps. If the home-owners chased us away, they were reported to the older gang members. Within a very short space of time, those unwilling to donate their empties to the cause received a personal visit from the riot organisers, warning them to co-operate unless they wanted their windows smashed in, or worse.

We added to our bottle supplies by stealing from the milk floats as they did their daily rounds. Some milkmen were sympathetic to our cause, and helped unload crates of empties. The older rioters who worked at the local creamery dropped crates of bottles over the fence into the long grass of the field beyond, to be picked up later.

When it came to petrol for petrol bombs, some people would buy it in cans, but that was risky: the garage owners took note of who bought petrol in this way, and informed the police. To avoid detection, petrol was siphoned out of cars into bottles, using plastic tubing. Bricks and stones were gathered and concealed in litter-bins in the locality of planned riots.

The Tartan Gangs also provided look-outs, and we learnt how to erect barricades quickly, using street furniture like benches and litter-bins, along with planks, crates and burning tyres. Later, when I was 15, I'd hold up buses and cars to block roads when the Army was known to be patrolling the neighbourhood, or when cars driven by Catholics thought to be up to no good had been spotted in Protestant areas.

Taxi-men from either community were no longer welcome in the other community. In Belfast, taxis had been used in a number of killings. Not only could they bring grief to a community, their drivers could also gather intelligence about the layout of our neighbourhood and feed it back to others with violence in mind.

At night, we acted as vigilantes, patrolling our estates, and looking out for anything suspicious. Increasingly, I was getting into trouble with Mum for coming home later and later. Often, to avoid such confrontations, I returned home early, pretended to go to bed and then climbed out my bedroom window onto the porch and down to the pavement. Later in the night, I returned to my room via the same route. The pull of my friends began to take precedence over what was expected of me at home.

It was frightening walking the streets at night, albeit under the supervision of an older man: drive-by shootings were well known, and more than once I and the boys I was with leapt behind garden walls when cars speeding our way slowed down as they passed by. But the excitement outweighed the fear, as did the sense of belonging and of doing something useful to protect my community.

When G., the brother of one of our Tartan leaders, T., was shot and wounded by the IRA – mistaken perhaps for T. – we went on the rampage in a series of riots. It was during one such riot that I remember a Catholic boy being kicked unconscious. It was the first time I saw someone fighting, then screaming, then still. In the midst of the chaos it stopped me short, but unlike the occasion when my friend's nose was bloodied, I was fascinated by the sight. Then I turned back to the battle. I was already becoming desensitised to violence.

In the beginning my involvement in the rioting was confined to weekends, but during 1970 I began playing truant from school. We called it 'mitching'. To avoid suspicion at home, I left as usual in the morning as if I was going to school, then took a detour across the fields to a place where we'd built a den out of old doors and scraps of wood. Here we ate crisps, tins of beans and bread, built fires and, as bombs began to explode in Lurgan, plotted revenge against the IRA and their Catholic sympathisers.

Our absence didn't go unnoticed. We were caught on a number of occasions by senior teachers who came looking for us. One particular man – 'Sarg', as he was known – was happy to wield a wooden bat against our buttocks if he found us truanting.

By the time I was in my last year in Lurgan Junior High, my concentration on school-work had lapsed, and I was moved down from the higher-grade classes to those for children of lower ability and achievement. I didn't care. School no longer mattered. I had far more important things to do. The murders of the Scottish soldiers had not only intensified my hatred for Catholics, but the Tartan Gangs they had inspired provided a means by which I could channel that hatred and feel that I belonged. As far as I was concerned, I was doing something to save my community from the bombs of the IRA which were going off in Lurgan with increasing regularity.

One flash-point was Wellworths, the shop in the centre of the town that for us marked the boundary between Catholic and Protestant territory. Catholics came into the store through the back entrance and we used the one at the front. Then we'd clash in the store, with shoppers running for cover. We'd lift hammers and screw-drivers and spanners, and running over the top of the counters, we'd throw them or fight with them. The police were always called to restore order. To many people in the town we were hooligans running riot, but they didn't know the enemy as we did.

Rioting was as much about finding a sense of identity and belonging, as it was about hating and hurting those who threatened my community. The more the older guys saw I wanted to throw stones and bottles, the more they allowed me to hang around with them. People who were outside that group ... well, I felt superior even among my peers. If I was selected to gather stones or bottles, and I knew where they were all hidden and others didn't, that gave me a sense of importance. Maybe, then, some of the older guys would tell me there was going to be a riot up in the town that night, and ask me to come with them. I felt I was one of the boys. There was a sense of bravado – a feeling that nothing could happen to me. I always felt I'd be in control of every situation, despite the huge element of fear.

It was from the Tartan Gangs that older men involved in paramilitary activity selected likely recruits. Units claiming allegiance to the UVF operated on our estate. We had some idea who the big boys were, but people kept quiet. If you wanted to join the UVF you might indicate your interest, but usually you were approached by them, not the other way round. In my case, neither I nor the men who drew me into paramilitary involvement had any intention of doing so at the time it happened.

It's hard to convey to people who have not lived through civil conflict how communities are affected by violence on their doorsteps, fear in the air, and rumours flying all over the place. Our politicians, most notably for me in the shape of my hero, Ian Paisley, were preparing us for the defence of our Unionist way of life, our desire to remain British. He wasn't afraid to speak out against anyone who threatened us. He was a minister, a man of God, so God, I reasoned, must be on our side. We would triumph. Boys like me weren't sophisticated in the ways of political rhetoric. If Paisley spoke of our community needing to stand up and fight for its survival, we took that literally. Looking at video clips of Paisley in full flow at that time, he states clearly that a time for armed resistance might well come. For me and the boys I ran around with, the IRA bombing campaign in Lurgan seemed a very good reason for armed resistance.

On housing estates like my own, ordinary men discussed the threat in our midst, and how they might protect their families. Some people became more involved in the political process, some joined the Royal Ulster Constabulary or the Ulster Defence Regiment, but others felt these responses were inadequate to stem the march of Republicanism and the bombs and shootings of the IRA. Neither were they prepared to behave like sitting ducks in the wake of that violence. Small groups began to prepare themselves for action. In the beginning paramilitary units on estates like mine were not set up in any formal way. More often than not, they were groups of friends – some with Army experience, others with access to arms and explosives, or to other people who could help supply them – who came together and aligned themselves with one or other of the Loyalist organisations of the day, like the UDA or UVF. Some people had a foot in more than one camp, legal and illegal.

It is not surprising that children growing up in this context might sometimes stumble upon things they shouldn't see. That's what happened to me. I can't give the details of my own experience. The men involved are long since dead, but their families aren't, and they've had to deal with enough pain already. Instead, let me tell you a story that captures how easily these things can happen with long-term consequences that, at the time, were unimaginable.

Picture a boy playing at home. In the course of his play he discovers a gun wrapped in a cloth, hidden beneath the mattress he was shifting in order to build a den. What a find! He knows he should put it straight back, but no one's around. For just a few minutes he can really take the part of John Wayne coming into town to sort out the baddies. That won't do any harm. He's so absorbed in his game that he doesn't see the passing tradesman who observes him through the window, leaping off his armchair-shaped horse in the sitting-room that has become a scene from the Wild West.

The tradesman reports what he's seen to the police. They visit the boy's home, question him and his family and search the premises. The boy denies ever playing with a gun. The police find no weapons. They leave, but their visit has alerted the men responsible for the gun to the boy's discovery. They know he'll know who hid it. They can't jeopardise their own operations. Lives depend upon the boy's silence. Although he reacted well to the police visit, he's still a boy and they're not sure his silence can be guaranteed.

The men are people the boy respects and trusts. They decide to draw him into their group, to strengthen his sense of belonging, and therefore his commitment to keeping quiet. He's delighted. They impress upon him the need never to speak of what he sees and does when he's with them, even with members of his own family. It makes him feel important and special. Now he's one of the big boys. That's how he feels. In reality he's just a 12-year-old child.

Chapter 4

In conflict people talk of peace, but do not under-stand it. It is less tangible than violence.
                              Alistair and Ruth in conversation

1970

The boy is sitting in a small, sparsely furnished room. He's working with explosives. The screw-thread of the home-made bomb before him must be cleaned ... very carefully. If any trace of explosive has been left in the thread, it might spark when the lid is screwed on and send the whole place up in smoke. He's alone in the room. The men who've taught him what to do are working elsewhere in the building, giving the impression of normality. He's proud that they trust him to do this task. He's no longer playing at being a hero, he is one ... And yet ... as the men left the room a few minutes ago, all he wanted to do was cry out, 'Don't leave me!'

I'm not the only teenager who, in the early 1970s, could identify with the boy in the story I've just told. His experience captures the contra-dictions that confront any child caught up in conflict. In Northern Ireland the breakdown of civil order and the explosion of violence into our lives radically shifted the parameters of what was considered normal. The extraordinary became everyday, but many of us were brutalised by and became brutal in that process.

The fear felt by the boy in my story was well founded. As 1971 drew to a close, Jack McCabe, an experienced Provisional IRA bomb-maker, was mixing explosives in his garage when his shovel hit the ground and caused a spark. The explosives ignited and McCabe was killed in the resulting explosion.

The IRA considered McCabe's mix of explosives to be too dangerous for use by its Volunteers, and ordered their men to dispose of the remain-ing 'Black Stuff'. It was duly placed in a car, driven into central Belfast and detonated. Out of McCabe's fatal error came the car bomb. It was welcomed by the Provisionals for its greater capacity to destroy life and property, while requiring fewer Volunteers to carry out the operation.

This deadly development was a grim herald for 1972, which went on to be the bloodiest year of the conflict to that date. Altogether, nearly 500 people were killed.

The intensification and escalation of hate and violence were mirrored in my personal experience through 1972. For me, that increasing hatred and the capacity to inflict hurt upon others were rooted in feelings of fear and impotence, and the experience of human tragedy within my own community.

On 7 January the *Lurgan Mail* proclaimed:

> A GRIM START TO 1972. Terrorist activity in the locality during the first few days of the new year, gives no promise of 1972 being any more peaceful than it's predecessor.

The article went on to catalogue two armed hold-ups, at least a dozen 'malicious' fires, rioting in the main street and at the flash-point between the Shankill and Wakehurst estates, and police and troops being called out to investigate a number of bomb scares.

Over in Londonderry on 27 January two RUC officers – one Catholic, the other Protestant – were shot dead while driving with three colleagues. They were the first policemen to be killed in the city during the conflict. Tension escalated. Three days later came 'Bloody Sunday' when members of the Parachute Regiment shot dead 13 unarmed Catholic civilians during a civil rights march in Londonderry. Another person died a few days later from his wounds. Less than a month after that, Lurgan's centre was sealed off by British soldiers and men from the UDR. Civil rights marchers protesting against internment, under the banner of the Civil Disobedience Campaign, brought the town to a standstill. All vehicles entering Lurgan were stopped and searched. 1000 troops and 400 policemen were on duty that day. Barbed-wire barriers were erected at the two points where the marchers were stopped. A helicopter scanned the area throughout the day and a huge fleet of military vehicles, including excavators, were much in evidence. The human cost of the escalating violence was emotionally expressed by an anonymous journalist on the front page of the *Lurgan Mail* on 25 February:

> With distressing regularity Lurgan's flashpoint between Shankill and Wakehurst estates erupts into violence. And ordinary, honest, work-

ing class people, people who perhaps have put life-savings into their homes and who have never thrown a stone in anger, are the ones to suffer. On both sides of the sectarian divide!

Roadways and gardens littered with the ammunition of riot and surprise attack, windows shattered then shuttered with hardboard and wire mesh, streets in total darkness from dusk to dawn. These are the visible signs of a fear that has gripped communities which together should be seeking an answer to the aching problem of co-existence.

They are contributory factors to the real tragedy of the appalling situation – the shattered nerves, the sleepless nights, the unhappy children, the uneasy daytime lull in hostilities.

Could not a fresh start be made? ...

Each side believes itself to be the innocent victim of the other and the hate and mistrust goes on ...

That's not how my mates and I saw it. Being caught up in potentially deadly conflict can paradoxically make you feel very alive in the moment, particularly when, with all the arrogance and ignorance of youth, you don't understand the consequences of these things, and you feel invincible.

By now, I'd ceased to distinguish, if I ever had, between the IRA and Catholics as a whole. In my mind there was no such thing as a good Catholic. How could I think otherwise? The only time I met Catholics was when they were throwing petrol bombs and other missiles at me during the riots.

By 1972 these confrontations were an almost nightly occurrence. Whenever there was trouble, word travelled fast to the local community centre where I and my friends often gathered. If we weren't starting a riot, then we were ready to join in any flare-ups between the two communities.

Occasionally my sense of being indestructible faltered when petrol bombs set my own shoes and trousers on fire, or I was hit by a hurled brick, marble, stone or billiard-ball, or by ball-bearings fired from catapults made from equipment taken from local building sites. Often the Army arrived to stop the fighting.

The soldiers were there to restore order, but many were far from neutral. I remember some of the men from the Black Watch, a Scottish regiment, turning their lapels to show us their Orange and Loyalist badges. They were our heroes, even when they were breaking up riots. They always seemed to deal with them from our side, telling us to clear the road, and firing rubber bullets as they faced the Catholic boys. We used to watch and cheer from the side, and do exactly as they said. We felt it was our Army, our police. They were opposing the IRA, not us, so we didn't target them – at least not in the beginning.

One Sunday I was hurt while trying to help my friend Stevie. I was in the town centre with another mate, Willie, when we came across Stevie surrounded by six Catholic lads. Stevie had a Protestant girlfriend who lived on the Wakehurst Estate. To get to her home, unless he was to take a long diversion, he had to walk through Catholic areas. On this occasion he'd been caught out. I was scared because we were outnumbered. It would have been easier to pretend we hadn't seen Stevie, but neither of us could walk away. We charged into the fray. While I was laying into one of our opponents, another boy came and kicked me in the face and genitals. The adrenaline of the fight kept me hitting out, and despite being outnumbered we saw off Stevie's assailants. Then the pain kicked in. I had to be helped to get up by my friends. It was at this point that the police from the nearby barracks came out to disperse the group that had gathered. They'd been watching from a distance. At the time, I couldn't consider the possibility that they weren't on our side, that they could have rescued Stevie even before we arrived and had chosen not to. Didn't I know men in the security forces who couldn't square their task of capturing and arresting UVF men in our community with their own desire to protect us? Sometimes we see what we want to see, until we can no longer ignore the evidence against our perspective. In relation to the army and police, that challenge was further down the line for me. For now I believed we were working together, and that the 'Tartans' and paramilitary group to which I belonged were simply doing what the security forces couldn't do in trying to prevent Republicans taking over and IRA gunmen and bombers getting away with murder. There was no doubt in my mind that as soon as I was able, I was going to join the Army. In preparation for such a time, alongside all the other activity, when I was 13, I became a cadet in the Air Training Corps (ATC).

The weekly ATC meeting was held in the Ulster Defence Regiment (UDR) camp next to my old primary school. We weren't allowed to wear our uniforms in the street because it might provoke an attack by Republicans or, worse still, IRA members. We changed when we arrived and spent the next couple of hours learning to drill, to recognise aeroplanes and discover how they worked, and to use and care for guns. When I was about 14, a group of us spent a week at RAF Halton in England. We returned home with the trophy for scoring the highest marks in the shooting exercises, swimming, drill and tidiness competitions. I wonder if our officers realised to what secret use some of us were putting the training they were giving us with guns.

After the weekly meeting was over, I changed back into mufti, and returned home for tea before taking to the streets in vigilante patrols or on the riot lines. The art of rioting was to know when to advance and when to hold back. The less experienced boys could easily lose sense of how their own side was reacting and as a result, suddenly find themselves exposed to enemy fire because the others had pulled back to re-arm or re-group or, on a bad day, retreat.

We learnt as we went along and became quite proficient. I could hit almost anything I aimed at with a stone or bottle. Always a cheer went up when a petrol bomb smashed and the flames went up people's legs. I can remember putting sugar in the petrol bombs so that when the petrol hit someone with flames, the fire would burn whatever the boiling sugar stuck to.

I was driven on by the rush of adrenaline, the will to inflict as much damage upon my Catholic opponents as possible, and the longing to impress the older lads. Reckless courage was greatly admired. There was one lad – I'll call him Colin – who was known to have one of the hardest kicks in football. We ran around together, although he wasn't part of my immediate circle. I remember in one of the riots, when the Catholic rioters were pushing forward and we were falling back because we'd run out of stones and bottles, Colin waited in an alley as 20, 30, 40, maybe even 50 Catholic rioters ran past his hiding-place. I thought, 'Fuck, if he gets caught, he's dead! They'll beat him to death.' When the crowd passed him, he ran out and joined the back of it, as if he was a Catholic. He ran right up through to the front, and just as he got there, he turned around and whacked the guy on the face with his belt buckle. Big cheers went up. 'Fuck me, did you see what he done?' we said. 'Talk about guts! That's fantastic.' We all wanted to touch him. The high points of a riot lived on in conversations long after the rioters had been dispersed by the security forces.

The death of my friend's father in March 1972 – the story with which I began this book – changed everything for me. It brought home the reality of death, and the danger that confronted me and my family. That so many people turned out for the funeral was an indication not only of the high regard in which the dead man was held, but also of the shock that came with realising we were no longer safe in our own homes. Anyone might break in and blow our brains out.

I can't remember now the exact sequence of events that followed the murder of my friend's father. What I do know is that after his death, school became totally irrelevant to my life. The move to Lurgan Technical College in September of that year was doomed before the term even started. At the age of 14, for the first time in my life I went to a school attended by both Protestants and Catholics. By then it was too late. Segregation and inter-communal violence had set in stone my hatred of Catholics. Why should I treat the Catholics in my new school any differently from the Catholics I faced in the riots? Sometimes they were the same people. We were enemies. Fraternising with the enemy was treason. I hated all the Catholic teachers on principle. My disruptive behaviour held them all at bay so they could never come close enough to challenge my perception. That's not to say I behaved better with the Protestant teachers. The truth is, by that stage I was beyond educating.

The focus of my deepest hatred was a senior teacher in the school under whose authority I came. I'll call him Mr K.. He was a Protestant married to a Catholic. To my mind he'd betrayed our community. He'd done what I refused out of principle to do.

Around that time I went to a disco where I met and danced with a blonde girl. She was lovely. She was with a group of Protestant girls. They all went to the same school. While I was with her one of my mates came over and told me she was Catholic. At first I refused to believe him. I didn't want him to be right, but another girl from the school confirmed it. Even then, I had to prove it by asking her myself.

'Are you a Catholic?'

'Why are you asking me that?'

'I need to know. It's important.'

'It's not important to me. Why's it important to you? I like you and I'm enjoying your company. Aren't you enjoying mine?'

'It's got nothing to do with that. Are you a Catholic or not?'

'Yes.'

'Right, that's it!'

And I walked away. I remember feeling gutted, but with my mates I was all, 'Yeah, that showed her!' Years later, when I was in prison, I thought about that girl, wondering what she'd felt, what, if any, influence my behaviour had upon her attitude towards Protestants, and how she'd dealt with that. I wanted to know what she was doing now.

Unlike me, Mr K. had crossed the line. In my adolescent eyes that made him worse than my enemy. Today I would in many ways see men like Mr K. in a very different light, but as a teenage boy with all the experiences

I'd had, the issue was clear cut. There were no shades of grey.

From the day I started at Lurgan Tech, I did everything I could to get expelled. It was with the conflict that I now identified myself. I knew I was going to join the Army, and outside on the streets a war was already being waged that gave me a sense of identity and purpose which couldn't be matched by anything education had to offer. Soon, unknown to most of those who knew and cared about me, I'd be a fully sworn-in member of the UVF. School was irrelevant.

My attempts to be excluded went well beyond the usual kind of teenage rebellion – smoking in the toilets, writing graffiti on the walls. I and my mates ignored all the Catholic pupils except to fight them in the corridors, and as we left school. Often the police had to be present at the end of the day to escort them to safety at the top of the town. The only usable school entrances at the time were at the back of the school which opened into a Protestant area. The front of the school was sealed off and the windows blacked out because the Army had set up what was known as Kitchen Hill Barracks in an old factory on that side of the school. There were road-blocks at either end of the street where it was situated.

Despite the fact that signs of the conflict came right into the school, I don't recall any attempt by teachers to address what was happening on the streets of Lurgan. I wonder now if it was policy not to talk about it, or how we felt about riots, violence and living under siege, yet that was the only real world for me. Why would I want to learn Maths and English when there were riots to be had up in the town? It was madness. Like setting a bowl of sweets and a bowl of vegetables in front of a child and asking them to choose one. What are they going to go for? The riots were here and now. They were real and exciting. They gave me a role, a purpose, an identity. School didn't.

I remember only one encounter at school that challenged my perceptions in relation to Catholics. When I first joined the Tartans we bought sweets from a local shop opposite Glenavon Football Club. It was run by a Catholic family called Smyth, but because it was in a Protestant area, and because it was the only shop open on Sundays, local people used it. To begin with I felt the Smyths were not bad Catholics, but as tensions increased, word was passed round that shops run by Catholics, and which sold Republican goods, should be boycotted. I loved a brand of crisps that were made in the South, but once the boycott was implemented, I couldn't buy them any more, nor go to the Smyths' shop. As my own hatred for Catholics deepened, I became involved with other Loyalists in intimidating the Smyth family, to the extent that they were forced to leave their shop and move to a Catholic area in the town.

While I was at Lurgan Tech, during one detention, I was made to sit next to one of the girls from the Smyth family. It was the first time I'd ever had to sit next to a Catholic. For some reason I broke my rule of ignoring Catholic pupils. We talked about what had happened to her family. I was hostile and tried to make fun of her, but I remember her as an intelligent girl who understood and defended her position far better than I was able to defend my own. What impressed me was that she showed no signs of being intimidated by me. Not that I could own such a reflection at the time. I couldn't accept that any Catholic had a positive quality.

You might think that since it was a mixed school, all the teachers would be committed to helping Catholics and Protestants live together peacefully. That wasn't the case. They could hold just as strong views as any of us. There was one particular teacher who was caught rioting. There were rumours that he'd been using a crossbow. He was a Catholic. The Head didn't sack him, so we gave him hell – wrecking his car, and throwing darts and big glass marbles at him during class when he was writing on the blackboard. We called him an 'IRA bastard'. He continued teaching after his arrest, but then suddenly disappeared. We were never told why.

When a local Loyalist paramilitary paper ran an article accusing Mr K. of bias against Protestant pupils, I brought it to school and was caught in the act of sliding it under his office door. As a punishment I was excluded from school. It was one of many times when I was banned from attending, but I never experienced that as much of a punishment.

I believe there was some truth in the accusation against Mr K., not only because I felt I was on the receiving end of his bias, but because I remember a time when Mum was so incensed by what she saw as him goading me that she came to the school and threatened him with her umbrella. My reaction was predictable, but Mum's was not. She was a quiet woman of faith. She didn't hate Catholics, and she wanted only to live in peace. She knew I could be a handful. When I did wrong at school, she always supported the teachers in their disciplining of me, but this was one of those rare occasions when she challenged authority because she perceived injustice.

Looking back, I feel a degree of sympathy for Mr K. that I didn't have at the time. We weren't only a handful; we were a danger to the school, the staff and the other pupils.

One day during a break, a friend and I went into the science lab and turned on all the Bunsen burners without lighting them. Then we walked out, closing the door behind us. Our aim was to scare everyone with the smell of gas. I can't remember how aware we were of the potentially fatal consequences of filling a classroom with inflammable gas. Perhaps I was. I felt like I was being mistreated in school so I didn't care about hurting people. The whole culture of violence in Northern Ireland, particularly as I was experiencing it on the streets of Lurgan, enabled me to think that we could do what we liked and that nobody was going to tell us how to behave. If they did, we'd make sure they felt the consequences. We became a law unto ourselves because we had no respect for the teachers. It was different in the paramilitary organisations. They were taking action for our sakes. We wanted to be part of them. We respected the leaders and obeyed the rules they laid down.

Our respect for anyone else had to be earned. On one occasion when I was following my favourite boys' flute band, we came under fire from IRA snipers hiding behind gravestones in a local cemetery. Everyone hit the ground. There was an Army Personnel Carrier (known as a PIG) close by. As the snipers fired, the soldiers taking shelter behind it shouted for us to crawl to them for safety. An RUC officer, who was also there, emptied a round of bullets in the direction of the graveyard, despite the Army unit yelling at him to stop shooting. Later he was disciplined for his action, but to us boys he was a hero. He was a Warrant Officer in my ATC unit, and from that time he never had any problems with me or the rest of the cadets.

Not so Mr K.. The Bunsen burner incident triggered a full-scale emergency evacuation. I relished the fact that Mr K. knew who had created the potentially life-threatening problem, but was unable to prove it.

On another occasion I openly wore a Loyalist badge, and because I wouldn't remove it when asked, I was excluded from school for another brief period. At the time I felt that if Catholics were offended by me wearing a badge which had the flag of my country on it, they should go somewhere else to live.

One of my exclusions involved the police. In certain classrooms, like the woodwork room, there were emergency 'STOP' buttons beside the machines, in case a pupil got into difficulty with them. When the button was pushed it cut the electricity, not just in that room but in the whole school. I pushed this button on a number of occasions, but escaped detection. Finally, to catch the culprit, Mr K. painted some form of invisible 'ink' on the 'STOP' letters on the buttons. The next time I pushed the button and cut the electricity supply, Mr K. lined everyone up and went along asking them to show their hands. I'd no idea about the ink.

When my hand was turned upwards, it revealed 'STOP' written like a mirror image on my palm.

Seeing the evidence, Mr K. turned and laughed, 'Look who it is! Look who we've caught. You're in trouble now, boy.'

I was excluded again. This time an official letter was sent to my parents. At home I said I'd been caught in the machinery, and pushed the button in a panic, but I was the only one who believed that story. Unfortunately for Mr K., being excluded from school didn't prevent me causing trouble there.

Every day I sat outside the shop opposite the school, looking into my classroom, smoking like I didn't have a care in the world, and distracting my classmates. Eventually Mr K. and one of his colleagues came out and told me I had to move. I refused. They went into the shop and asked the shop-keeper to stop me using his shop-front in this way. The shop-keeper refused.

'It's a free country. It's my shop. He can sit there all day if he wants.'

The police became involved. They couldn't move me on, but told me I should be in school.

'I want to be,' I said, 'but they won't let me.'

An education officer became involved and the police visited the school to say that by law I had to attend. If I were prevented from doing so, the Headmaster could find himself in court. I was allowed into school the next day. I was told to sit in the lecture theatre, but only the metal-work teacher was prepared to teach me. He was the one teacher for whom I had any respect. All he wanted to do was teach us how to use tools and make things, and to feel good about ourselves.

I feel a lot of sympathy now for the teachers trying to teach us in an environment of violence. It must have been all but impossible. How do you get young men to listen to you in a classroom when, as far as they're concerned, their whole world outside is falling apart?

Although my parents weren't aware of every time I was excluded – I would pretend to go to school as usual – they were increasingly worried by my behaviour, the attitude of the Headmaster, and the impact of being in a religiously mixed school where contact, far from creating under-standing, all too frequently led to conflict. By the end of my first year at the Tech., Mum was sufficiently concerned to consider drastic measures. She had a sister living across the Irish Channel in Drumchapel, a town just outside Glasgow. After consulting with her, they agreed that I should go and live with my aunt until I left school. More than anything, Mum wanted me to be away from the violence that she feared was sucking me into a downward spiral, despite her best efforts to keep me on the straight and narrow. When Dad returned from work, all the arrangements had been made. During the summer holiday of 1973, my bag was packed, and I set off with Mum on the ferry to Scotland.

Mum saw the move as a means of saving me from the conflict. I saw it as a big adventure. For both of us the coming weeks would fail to fulfil our expectations.

Chapter 5

It is well that war is so terrible else we should grow too fond of it.

General Robert E. Lee

1973

It was a song that finally brought me back to Lurgan from Scotland. It highlighted my homesickness for my family and friends.

To begin with I liked living with my aunt. Everything was new. Coming from conflict-ridden Northern Ireland, which was invariably headline news, gave me a certain kudos among my new classmates. The teachers said that if I'd managed to survive living in the Province, then I wouldn't have any trouble coping in Scotland. That made me feel special and I settled in well.

The boy who became my closest friend lived next door to my aunt. His family was Catholic. To begin with I was a little wary, but here in Scotland it didn't seem to matter so much. He wasn't a threat to me. He'd nothing to do with Northern Ireland and we got on really well.

My aunt also had a lodger. He was a soldier in the Black Watch. In my eyes that made him someone to look up to. I liked him talking about his Army experience, and he connected me with home: in Lurgan my mates and I had got to know the names of the soldiers from the Black Watch who were serving in the town. These were the men we felt were on our side.

My new teachers were wrong, of course. Once the novelty of being away from home in a new place had passed, I had great trouble coping in Scotland. I missed my family and my friends, and I missed the conflict, the fighting, the sense of belonging and of doing something worthwhile. I had nowhere to focus my energy. I was an outsider temporarily set in this community, so there was little incentive to make myself at home.

A couple of my Lurgan mates kept in touch with me. They told me about their involvement in the ongoing riots. I was homesick for it all. 'Normal' life wasn't half so exciting and school was a struggle: I'd missed so many lessons in Lurgan that none of the work came easily. I started playing truant again.

The song was the final straw. My best mate sent it to me. It was based on a true story about a British soldier from the Parachute Regiment. Sergeant Michael Willetts was blown up in May 1971. His story was turned into a haunting song by Harvey Andrews. I can see now that the song was a protest against the senseless waste of human life in conflict, and a condemnation of the hatred on both sides of our struggle. At the time I didn't notice that. I was simply moved by the heroism of the soldier and, of course, I saw him as 'one of us'. The ballad was called 'The Soldier':

In a station in the city a British soldier stood
Talking to the people there if the people would
Some just stared in hatred, others turned in pain
And the lonely British soldier wished he was back home again

Come join the British Army! said the posters in his town
See the world and have your fun come serve before the Crown
The jobs were hard to come by and he could not face the dole
So he took his country's shilling and enlisted on the roll

For there was no fear of fighting, the Empire long was lost
Just ten years in the army getting paid for being bossed
Then leave a man experienced, a man who's made the grade
A medal and a pension, some memories and a trade

Then came the call to Ireland as the call had come before
Another bloody chapter in an endless civil war
The priests they stood on both sides the priests they stood behind
Another fight in Jesus' name the blind against the blind

The soldier stood between them between the whistling stones
And then the broken bottles that led to broken bones
The petrol bombs that burned his hands the nails that pierced
    his skin
And wished that he had stayed at home surrounded by his kin

The station filled with people the soldier soon was bored
But better in the station than where the people warred

49

The room filled up with mothers, with daughters and with sons
Who stared with itchy fingers at the soldier and his gun

A yell of fear, a screech of brakes, a shattering of glass
The window of the station broke to let the package pass
A scream came from the mothers as they ran towards the door
Dragging children, crying, from the bomb upon the floor

The soldier stood and could not move, his gun he could not use
He knew the bomb had seconds and not minutes on the fuse
He could not run to pick it up and throw it in the street
There were far too many people there too many running feet

Take cover! yelled the soldier, Take cover for your lives
And the Irishmen threw down their young and stood before
    their wives
They turned towards the soldier their eyes alive with fear
For God's sake save our children or they'll end their short lives here

The soldier moved towards the bomb his stomach like a stone
Why was this his battle, God, why was he alone
He lay down on the package and he murmured one farewell
To those at home in England, to those he loved so well

He saw the sights of summer felt the wind upon his brow
The young girls in the city parks how precious were they now
The soaring of the swallow, the beauty of the swan
The music of the turning earth so soon would it be gone

A muffled soft explosion and the room began to quake
The soldier blown across the floor his blood a crimson lake
There was no time to cry or shout there was no time to moan
And they turned their children's faces from the blood and from
    the bone

The crowd outside soon gathered and the ambulances came
To carry off the body of a pawn lost to the game
And the crowd they clapped and jeered and they sang their
    rebel song
One soldier less to interfere where he did not belong

50

And will the children growing up learn at their mothers' knee
The story of the soldier who bought their liberty
Who used his youthful body as the means towards the end
Who gave his life to those who called him murderer not friend

When I heard the song, I cried. I was choked by the bravery of the soldier. His story reminded me of what really mattered to me, of where I belonged, and it wasn't Scotland. I wanted to go home. To that end my behaviour became increasingly disruptive. When my aunt could no longer manage me, my Mum came and took me home to Lurgan. It was the best Christmas present I could have had.

It was great to be back. I had experiences to share with friends who'd never travelled much beyond Lurgan, let alone been away from the Province. I felt special again. Much to the concern of my family, I slipped back into my old ways. For a while they discussed sending me to live in Australia with my sister and her husband who were about to emigrate, but in the end they decided to wait until my schooling finished. It's one of those decisions that families make and then, when what they most fear finally happens, they blame themselves for not having chosen differently.

As far as I was concerned, the only reason to see school out was to show Mr K. that the likes of him couldn't get rid of me, and to cause as much trouble as I could when I was there. At the time I thought all my behaviour was entirely justified, but looking back, I think it was symptomatic of a boy trying to behave like a man in a situation of conflict that no child should have to experience. Why do we expect children to behave normally when what's happening around them is entirely abnormal?

After my return from Scotland, the school no longer pursued the matter when I played truant, perhaps because my time there was almost over and life was so much easier for the teachers when I was absent. In the classroom I felt invincible. On one occasion, when I felt I was being picked on by a teacher, I told some of the older boys I ran around with outside school. They turned up the next day, walked into the classroom of the teacher concerned and beat him up, threatening him with further violence if ever he picked on me again. No wonder none of the teachers wanted to teach me!

On another occasion, as was the custom at that time, Mr K. was going to cane me for something I'd done. When I went into his room, he turned on a tape recorder, so I was monosyllabic in all my answers to his questions. When he told me to put out my hand to be hit with a dowel rod, I refused and got up to leave. As I turned towards the door, he hit me on the back of my legs. I grabbed the cane, snapped it across my thigh and threw it at him.

During my times of exclusion I worked at a local warehouse where my Dad had found me a job. It gave me cash in hand, and there was still plenty of time to do the UVF work with which I'd become involved. By that time I was no longer working with the men who'd drawn me into their group after I'd accidentally seen more than was good for me. That change of allegiance was brought about by three key factors – the impact that the murder of Peter's father had upon me, the actions of the British government, and a major reorganisation of the UVF.

On 24 March 1972, in response to increasing violence across the Province, Edward Heath, the British Prime Minister, announced the suspension of the Stormont Parliament and introduced Direct Rule from London. A new Northern Ireland Office was created, run largely by English civil servants under the authority of a Secretary of State for Northern Ireland. It was a bitter blow for us. We saw it as a sign of the ongoing weakness of the British government in the face of IRA violence.

On the same day, the front page of the *Lurgan Mail* reported a terrible example of that violence – the death of the young mother of an 18-month-old baby, who was killed when a bomb went off in the ladies' toilets in Market Street, the main shopping area of the town. The following week the town centre was torn apart by riots. We wrecked the windows and doors of shops and businesses, and roamed virtually unhindered from one end of the main street to the other. Barricades were hurriedly erected at a number of points, with rubble from a nearby bomb-blasted pub and wooden seats blocking off one street.

The problem began when a crowd of us were confronted by a detachment of troops in Land Rovers. It was exacerbated because many schools were closed due to a two-day strike that had hit local businesses and shops, and cut off heating and lighting in some areas. The strike was a protest against the internment of the first Loyalists. It provided us with an unexpected opportunity to vent the anger we felt about the increasing bombs and shootings, and we exploded through the town centre.

Shortly after the strike, in response to the bombing, the parking of unattended cars in the main street and several of the streets leading away from it was prohibited, but if this was meant to deter bombers, it didn't succeed. On 9 June the *Lurgan Mail*'s front-page headline proclaimed,

'TOWN IS BLITZED', and the accompanying report described the town centre as a 'scene of utter devastation following the second terrorist car bomb explosion within 24 hours.' Later that month the 'Provies' (IRA) announced a truce, but less than a month after that, bombers left a trail of destruction when five bombs went off in the town within the space of a week.

The security forces were unable to prevent the bombing, and their increasingly intrusive attempts to gain intelligence about paramilitary activity on both sides of the conflict were causing resentment not only on Catholic estates, but also in my community. Houses were sometimes searched, and men taken away for questioning about their activities. My own home was searched on more than one occasion.

Once when the Army arrived, they were clearly looking for guns. They knocked down part of a hollow wall in the house, and dug up the whole garden. I thanked them for the latter – Dad had been telling me for some time to weed the garden. I enjoyed taunting the soldiers, particularly in front of the crowd of neighbours who had gathered outside in support of my family. Women who'd had similar experiences came up to sympathise with Mum.

Increasingly, people on our estate began to feel that not only did they have to find ways of defending themselves from the violence of the IRA, but the very people we looked to for security were making our lives even more difficult.

These thoughts clashed with the way I looked up to the soldiers in other situations. The same contradictions appeared in relation to the police. When any RUC or UDR men were shot dead, my friends and I mourned and promised revenge. Such men were our neighbours and sometimes our friends, but they were also the upholders of the law which we were increasingly breaking.

Things came to a head early in August, when there was a confrontation between a Protestant crowd, including myself, and the security forces. We stoned the homes of five RUC men on our estate. William Whitelaw, the Northern Ireland Secretary of the time, condemned the attacks, but failed to understand the anger, fear, impotence and sense of injustice that had provoked them. It was the reorganisation of the UVF that provided the channel I needed to release these powerful emotions.

On 1 July 1972, Gusty Spence, a key figure in the UVF, was given 48 hours' prison leave to attend the marriage of one of his daughters. The UVF leadership at the time didn't want him to return to Crumlin Road Prison, where he was serving a life sentence for a murder he's always professed he didn't commit. They were struggling to respond in the face of increasing IRA violence, and to keep control of their own organisation. They needed Gusty on the outside of prison. He insisted that he was duty-bound to keep to the terms of his leave, and wouldn't do anything himself to scupper his return to jail. As his nephew was driving him back to prison on the Sunday, two other cars pulled in and sandwiched the car between them. Hooded men broke the nose of Gusty's nephew as he struggled to resist their intervention. They seized Gusty, bundled him into the back of one of their vehicles and sped away. At first the RUC thought he'd been captured by the IRA, but he had in fact been picked up by our own people. He wasn't rearrested and sent back to prison until the November of that year.

During his time of freedom Gusty reorganised the UVF along the lines of the original UVF battalion structures and leadership patterns. He introduced a uniform and set about re-equipping the organisation. Members stole guns from anywhere they could. On 23 October 1972, an armed UVF unit carried out their most successful procurement of arms when they raided the Territorial Army depot in Lurgan where I attended the ATC.

Lurgan was a key UVF stronghold. The rival Protestant paramilitary group, the UDA, were very much a minority group in our area. Loyalist and Republican paramilitaries were highly active in County Armagh. The regular riots in Lurgan were noted in government despatches as the worst that existed outside Belfast. Perhaps for those reasons a new and, within paramilitary circles, well-known man came to head up the UVF in our area. With his appearance, some of the men who'd been operating locally under the UVF banner stepped away from the action. I, on the other hand, following the death of Peter's father, wanted to increase my involvement. A friend and I approached the new UVF man, asking if we could join the organisation formally. We were turned down on a couple of occasions because we were too young. Then, one day, we were asked to hide some guns – not an unusual request to be made to young boys who'd already proved their worth in the Tartan Gangs and on the riot lines. We took the weapons and concealed them, but not before I'd used one to help me lay my hands on some money, which I handed over to the UVF leader, once again asking to join the group. This time we were told to go to a certain place at a certain time where we were interviewed by masked UVF men.

We were asked if we understood what it meant to become involved in the UVF. We were told that we might not be able to run around with the mates we already had, that we couldn't tell anyone we were involved, that we'd be in trouble if we did, that we couldn't go out and get drunk because we might say things we weren't meant to say. We were told that we might be asked to do things where we might be arrested or shot. We were given a week to think about this and told to come back at the end of that time if we still wanted to join.

I returned within a few days, committed to becoming a member. I was taken to another location where, in an upstairs room, I was brought before a number of masked men sitting behind a table draped with a Union Jack and an Ulster flag, upon which lay a Bible and a gun. With the Bible in my hand, I read out the oaths of allegiance, swearing loyalty to Ulster and to the UVF, and committing myself to fight any enemies, to never betray my comrades and to always obey orders. As I was sworn into the 3rd Mid-Ulster Battalion, I felt proud to be doing something to protect my community, to be standing alongside other men of action who weren't, as I saw it, prepared to sit by while the IRA tried to bomb us out of our British heritage, a heritage that we were no longer convinced the British government wished to maintain.

I was clear about my purpose. It was the protection of my family and the Unionist way of life and faith that was central to my community. This involved countering any attack by Republican paramilitaries, retaliating with greater violence, deterring Catholics from supporting the IRA, and resisting any move that might weaken the Unionist position in Northern Ireland.

The nature of UVF activity is well known – the making and planting of bombs and incendiary devices, protecting local communities and well-known individuals, creating diversions for major operations, gathering intelligence for specific shootings, or choosing random targets to remind Catholics that while the IRA was given support by them, none of them were safe. Robberies were carried out solely to fund paramilitary operations. Those who undertook robberies for personal gain were severely reprimanded and punished.

With my friend, I became a member of a small unit that worked together, usually in isolation from other units: the less any unit knew about what other units were doing, the less they could say if they were caught and interrogated, either by the security forces or by the IRA. When an operation was to take place, other units might be informed not to do anything that could interfere with the success of that operation, but the exact details of it were known only to the leadership and the unit members carrying out the action. If there was to be a shooting, for example, then it would be unhelpful to have rioting in that locality, drawing troops and police to the scene.

Necessity made us imaginative in the materials we used to make weapons. Condoms made reasonably accurate timing devices in incendiary bombs. Explosive powder would be placed in a cigarette packet. Near the intended target we'd put acid into a condom. It took about 12 minutes for acid to burn through one condom. By altering the number of condoms used, we had some idea of how long it would be before the acid burnt through the rubber and ignited the explosives. The packet was sealed and placed innocuously among goods on sale in a shop, or left without drawing attention in a bar or other public place.

Intelligence gathering might take weeks of watching a potential target go about their daily business. Sometimes observation needed the cover of darkness. Not every plan was implemented, because events across the Province were moving so quickly and other operations might take priority and require the cancellation of my unit's work.

I remember hiding in a ditch in the pouring rain on a dark night, waiting to carry out a particular operation. At the last minute another member of my unit came by, calling out my name. I was told the operation was off. I was furious. I was all psyched up for action.

After my return from Scotland, there was a lot of action, but not quite of the kind I'd anticipated. While I'd been away, on 17 November 1973, the UVF leadership had declared a ceasefire, intending it to last until the end of the year. If our demands were not met during that time, we'd renew our military campaign. The political situation unfolding during 1973 was one which appeared more favourable to Republicans than to us Loyalists. Earlier in the year elections had taken place for the new Northern Ireland Assembly. On 21 November, just four days after the ceasefire was declared, members of the Unionist Party under the leadership of Brian Faulkner, the Republican SDLP led by Gerry Fitt, and the Alliance Party agreed to share power in a devolved government. My hero, Ian Paisley, and his colleague William Craig were appalled. Despite the split in the Unionist party caused by the agreement, Faulkner went on to attend the first Anglo-Irish conference since the partition of Ireland. The talks opened on 6 December in the Civil Service Staff College in Sunningdale, Berkshire. The 'Sunningdale Agreement' that emerged from these talks proposed a Council of Ireland made up of Ministers drawn from the two jurisdictions, and a consultative Assembly comprised of members of the Northern Ireland Assembly and the Irish parliament in Dublin.

It was an agreement drawn up far away from the violence tearing apart our communities in Northern Ireland, and a million miles away from what was acceptable to those of us who were followers of Paisley and Craig. In our ceasefire statement, the UVF declared that we'd work with all who opposed Sunningdale for the restoration of 'a democratic system of government' – namely, majority rule. If that was not forthcoming, then we'd return to armed struggle. Our leadership also pointed out that the UVF were responsible for 97 per cent of the Loyalist violence, with the exception of sectarian killings. We were also responsible for detonating 200 bombs in comparison to the 300 exploded by the IRA.

It was into this political ferment that I returned from Scotland. On 4 January 1974 the Ulster Unionist Council rejected Sunningdale by 427 to 374 votes. Faulkner resigned. In England, as a result of the miners' strike, Heath's government called an election for the following month. The United Ulster Unionist Coalition, fighting on the basis of 'Who runs Ulster?', won 11 of the 12 Westminster seats. The lost seat was won by Gerry Fitt, whose constituency of West Belfast had a large Nationalist majority.

Despite overwhelming Unionist success in the election, the issue of power-sharing was not resolved, so we returned to violence, shooting Catholics and, in the face of the IRA's bombing campaign against the security forces in the Province and in England, restarting our own bombing operations. In the next couple of months two bombs went off, killing six Catholics in two bars in Belfast.

Units from my own battalion of the UVF were said by some to be responsible, together with UVF men from Belfast, for exploding three bombs in Dublin and one in Monaghan on 17 May 1974. Other sources suggested that the security forces were implicated in the bombings. Thirty-three people were killed in the blasts. The combined death toll was the largest loss of life in a single day in the conflict.

For those of Brian Faulkner's persuasion, just three days before the Dublin and Monaghan bombs there had been a glimmer of hope for a political solution when the Northern Ireland Assembly rejected a Loyalist opposition motion condemning power-sharing and the Council of Ireland. It was snuffed out that same day when, in the evening, a group called the Ulster Workers Council (UWC) announced a general strike. This development came as a surprise to many people on the receiving end of the news, but it had been carefully planned over a number of weeks. It was organised by groups including not only trades unionists but also Loyalist politicians and paramilitaries. Its purpose was to bring down power-sharing and Sunningdale once and for all.

When the strike began on 15 May, there wasn't mass support for it. A similar strike called the year before had resulted in five deaths in one day, and no one wanted a repeat performance of that violence. The organisers of the new strike were determined to prevent it this time, although there was intimidation of some workers in the first few days. Shipyard employees in Belfast were told their cars would be vandalised in the car park if they worked. Shops were threatened with fire-bombs if they remained open. People were turned away from work at gunpoint, or at manned barricades. Whenever the Army moved in to dismantle the barricades, those manning them melted away, only to return when the Army had gone. This avoidance of confrontation worked. By the fourth day the strike had taken hold, and had general support in the Unionist community across the Province.

The Workers' Strike had a major impact on me. Although it only lasted for two weeks, in my memory it seemed to go on for months. Perhaps that's because the Sunningdale Agreement provoked public disorder in Loyalist communities for several months leading up to the Workers' Strike, in the form of increased rioting and the erection of barricades. When the strike came into effect, our Community Centre became a hive of extra activity. Local people banded together to make sure that food parcels went out to those in need, like the elderly and infirm, and that they didn't run short of coal. Farmers brought in churns of milk to be shared out. Soup and sandwiches were always available. I remember raiding some food stores and delivery vans to get food for those who didn't have enough.

The community spirit of that time is how I imagine it was like in the Blitz. We didn't feel under siege because we felt in control of the strike. It was due to Unionists that the electricity was off. We'd brought everyone out of work. This was our country and we were showing our power. No factories could operate unless we said so. No shops could open without our permission. We exempted certain businesses from closure like food suppliers, chemists, post offices and newsagents. The movement of petrol and oil supplies was banned. All petrol pumps in both communities were closed down. Nobody could drive their car on the road without our say so.

A week into the strike, I remember a meeting being held in the Community Centre, organised by the County Armagh Save Ulster Campaign and the Loyalist Workers' Council. My Dad was among those on the stage leading the meeting. It was attended by more than a 1000 people who spilled out onto the road. They were unanimous in supporting the strike action, and committees were set up to deal with particular aspects of its impact, such as the ongoing care of vulnerable groups. Paramilitary leaders also offered at that meeting to take action against any 'hooligan element'.

The sense of power was great. It was the complete opposite of how my community so often felt in the light of IRA bombs and shootings. One encounter during the strike also gave me a taste of personal power that I greatly relished. Perhaps it was one of the incidents that had prompted the complaint against a 'hooligan element'. If it was, I couldn't have cared less because it gave me so much satisfaction at the time.

One day during the strike I was manning a barricade when it was approached by a car driven by Mr K.. The lads and I were all masked, but as his car drew to a standstill I repeated his own words to me when I'd been discovered as the boy setting off the alarm system in school:

'Look who it is. Look who we've caught. You're in trouble now!'

I didn't care if he recognised me. I was the one in control. Not him. He was now in my territory. By the time we allowed him to drive away, his car had been wrecked – mirrors and lights broken, paintwork scratched, tyres slashed.

Whatever my family might have wanted, as far as I was concerned my school career was well and truly over.

Chapter 6

A great many people think they are thinking when they are rearranging their prejudices.

William James

1974

The Workers' Strike brought down the Stormont Executive. In Lurgan we celebrated our success with a mass turnout of Loyalists, all pouring into the town centre to hear Ian Paisley reiterate his pledge not to sit down with Republicans to discuss the future of Ulster. He looked ten feet tall and we thought he was great. It was a euphoric time, but it didn't last.

Now that I'd finished with school, the question of what to do next became more pressing. I knew from my job at the warehouse that I didn't want to spend my life on a production line. The money might be good but the labour was boring and demoralising. I'd developed a taste for adventure, excitement and danger. This was the moment to fulfil my dream of becoming a soldier in the British Army. That dream might have become a little tarnished by the reality of soldiers doing house searches in our community, or chatting up little kids on the street to see if they could trap them into saying their daddy had a better gun than the soldier's, but in times of conflict it's easier to put aside than address the contradictions that cast doubt on dearly held views. Start questioning, and things begin to fall apart round your ears. When everything else in your life is chaotic, rocking the boat further isn't a great idea.

My friend and I were directed by the Army Careers Officer at the local TA Camp to Palace Barracks in Belfast. There we were interviewed, and had medical checks and fitness assessments. I passed muster but my friend was turned down because of the political tattoos on his arm. It was a blow for both of us. I'd been looking forward to training with him and, for all my bravado, I found reassurance in the thought of having someone from home with me in England.

While all this exploration was going on, the rest of my life had returned to 'normal'. With the breakdown of the UVF ceasefire, there was plenty of work to be done, and the usual rioting was back in full spate. One incident on the riot line had far-reaching consequences for my Army career.

One Saturday afternoon there was a major riot in the town centre. The police arrived in force to break it up and restore order. They ran into the crowd, grabbing people and trailing them off into their Land Rovers. One of my friends was caught and dragged away. The rest of my mates and I followed in hot pursuit, pelting those protecting the vehicle he'd been thrown into with stones, petrol bombs and sticks. In the ensuing scuffle I was able to climb in to free my friend. Between us we overpowered the guarding officer, but as my friend ran for it, I was caught. Later, at the police station, I was charged with obstructing the police in the course of their duty, and with disorderly behaviour. I was released on condition that I report regularly to the police barracks so that they could keep tabs on me. During one of those visits I told them about being accepted by the Army for basic training in Sutton Coldfield, England. When the date of my court appearance came up, it clashed with the time I was due to be away. Recognising that the Army might be just what I needed to help me find a way out of the conflict in the Province, the police told me to leave for England as planned. I need not appear in court. I would probably get a fine, and they would notify me about that when the time came.

On the boat over to England, I met up with a Catholic lad from Dublin who was also on his way to do basic training at Sutton Coldfield. We got on well together. Both of us were a little nervous about leaving home and finding our way to the General Service Corps base. When we arrived at the Camp we were assigned to different houses. I shared a dormitory with three English recruits, one of whom was black. It was my first encounter with a black person. My room-mates had already been at the camp for a couple of weeks, and I felt very much the new boy.

The following day I had an Army haircut and collected my uniform. I was asked which regiment I wanted to join and said, 'The Black Watch.' That was my first mistake. Scottish regiments, it seemed, were looked down on by the English soldiers questioning me. After this interview there were a number of sessions on procedure and, with other new recruits, I was shown around the base to the NAAFI, where I could go, and the Officers' Mess, which was out of bounds. I felt very intimidated by the men in the NAAFI. The bravado for which I was well known among my friends and opponents in Lurgan, failed me in this unfamiliar environment.

I quickly became conscious that it was a distinct disadvantage to have

61

an Irish accent. The men around me didn't distinguish between lads from Northern Ireland who were British, and those from the South who were Irish. We were all seen as Irish. This confused me greatly since I'd always seen myself as British, yet here were my 'own kind' not accepting me as one of them. I noticed how I and the Dublin lad I'd met on the boat coming over were constantly stopped by NCOs and made to do press-ups wherever we were, and for no apparent reason.

I had no problem coping with the training. I was fit. I knew how to handle weapons. I was familiar with explosives. I knew how to drill. But I didn't know how to handle the anti-Irish prejudice that followed me wherever I went in the camp. This became particularly acute when on 5 October 1974, during my basic training, a bomb planted by the IRA went off in a Guildford pub, killing four soldiers, and on 21 November, the Birmingham pub bombings killed another 21 people. Entering the NAAFI after the latter bombs, I had full Coke cans thrown at me so that they exploded against the wall behind, and taunts of 'Irish bastard' met me wherever I went.

Perhaps I might have got through the backlash of those bombings and finished my training if other circumstances hadn't prevented me from progressing further. One day I was summoned to see the officer in charge of the recruits. He read out a letter he had from the police in Lurgan, notifying me about the fine I had to pay as a result of the court case concerning my arrest at the riot. As a legal document, this letter should have been addressed to me. That the officer had it suggests it had been intercepted by the Army authorities – perhaps, in the light of the Birmingham and Guildford pub bombs, as a symptom of heightened security. I can only say that other soldiers who had fallen foul of the law were sent letters directly from the police dealing with their cases and, unlike me, they weren't forced to resign, even though some of the charges against them had been more serious than those against me.

The officer was furious that I hadn't filled in details of my arrest when I'd applied for the Army, although, as I told him, the offence hadn't been committed at that stage. The officer made it clear that the Army wasn't the place for someone like me who was prepared to obstruct the security forces in the course of their duty, and that he didn't want me in the Army. He informed me that he'd be drawing up discharge papers for me to sign. These would say that I'd decided the Army wasn't for me.

At first I refused. In the face of this resistance, the officer threatened to make my time as hard as he could make it. Feeling isolated and alone, unable to talk to family, and having been the butt of a fair amount of bullying already, I wasn't sure I wanted to endure further torment. The officer also threatened me with dishonourable discharge if I didn't comply with his wishes. This, said the officer, would follow me all my life and preclude me from getting any other worthwhile jobs. I believed him. In the end I felt I had no option but to sign the papers.

I was deeply shaken by this turn of events. This treatment wasn't what I had expected of the British Army. I thought I'd be welcomed in with open arms. I was a loyal subject, committed to the Crown and to everything British, and yet I was treated as an unwelcome foreigner. I left without ceremony, disorientated and aggrieved. At the railway station I had no idea what train I was supposed to catch. A friendly station manager, hearing my accent, suggested I'd be safer if I didn't take the train coming into the station, which was crammed with Birmingham City football supporters. When I got on the next train I tucked myself in a corner, afraid to speak to anyone. Travelling on my own on the boat also scared me. Put me on a riot line and, although I'd be frightened, I'd know what I was about and get stuck in, but that journey home was a nightmare.

Eventually I arrived in Belfast. I had no idea how to get from the docks to the station. When I finally reached it, I discovered I'd come to the wrong one. I wandered across the city, trying to follow the directions I'd been given to get me to the Europa Hotel, which was near the right station. On the way I became lost and strayed into Republican areas. With my Army crew-cut and green kit-bag, I was lucky not to be lynched. I arrived back in Lurgan exhausted and bewildered. Only then, when I was back on home territory, did I begin to think clearly again and finally rang my parents.

In the light of my experiences in Scotland and in England, I realised that I felt safer and more secure at home, despite all the violence in Lurgan, than I did when I was away from it. I knew what the 'rules' were. I was glad to be back with people who loved me. I felt deeply angry and bitter about my treatment at the hands of the Army. My anger was shared by the recruiting officer in Lurgan. He made a formal complaint about what had happened. As a result I received a written apology from the Army base in Sutton Coldfield. The letter said that the officer responsible for my discharge had overstepped the mark and been disciplined. There was also a cheque enclosed covering the pay I'd lost, including a pay increase. Finally, I was invited to return to Sutton Coldfield to continue my training. I refused. My dream of following my father's footsteps into Army life had turned out to be a nightmare I was not prepared to repeat.

The only place I felt I belonged now was among my own people in Northern Ireland. They were the only ones I could trust. As for the soldiers on our streets, in the light of my experiences in England, they'd become my enemy as well.

That reality was painfully brought home to me in the wake of what became known as the Miami Showband Massacre. At the end of July 1975 the Miami Showband, a Dublin group that was one of the most popular bands north and south of the border among both Protestants and Catholics, was returning home after a gig in Banbridge. Near the border town of Newry they were stopped at a checkpoint by men in Army uniform. They were ordered from their van and told to put their hands on their heads and stand in a line facing away from the van into a field. The 'soldiers' were in fact UVF men from the Mid-Ulster Brigade. The plan was to plant a bomb in the van, put the band back in and send them on their way. The bomb would go off on the other side of the border, and the band would be accused of smuggling bombs for the IRA. Instead the explosives went off accidentally as the men were putting them in place, killing two of them instantly. Another UVF man ordered that there should be no witnesses. Three of the band were shot dead and another was seriously wounded. The fifth member had been blown through a hedge by the force of the explosion. He hid in a burning ditch before escaping.

Following the Miami Showband Massacre, military activity in Mid-Ulster increased. One evening a friend came running to the Community Centre to tell me that an Army PIG was parked outside my house and soldiers were searching it for guns. I ran home to support Mum. The dog was barking in the garden. Neighbours had gathered outside. One of them had been arrested and questioned on an earlier occasion. He'd been roughly treated, so he'd come across to offer support, but the soldiers wouldn't let him in. A soldier was guarding Mum and one of my brothers in the living-room.

'I haven't been here long,' said the soldier, trying to make conversation, 'but it's a lovely country.'

'You're fighting for a country that you don't know anything about,' I said to him, feeling utter contempt.

When the search was completed, I was taken away for questioning. I was pushed onto the floor of the PIG. The soldiers rested their boots on me. As the vehicle was driven away gunshots ricocheted off the sides. They were fired by men sympathetic to the UVF. With each shot, the soldiers' boots pressed down harder upon me. I felt alone and afraid.

I was taken to Kitchen Hill Barracks. While I was there I was made to walk in a darkened room between two lines of soldiers shouting loudly to disorientate me, and kicking and hitting me as I passed by. As soon as I was able, following advice I'd been given by other UVF men, I asked to see the Army doctor. I was taken to another room. The medical officer who arrived was a big, intimidating man. He told me to take off my clothes. I was scared and refused, but the doctor told me I had no choice now.

At one point during my time at the barracks, I was made to stand with my hands and fingers spread out on a hot radiator. The pain made me pass out a couple of times. Then I was told to sit on the floor with my back straight, my legs stretched out in front of me, my head upright, my arms unbending, with my hands on my knees. It was a very tense position to be in. Every time I relaxed my arms, my body sagged, and I was hit on the back with a baton.

While all this was going on, a local Justice of the Peace, Alistair Black, came with his son to see my parents. He told them to let him know if I hadn't returned home by five in the morning. The Army could only hold people for a limited period of time before either releasing them or handing them on to the police.

After questioning, I was told that the Army were going to take me to the Catholic end of town and leave me there at the 'mercy' of the local men. I was very frightened by this. As threatened, they drove me to the Republican estates, but thankfully didn't stop there. I was finally dropped off on the Grey Estate, badly bruised and very shaken, but also feeling proud that I had suffered for the cause. My hatred for the Army was well and truly set through that experience. I was not alone in this regard.

Relations between local Loyalists and the Army became increasingly strained as the year went on. On 23 October members of the UVF released a statement via the *Lurgan Mail* saying:

> Due to severe harassment of members of the Force and their families and of innocent Protestants, the brutality against them, and the searching of their homes in 'B' Company's area, Lurgan, the Third Mid-Ulster Battalion staff have decided to retaliate against what we now call the Occupation Forces in Protestant areas, whether they be on or off duty. This also applies to those who work for 3 Brigade (Kitchen Hill), those attending discos at the camp and to those who serve tea to them on our estates.

A couple of days later on a Sunday evening, the first ever gun battle on a

Protestant estate in Lurgan took place on the Grey Estate. According to the *Lurgan Mail*, it was sparked off 'when a crowd of youths and men launched several stone-throwing attacks on passing Army Land Rover patrols in Pollock Drive.' The paper said it was evident the attack had been planned, because 'hundreds of bottles had earlier been gathered at the community centre and young girls were observed gathering milk and beer bottles in large sacks.' When the patrol tried to surround the 50 or so rioters, they came under further attack. They were joined shortly afterwards by two Army Saracens, a PIG and a large force of troops. The Army took up positions in Dickson Primary School and at the Community Centre. They also charged the rioters. There was a black-out on the Estate. The rioters smashed street-lights and ordered drivers to switch off their headlamps. People in their homes turned off their lighting. Everywhere there was chaos as the road quickly filled with broken glass, and the crowd taunted the Army. The journalist reported that within seconds of the Army taking up positions in the school, gunmen shooting from different positions at different times opened up on the soldiers, injuring one of them in the abdomen. A woman watching the scenes from her living-room was grazed in the neck by a stray bullet. To this day houses by the school bear pock-marks where the bullets hit.

As the situation became less dangerous, onlookers flocked to the scene, jeering at the troops as they moved away. The gunmen melted away into the night. The Mid-Ulster Battalion of the UVF admitted responsibility for the gun battle. Some weeks later, I would be charged with shooting the soldier.

Chapter 7

All things are subject to interpretation. Whichever interpretation prevails at a given time is a function of power and not truth.

Friedrich Nietzsche

1975

Violence is seductive. The sense of power that comes from using it to keep another person or community in their place is addictive. Preparing for an operation one day, I came across a group of rioters whose presence was potentially detrimental to the success of the task in hand. When I asked their leader to leave the area, he refused. Only when I put a gun down his throat, and told him he was getting in the way of people who wouldn't take his resistance kindly, did the group rapidly apologise and withdraw.

'We didn't know you were working for your man,' they said with grovelling respect tinged with fear – 'your man' being the key UVF leader in the area. By association, I suddenly became one of the big boys in their eyes: someone not to be messed with. That felt good.

Years later, speaking at a conference about child soldiers, I found others who shared my view that the younger the age children become combatants, the harder it is for them to reintegrate into normal life precisely because of the satisfaction that comes from the power they discover through violence. As a teenage paramilitary, I and those I worked with were eager to do more and more. Not only did we carry out orders, but we suggested acts of retaliation in response to IRA bombings and shootings. To those brutalised by civil conflict, the immediate response to murder is to retaliate with more vicious murders – the hijacking of a bus perhaps, at a time and place when its passengers will all be Catholic. Then we can shoot the lot of them. That's the way to do it.

I never questioned the hatred that fuelled my actions. I believed ours was a just cause; that right was on our side; that *God* was on our side. Caught up in the fight, there was no time or desire to ask the questions that later haunted me about my involvement in violent acts. I had no doubt that those I hurt deserved their punishment.

It's not my intention to justify violence, but I want to tell you about two incidents that might help you understand the mind-set I had at the time they happened. In the first, I was with my friends going from house to house on the Grey Estate, collecting for UVF prisoners and their families. At one house the occupant came out and ripped up in front of us the note we'd delivered earlier informing residents that we'd be calling. He screwed up the bits and threw them on the ground, telling us he had no intention of supporting our 'cause', which he believed to be utterly wrong. To us, this was the ultimate insult. As far as we were concerned, it was people like this man who enjoyed security on the Estate because other men were prepared to defend it and pay the price of that action by being killed or imprisoned, while he condemned them and did nothing to help. We picked up the pieces of the note, went back to report the incident to the local commander, and returned later with others to the man's house. We forced our way in, dragged him out, beat him senseless and stuffed the ripped note down his throat, forcing him to eat it.

In the second incident, the local UVF had been summoned by the neighbours of a man on the Estate who was beating up his wife out in the street, in front of children, and verbally abusing anyone who tried to stop him. This wasn't the first time it had happened and they wanted action. It wasn't uncommon for residents to appeal for assistance in such situations to the dominant local paramilitary group rather than the police. They felt the former were more likely than the latter to be effective in dealing with some problems, and many had become wary of the RUC because of what was seen as their 'heavy-handed' action in Loyalist communities.

I was among those who went down to warn the man that his behaviour wasn't acceptable and had to stop. The husband agreed to this request but within a couple of days his wife's screams were heard once more as he laid into her. With a number of the bigger boys, I returned to the house and gave the man a good kicking and beating.

I can remember him crying and screaming for us to stop, and I thought it was funny. I said, 'You're not the big guy now, are you, now you're not kicking a wee girl all over the street, with her begging you to stop and you carrying on. How does it feel to be on the other end of the boot?'

I had a real sense of justice. I felt he got what he deserved.

When I recount these two stories to friends who haven't experienced extreme conflict, it produces an interesting response. They tend to be repulsed by the first incident, but feel some sympathy for my reaction to the second man who kept beating up his wife. However much they don't want to admit it, they feel some sense of satisfaction, and even justice, in him being given a taste of his own medicine. Because of how he treated his wife, they identify less with him than the man who refused to give money for paramilitary prisoners and their families. It's always easier to hurt and to justify violence against those we consider to be 'not like us' – people we think of as inhuman or less than human. If you get some sense of understanding, or even sympathising with the use of violence in one situation, then the question becomes, when is it appropriate to use violence, and to what degree? Taking the step of seeing the use of violence as valid or necessary wasn't difficult for me, growing up as I did with conflict erupting on the streets where I lived, and people I knew being murdered in their homes. The degree to which I was prepared to use it steadily increased as I became acclimatised to its impact and experienced its extremes. Once it was part of my way of life, I remember only one occasion when I was disturbed by its use.

As a member of the Tartans it was obligatory to attend regular meetings in the Community Centre. These gatherings were concerned not only with disseminating news about what was happening locally and more widely in the Province, but also with disciplinary matters. On one occasion a young man of 18 or 19 – I'll call him Rick – was to be disciplined for not attending meetings despite being told to do so. Of the 50 boys and young men present, four were picked out to give Rick a punishment beating that was to last for one or two minutes. During that time the lights were switched off. When they came back on, Rick was lying on the ground battered, bruised and bleeding. What disturbed me was that we all went along with it, even though Rick was one of our own and, perhaps more significantly in terms of my reaction, he was a good guy. Not only that, but in my opinion at least one of the men who carried out the beating seemed to enjoy it. My memory is that Rick drifted away from the gangs and the type of violent behaviour that existed in those mad times. I've often wondered how he was affected by the rough justice inflicted on him by those who were supposed to be his friends.

That one incident aside, I never questioned the rightness of using violence in my own context. I returned from my abortive attempt to join the Army disillusioned and angry. I felt very much that it was us Loyalists against the rest of the world, and the rest of the world now included British soldiers and the RUC. I threw myself into UVF activity with a vengeance. At the time of the gun battle on the Grey Estate, I was working on another operation. News had been passed to my cell that a local Protestant had been threatened by a Catholic fellow employee. He'd been told that if he didn't leave his job, then he'd be shot. When I heard this I was furious. I decided that I'd do to the Catholic what he had threatened to do to his Protestant colleague. We spent two weeks on surveillance and planning, watching our target going about his daily business, checking his routines, working out how we'd get him.

On 29 October, just a couple of days after the gun battle, we drove in a stolen car to his home. I was scared, but I was also utterly focused on the task in hand. At such times it's as if you go into a different level of consciousness where all extraneous information is filtered out. On an everyday basis, hate motivated me to take revenge for all that had been done to my community, but in the act of killing, the hate disappeared. I'd demonised my victim sufficiently to feel nothing for him or the value of his life. This was just a job that needed to be done.

Only our driver was visible to those outside the car. The rest of us were masked and crouching on the floor of it. We drove round the block once, past the house of our intended victim. As we came round again to make a left turn into the man's street, a police wagon appeared from our right. It had turned out onto the road from the nearby Kitchen Hill Barracks. Our driver decided to do the circuit again, giving time for the police wagon to leave the area. It stopped at the next set of traffic lights. I wondered if it was a set-up. On the floor we felt panic as the driver told us what was happening.

When the lights turned to green the wagon turned left. Our car followed. We could have driven the other way at this point but we were determined to carry out our plan. At the next set of traffic lights, the police drove straight on while we turned left again to go back round to our target.

When we reached the home, I got out. In a split second of looking round, I noticed a young boy outside the front door of the next house. He was the younger brother of my target. If he'd been older, I might have shot him too. I didn't have time to break into the house. That was more dangerous anyway. I ignored the child and went straight to the front window, where I could see the shadow of someone inside against the blind. I fired five shots aimed in a tight circle at that person. Then I turned and jumped back into the car.

'I've scored,' I said as we drove away.

Those are the facts of it: cold, hard facts. In the space of a few short seconds I had crossed a line, and there could be no going back. Back then, my cry was one of triumph. It would be some years before I'd fully own the tragedy of it all: a life cut short, his family and my family torn apart, and a legacy of darkness for me from which I think I will never be free.

Immediately after the shooting, we dumped the car, off-loaded the gun, and went to a disco in the local Community Centre to establish an alibi. Our hands were stamped on the way in, but the place was so busy I felt confident no one would register at what time we arrived. After a short time we left and went for a Chinese take-away before returning to the disco. If someone said later that they hadn't seen us at the disco, we could say we went out to the Chinese restaurant, and that could be verified.

Finally I went home, and lay on the settee to wait for the late-night news. It confirmed that I had indeed killed my intended victim. Not that I'd have cared much at that time if my shots had ended the life of anyone else in his family. My parents were devastated. They knew the family of the dead man, some of whom worked in the canteen of the factory where my Dad was a foreman.

Their reaction to the news meant little to me, but seeing something I'd done reported on the television hit home. While we were carrying out the operation, getting rid of the evidence and establishing an alibi, my mind had been utterly focused on those tasks. Now the world opened up again. Other reactions came into sharp relief. Once the adrenaline rush wore off, I felt exhausted, yet sleep eluded me. When finally I went to bed, I lay awake feeling frightened by the enormity of it all, worrying what would happen if I didn't wake up: in one small corner of my mind I wondered if God was angry with me for what I'd done.

Dark thoughts on a dark night, but the next morning I couldn't wait to get out and meet up with the boys to talk about what had happened. I didn't tell those who didn't know that it was me who'd pulled the trigger, but as the others talked about a Catholic getting what he deserved, I revelled in that fact. Some of our parents were anxious. They feared there'd be retaliation, but I didn't care. We'd sent a message to the other side: if you threaten Protestants, we'll protect them, and we'll deal out double the measure of terror that you try to inflict upon us.

I'd also proved something to myself. Throughout my teenage years I'd been testing myself, going into uncharted waters, needing to prove that I was prepared to go all the way – otherwise it was all just talk, and I was contemptuous of that. I wanted my UVF leaders to know I wasn't dead weight. I was useful, I was prepared.

While I was with the boys, I received a summons from the local UVF leadership. They knew I'd been going to act, so when the news came through, they knew it was me. I was ordered not to run around boasting about the operation. It was regarded as a job well done, but if the UVF came to hear that either I or any of the other members of my cell were talking about it to others, we'd be dealt with severely.

The killing was reported in the paper and life went on as usual. Away from a conflict zone, any killing makes headline news for days, but when you live with shootings and bombings going on all the time, that's not the case. It becomes old news very quickly. Even those who aren't caught up in violent action become desensitised to it in some way. They may be shocked for a short time, but then they just get on with life because that kind of thing is happening all the time.

As for me, I was on a roll. I felt invincible. The week after the shooting, there was an armed robbery at the Post Office in Queen Street. It was the second raid the staff there had experienced in the space of three weeks. The robbery took place just before 1 p.m. and the raiders made off with the money in the direction of Lurgan Park.

While the robbery was in progress someone had raised the alarm. A patrol rushed to the scene and then, with other Army vehicles, they converged on the park. One of the gang members escaped detection by hiding in the lake. The gun used in the hold-up was later found hidden in bushes at the water's edge.

When the security forces arrived, a mate and I were walking along one of the paths not far from the children's play area. We were surrounded by police and soldiers. I was thrown on the ground and the muzzle of a rifle was forced into the back of my neck. A policeman sat on my back with his gun at my head.

We tried asking what all this was about and shouted at the security forces about how they were treating us. We were arrested and taken to Lurgan Police Station. We were so naïve, yelling from our separate cells, urging one another to keep quiet and say nothing to the police. After a short while my friend was taken to another station. Another lad was arrested the same day, then a fourth on the following day. I denied everything, and demanded to see a solicitor. The request was ignored. My parents were informed I'd been arrested, but they weren't allowed to see me. To begin with I was scared, but cocky while I was being questioned.

In the immediate days after the robbery sniffer dogs found the gun. Ballistics tests linked it with the killing I'd committed the week before, but I was saying nothing. I slept badly. I was moved to Banbridge Station, then to Moira, and then back to Lurgan. Different people questioned me.

They brought in statements supposedly signed by the other lads. I assumed these were fakes.

I remember being in a room during that time with five or six police officers. They kept turning the lights off and stamping their feet in the darkness. When that happened I'd crouch down and cover my head with my hands. Then the lights would come back on, and they'd laugh at me huddled down and squinting in the light. They were trying to frighten and humiliate me. I didn't know if it was night or day. When I was asleep, they woke me. I became exhausted and disorientated. Everything was muddled. When I was questioned, one man would play the good guy, and another would be the nasty guy. Sometimes I responded by denying the accusations, but mostly by that stage I kept silent.

Then, on the third day an officer came in and said, 'I've scored! I've scored!' and I knew they had accurate information now about the killing. They started questioning me about other offences, including the shooting of the soldier during the Grey Estate gun battle. All the time I was trying to clarify what they knew and what they were guessing. Finally, they wrote out a statement, asking if I agreed to it. As I signed it, I felt huge disappointment in myself, and a sense of resignation that I was going to prison. Later, when my solicitor was at last allowed in, he told me that if I'd held out against signing anything for a few more hours, the police would have had to release or charge me. I was gutted when I heard this, but it was too late.

I was charged with membership of an illegal organisation, possession of a gun, armed robbery and murder.

If I'd been living any kind of childhood, however abnormal, it was now well and truly over.

Chapter 8

*We are all exceptional cases ... Each man insists on
being innocent, even if it means accusing the whole
human race, and heaven.*

Albert Camus

1975–76

I'll always remember the first night I spent in a cell on the UVF wing of
the Crumlin Road Prison. I was sharing it with Raymie Crozier, a member of the unit involved in the Miami Showband Massacre. The radio was
playing as we lay on our bunks. The Christmas number 1 came on:
'Bohemian Rhapsody' by Queen.

> Mama just killed a man.
> Put a gun against his head,
> pulled my trigger,
> now he's dead ...

Words and music by Freddie Mercury © 1975; reproduced by
permission of Queen Music Ltd/EMI Music Publishing Ltd.

I wept silently into my pillow. If Raymie heard me, he gave no indication.
I was glad of that. It was the first time the enormity of what I'd done
struck home. Other kids my own age were all with their families preparing for Christmas. I was behind bars, suddenly uncertain about the
future. Perhaps there was also an element of relief in those tears. I'd been
in the prison for a couple of weeks, largely kept in isolation, waiting for
permission to join the UVF wing. It took that length of time for the UVF
commander on the wing to check with UVF leaders outside the prison
that I was there because of politically motivated paramilitary activity.
Sometimes men who'd been accepted onto the wing were put out when it
was discovered later that the armed robbery they'd been involved with
had been for personal gain and not for the organisation. Then they were
slapped around before being evicted.

Crumlin Road Prison wouldn't look out of place in a Dickens novel. Built in 1845, it was solid, stark and grey, and to my 17-year-old self, scary. Getting out of the police van on the day I arrived, I found myself in a courtyard with massive walls that loomed over me. I was surrounded by uniformed guards and taken for 'processing'. The prison officers (known to prisoners as 'screws') saw me as source of fun and taunted me through my initiation into prison life. I felt intimidated and alone. My personal effects were logged and removed. A strip search was followed by a shower and then I was covered in white delousing powder and given bed-linen and basic toiletries. The place echoed with noise from other parts of the prison. The sounds of shouting, keys rattling and metal doors clanging shut reverberated around me.

After seeing the Governor, I was sent to a cell in a sectioned-off area of the Annexe known as 'behind the wire'. During my time there I was able to wear my ordinary clothes. Remand prisoners were entitled to three visits a week, sometimes more, and could receive food parcels. It was while I was 'behind the wire' that I saw my parents for the first time since my arrest. Visits always happened in the presence of the screws, so they were often awkward, unnatural encounters. My memory of those visits is that the seriousness of what I'd done hadn't sunk in. I told Mum and Dad that I was innocent, and that I'd been forced to sign my statement under duress. I was convinced I'd be able to talk my way out of it. I had absolutely no sense of the agony they were going through, and they didn't let on. All this was uncharted waters for them, but they kept the conversations hopeful and hid the devastation they felt.

While visits were difficult, they were a welcome break in a daily routine that saw me locked in my cell for 23 of the 24 hours. First thing in the morning, when the door was unlocked, I 'slopped out' and washed. I ate all my meals in my cell. We had one hour of exercise every day, walking around a small yard. I wasn't allowed to walk with anyone else or speak to them. Apart from that there was nothing else to do except wait for news.

The UVF wing was utterly different from life 'behind the wire'. Discipline exerted by the UVF leaders was strict. On my arrival I was interviewed by Bobby Spence – Gusty's brother. He wanted to know if I'd given the names of accomplices or information that would be compromising to UVF operations outside the prison. There was a stigma attached to those who'd given statements. It suggested you weren't tough enough to keep your mouth shut, and that you'd let others down. I was conscious of my own disappointment in myself for signing a statement, but relieved that I hadn't implicated anyone else in what I'd said or what had been written in my name.

There was a tension here for Loyalist paramilitaries that I don't think Republican paramilitaries experienced. For the latter, the authorities in the Province, including the security forces, were the enemy, the oppressor. Resistance against the British State was a major theme in the history and identity of Republicans. For Loyalists like me, who'd been raised in church-going families and taught to respect the police, this wasn't the case. The RUC was on our side. It might have failed to be effective but it wasn't 'in our blood' to see the police as the enemy. It didn't sit easily with us. The conflict in Northern Ireland moved many men to illegal armed resistance who would never have broken the law in times of peace. Many Loyalist paramilitaries under police interrogation were encouraged to 'get things off your chest', and 'to clear your conscience'. That approach recognised the inner conflict felt by some as a result of the gulf between their upbringing, and the actions they'd taken in response to the violent Republican threat they lived with on a day-to-day basis. They wrestled with the sense of having done wrong.

Co-existing in contradiction to this reaction there was also a definite hierarchy among prisoners relating to the severity of the offences committed and where you lived in the Province. I looked up to the Belfast UVF men, particularly those charged with multiple murders. They were the big, serious offences. It's a crazy notion, as if just committing one murder was of little consequence. It's another example of how conflict distorts our humanity.

Because of my age, Bobby Spence took me under his wing. He quickly involved me in making handicrafts. I painted hankies, made badges, and drew pictures of Disney characters, all of which were taken by visiting relatives and sold through the organisation.

Once more I felt part of things. I was one of the boys. Because it was a remand wing, there was a lot going on. Legal teams came and went. These visits were hugely important to most of the men, as they talked through their defence and discussed evidence. There were conversations about court cases that were in process, and what verdicts were reached. One young man who was going to court was convinced he'd get out, so he gave away his cigarettes, but he was brought back at the end of the day and wanted his cigarettes back. He was finally released. I remember him because within a couple of weeks of his release he was dead – murdered by the IRA.

My own barrister was disturbed by how I and my friends hadn't grasped the enormity of what we'd done. We were always cracking jokes and fooling around. 'Even if we do 20 years,' we said, 'we'll still be in our thirties when we get out ...'

I had little sense then of the space men needed to sort out their thoughts. I was so unaware of myself, let alone anyone else. For the most part, this was still a big adventure. I wasn't married or a father, and I was oblivious to the ramifications of that for other people. In short, I was a typical teenager, selfish and thoughtless about the experience of others. Sharing a cell didn't bother me. Men are used to peeing with other men around and bodily noises are a source of amusement to teenagers. Crapping was more problematic. It was degrading and dehumanising to do that in company, but not embarrassing. Sometimes we did it into paper and threw it out the window so it wasn't in the cell. Orderlies from the non-political wings were forced to clear these parcels up from the yard below. If you were caught, you were charged.

Days on the wing began at 7 a.m. with slopping out and washing. There was a great deal more freedom of movement than I'd experienced in the Annexe. I could eat in the canteen or in my cell, and was free to mix with other remand prisoners on the wing, eating together, doing art-work, discussing cases, or making music. There was no moment of the day when I wasn't learning something new. There were also regular visits to Belfast Magistrates' Court. Standing before the judge, I'd learn how my case was developing and whether the police were ready to go ahead with the trial. If they weren't, then I'd be remanded for another month. When they were, the trial date was set.

At one point during my time on remand, over-crowding in Crumlin Road meant that I was transferred for a short time to a remand com-pound at Long Kesh Prison. The compounds, along with the later, infamous 'H' Blocks, eventually became known publicly as the Maze Prison. It was situated by the village of Maze just outside Belfast. Before becoming a prison, Long Kesh had been an Army barracks. The com-pounds were segregated so that no compound had more than one para-military organisation represented among its prisoners. All the men in Compound 6 were UVF members under the command of the most senior UVF man present. The compounds had far more space than the wings in Crumlin Road, but there was less opportunity to be on your own. We all slept in a Nissen-hut dormitory, rather than being locked in a cell at night. Perhaps that's why the older men found me more of a nuisance than when I'd been on the remand wing in Crumlin Road.

With Jackie, another teenage prisoner, I was always getting into trouble and ending up on 'fatigues'. Fatigues included cleaning paint off windows with razor blades, cleaning down the shower-block, and brushing up the yard. Our offences were talking after lights out and disturbing others, not making our beds properly, having dust on our lockers, doing practical jokes like turning cold water on men who were showering, and making 'brew'. Brew was a beer made from fruit, sugar and smuggled-in yeast. We made it in a gallon container hidden in a locker under clothes. The pressure had to be released every so often and we'd forgotten to do that. As our UVF officers were doing their daily inspection, the container exploded, covering anything in the near vicinity with sticky liquid, and filling the air with the heady smell of fermenting fruit.

We were always cheeky to the older men. We talked back at them and were so unaware of what was or wasn't acceptable that on occasion one or two of them became so furious with us that they lashed out and had to be restrained by others. For them, the uncertainty of life on remand heightened the emotion they felt about being separated from wives and children. All of that passed over my head. They were probably greatly relieved when I was moved back to the UVF remand wing at Crumlin Road.

I and my co-defendants were finally brought to trial in the May of 1976. Before the trial I was scared, but I tried not to show it. There was a tunnel under the Crumlin Road linking the prison to the Court House. It was a long, cold and dank arched passageway. Each day of the trial we were brought back and forth along it. In the court-room were our families and the family of our victim. There were lots of people in the public gallery as well as all the staff of the court. On the outside I was cocky and arrogant. Inside I felt only fear. In the formality of that setting the seriousness of what I'd done began to sink in. I was glad to be with my co-defendants. Like all boys of my age, there was a feeling of strength in numbers, and of not wanting to appear weak in front of mates, so we egged each other on. It must have been cruel for the murdered man's parents and siblings, but we didn't care about that. Not then.

The trial went on for a week. I remember being in the witness box, denying some things and claiming that my co-defendants didn't know I was going to shoot the man. That assertion was rejected. During the recesses we were put in the court cells. I was very 'gung ho' about it all. When I was found guilty of murder, I accepted it. I didn't feel crushed. Lots of other men had passed this way because they'd been prepared to stand up to their enemies. I thought, 'Fuck this – this is what happens.'

Because I was a juvenile at the time of my arrest, I was sentenced to be detained at the Secretary of State's pleasure. Unlike adult convictions for murder, no minimum sentence could be set. During sentencing I shouted at the police, calling them liars. I felt no remorse.

After sentencing I was taken to the holding cells where I had one hour with my parents. In that space I felt overwhelmed. We were very formal with each other. The presence of the police and screws prevented any other kind of interaction. Maybe that's just as well. I didn't want to be seen to fall apart, and what could my parents say? We hugged and kissed and said we'd be in touch.

Such contrasting emotions in such a short space of time! One minute I was the hard nut abusing those in court, and the next, I was struggling not to crack up with my parents. Perhaps they were just different expressions of the same emotion – fear.

Over the coming years I would become intimately aware of the co-existence of diametrically opposed thoughts and feelings, but to the prison authorities I was clearly bad through and through. As the Assistant Governor of Crumlin Road Prison noted in his written report about me on 19 May 1976:

> ... I can find nothing good to say about this young man. He is clearly committed to the UVF leadership and was convicted on a 4 year concurrent term for being a member of the organisation.
>
> I'm sure that his detention in custody should be a disciplined one. However I'm also sure that he would seek only to be 'with his mates' in compounds in the Maze.
>
> I recommend that he be sent to the compounds and kept there for a considerable length of time since at this stage he does not appear to have considered that he is a danger to a law abiding community.

Had I been 18 when I committed the offences for which I was arrested, I'd have been regarded as a political prisoner and sent immediately after sentencing to the Long Kesh compounds, but my age and the time of sentencing complicated the situation. On 4 November 1975, the Secretary of State for Northern Ireland had announced that 'special category status' was to cease. This meant that any paramilitary prisoner convicted of offences committed after 1 March 1976 would now be treated as an ordinary criminal. This ruling provoked riots and hijackings in the weeks following its announcement. In April 1976 the IRA murdered a prison officer. It was to be the first of a series of such murders by the Provies (Provisional IRA).

I was sentenced in May of that year. Because of the changes imposed by the Secretary of State, I had to claim political status by filling in a petition to him. I was kept 'behind the wire' for the month or so it took for the Northern Ireland Office to process this. During that time the screws tried to make me wear the young offender's uniform allocated to convicted prisoners, but I refused. They wouldn't allow me to wear my own clothes, as was the privilege of a prisoner with 'special category status', so I spent those weeks in limbo wearing only my underwear and a blanket. It was very cold.

It was during this second period of time 'behind the wire' that I was brought to court for my trial relating to the shooting of the soldier during the gun battle on the Grey Estate the previous October. When I arrived in the court-room something didn't feel quite right. There were no witnesses and no soldiers present. During the first break, when I was taken to one of the holding cells beneath the court, I talked about this with one of the other men there.

'That's odd,' he said. 'You should refuse to recognise the court when you go back.'

So that's what I did. My barrister was really unhappy with this unexpected move on my part. By law my action required a plea of 'not guilty' to be entered on my behalf. Such a plea put the onus on the prosecution to prove its case. This meant they would have to bring forward witnesses. The court was adjourned. The officers accompanying me back to the prison were furious. They dragged me away from the court-room and pushed me down the stairs to the passage linking the Courthouse to Crumlin Road Jail. A few weeks later my barrister told me the case had been dropped. By then my status as a political prisoner had been granted and I'd been moved to the compounds at Long Kesh.

The view of the prisoners there was that the security forces didn't want to pursue the case because it would have meant exposing people they had working under cover. There'd been speculation among local people at the time of the gun battle that a secret Army unit had been operating in the roof of a house on the Grey Estate, near Dixon's Primary School. The couple living there had recently come over from England with their kids and bought a chippie. Why would anyone move to Northern Ireland during the conflict?

For the next 12 years prison took away my freedom, but it also opened up my world.

Chapter 9

I know well what I am fleeing from but not what I'm in search of.

Michel de Montaigne

1976–81

One day, while sitting in the study hut in Long Kesh, I looked out the window and was startled to see in the compound a wee, fragile, bent old woman who was vaguely familiar. When I remembered why I knew her, I panicked. The last thing I wanted to do was meet her again. Her name was Mrs Blackthorn. She was a missionary who'd worked all over the world. Just after the riots on the Grey Estate and before I was arrested, I was at a mate's house with a group of friends and some girls who were sympathetic to the UVF. While we were larking around, a leaflet dropped through the letterbox. It was about the soldiers stationed in the Province and how they were away from home, doing a dangerous job that separated them from their loved ones. According to the leaflet, they needed all the support we could give them. I was furious.

'Who the fuck's giving them leaflets out?'

I ran from the house and searched all over the estate for the culprit. I eventually caught up with Mrs Blackthorn, complete with bag of leaflets, at the Community Centre. I snatched the bag from her hand, ripping it away from her fingers. I threw it into the bin, demanding who the fuck she thought she was. She told me her name and how she visited soldiers in barracks all around the Province.

'I'm also on the Board of Visitors at Long Kesh prison. I know Gusty Spence.'

'I don't care who the fuck you know. You shouldn't be giving them leaflets out.'

I gave her a mouthful of abuse. As I stalked away she said, 'I'll pray for you, son. I'll pray for you.'

Now, here she was in the compound. When I sneaked another look, she was talking to one of my mates and he was pointing to where I was. Next minute she was in the study hut.

'I suppose you don't want to talk to me.'

'No, I don't fucking want to talk to you.'

'Well, I've been talking to G. and he's sorry for what you all did. I don't suppose you want to say you're sorry.'

'No, I don't want to say I'm fucking sorry.'

My rudeness didn't deter her. She kept coming back to see me. A few years later I'd be moved by that, but it wasn't what I wanted as I sat in the study hut. I was embarrassed by how rough I'd been with her at the Community Centre. Just what damage I'd done to her at the time I didn't learn until I was further down the line in solitary confinement in one of the 'H' Blocks. Her reappearance and words then threw me into confusion, and probably were one of the life-lines that helped me claw my way back to humanity, but during my early days in the compounds of Long Kesh she was nothing more than an unwelcome intrusion.

For the first few years of my imprisonment I felt I was where I belonged. I was doing time with men who, like me, had been fighting for a cause. I felt no remorse for the murder I'd committed. Death is part of war, and I felt we were caught up in a civil war, fighting for the survival of our community. If I was sorry for anyone at all, it was me, not my family or the family of the man I'd murdered, whose lives I'd wrecked. Not that I spent much time wallowing in self-pity. In prison self-pity undermines your capacity to survive. I had moments of thinking about not getting out for a long time, and wondering what my family and friends were doing, and thinking about girls. Then I'd get emotional, particularly at Christmas. That was no use. It didn't fit with the tough image I tried to project. There was no room here for the gentle side of the young boy I'd once been. Just like there hadn't been room for him on the streets of Lurgan. Any thoughts that made me feel emotionally vulnerable had to be pushed down. I needed to learn to survive in this new world of prison life.

To begin with I was in Compound 18, where most of the guys came from outside Belfast. On arrival I had to go before the UVF command structure in that compound to learn the rules. I also had to tell the commander about myself, and I was told to get my hair cut.

The UVF leaders ran each compound along Army lines. We operated rather like a prisoner-of-war camp. Apart from first thing in the morning and last thing at night, when the prison officers came in to lock up or unlock the huts and to do a head count, they had little to do with our daily life, unless there was trouble.

A compound contained three Nissen huts and a shower-and-toilet block. One of the huts was split in two. Half of it was a dining area. The remainder was used as living and sleeping accommodation. In summer the huts were like ovens. In winter they were freezing, and when they weren't freezing they were damp, with condensation running down the walls. The small heaters were completely ineffective, but they worked brilliantly as toasters.

By the time I came to Long Kesh there was a study hut in each compound (or 'cage', as it was sometimes called). There were about 80 men per compound. Every man had a uniform provided either by his family or the UVF. It consisted of black trousers, a black shirt or polo-neck jumper, black socks and shoes, and a belt with a UVF buckle. The uniform was topped off with a black beret with a UVF badge pinned to the front. Once a week we paraded with a colour party. At other times we had drill practice out on the exercise yard.

The screws unlocked the huts and did a head count at 7 a.m. every morning. By 10 a.m. all the men had to be up, washed and shaved, with their cubicles cleaned out and dusted, and their bed-packs made up according to UVF regulations. Those who failed inspection were put on fatigues, which usually meant having extra cleaning duties. Between 10 a.m. and noon everyone carried out their assigned tasks for the day. These included periods of exercise and study, alongside cleaning the compound throughout to military standards. The toilets and shower block were scrubbed daily with carbolic soap and disinfectant. Smokers cleared the exercise ground of cigarette stubs. The kitchen area was to be left spotless by anyone who used it.

Each compound had a quartermaster who kept an inventory of all the food, cooking utensils and furniture in the huts. A compound administrator dealt with any requests to see the prison governor or professional staff like the prison doctor, dentist, welfare officer and education team. He monitored closely any contact we had with the prison world beyond our own compound. Drugs and their abuse were actively opposed by the UVF leadership. The administrator would check any medication coming into the compound, and prevent its release if it was any form of sedative or anti-depressant. Each compound had its own appointed welfare officer to help men with marital, social or family problems, and there was an education officer responsible for all library requests and study courses.

Education was a key part of prison life under the leadership of men like Gusty Spence. They considered it crucial for us to develop our minds, as well as finding some form of distraction to pass the time. Every man who came into the compounds was asked why they were there. This wasn't a question about what action had landed him in prison, but to make him think about the wider conflict, and its context in the history of our divided island. I'd never done that before, not least because I'd been too busy trying to cope with the present moment in a town where riots, bombs and shootings were happening on a daily basis and people in my community didn't feel safe.

The debates we had about the use of violence and the suffering it brought would have surprised people in the outside world who saw us as mindless and heartless terrorists. Unlike me at the time, many of the older men had become involved in violence very reluctantly. They knew the human cost, but they couldn't see any other way of protecting their way of life. Group discussions were a regular feature of the education programme. If you couldn't argue your point properly you were shot down in flames. It was a competitive process that was merciless to any man whose argument was weak. If another person got the better of me I'd go away and think through where I'd failed. I wouldn't make the same mistake again. I'm grateful for that tough discipline. For the first time in my life I had the opportunity to reflect on my experience instead of simply reacting to what was going on around me. It's made me much more precise in my analysis of various issues. It means today that I tend to see the questions that need to be asked and the issues that aren't being properly addressed, which others either miss or avoid. The downside of this is that on committees I'm sometimes seen as a thorn in the flesh. I won't settle for lazy arguments, particularly when the safety of others is jeopardised by lack of attention to detail.

In Long Kesh, lunch at noon was followed by a rest period. From 1400 hours to 1600 we continued with our duties. Beds could not be made up and used before 1600. This was to prevent men from cutting themselves off from prison life when they were depressed by staying in bed all day. There was a head count at 2100 and lights went out at midnight, after which time there was to be no talking.

Although some men kicked against the discipline and structure of the day, I valued it. It helped to contain me, and it prevented bullying. When men fell out they either had to resolve the issue through talking, or they went to the gymnasium with boxing gloves and a referee and fought it out. Fighting in any other way was an offence. There were a couple of occasions when I came to blows with other prisoners outside the gym. Luckily the leaders didn't get to hear about it.

One of my jobs was to collect food from the lorry that came each week. If we had plenty of one food type, I would barter for more of another.

There'd been a time when meals arrived at the gate ready prepared, but they were so disgusting that the UVF camp command officers negotiated for fresh food to be delivered. We cooked it ourselves, either individually or as a small group of friends. This meant we could demand better food because the prison no longer had to pay for the meals to be ready made.

Alongside prison food, once a week we were allowed food parcels from home. Whatever we received, we shared with friends. Steak was cut up so everyone had a piece. Salad, chicken, cake, fruit – you name it, our families sent it. At Christmas turkey was on the menu with all the trimmings. At that time it never occurred to me that Mum and Dad might be going without in order to provide for me. They were allowed to visit once a week, but they never said anything about the difficulties they endured as a result of my actions and imprisonment.

In the beginning I looked forward to visits, but they weren't always easy meetings. We were collected in a van and taken to the visitor block where there were small cubicles. Prisoners were separated from their visitors by a table fixed to the floor. A prison officer was present at the back of the cubicle. Some just looked in every so often. Others watched the whole time. There was little sense of privacy.

Another of my jobs was to collect the post through a hole in the wire, and then to hand it out. All the mail was checked by prison officers. One day I saw one of them opening the letters, smelling them and looking at photos he found in some of them. I mentioned it to our commanding officer, who reported it. The prison officer was removed from any work relating to our compound. If he'd come in after what I'd seen, he'd have been beaten up. Mail was very important.

To begin with I wrote and received lots of letters. In Loyalist communities like my own, both in Northern Ireland and in Scotland, there were people who saw political prisoners as heroes. They held fund-raising events for prisoners and their families, and they were happy to write to us. I received letters not only from family and friends, but also from the sisters of other prisoners, and sometimes from people I didn't know.

Longed-for letters were a double-edged sword. It wasn't easy for those outside to write about what was happening in their lives when they knew I couldn't be part of that or do anything about any difficulties that might arise for them. I analysed every word and tried to read between the lines as well – never a good idea when there was no immediate chance of checking out what I thought was or wasn't being said.

Sometimes a married man received a 'Dear John' letter telling him that his marriage was over. That kind of news always had an impact in the compound. The married men in particular felt for the person concerned, and wondered about the strength of their own marriages. It wasn't until later that I thought about how tough life was for the wives outside, living to all intents and purposes as single mothers, unable to claim benefit because their husbands were in prison, and often unable to find work for the same reason. They lived with the stigma of their husbands' actions, often trying to raise children and feeling fearful about their well-being. They couldn't easily socialise, particularly with men, without stirring gossip. I guess at the time I felt more sympathy for the men because I witnessed the impact of marital break-up on them first-hand, whereas the experience of the wives was distant from me.

Sometimes letters contained news of a family death and a funeral that couldn't be attended. We came to know when the men around us needed space to deal with bad news and disturbed emotions. There was little privacy, but it was accepted that if someone went off to the study hut when no lessons or groups were being held there, they should be left alone. Others pounded out their emotions by running round the exercise area, or working out in the gym. Like many of the men, I responded to the lack of quiet, private space by learning to filter out noise around me.

As a young prisoner, the letters that caused me the greatest *angst* came from girls. Not surprising, really. Apart from 'talk', there wasn't a lot I could do in prison to build a relationship. At times I became too dependent on my mail. I'd wait for letters from certain people. When they came I always read the last line first. How the writer signed off gave a good indication of the contents. If the goodbye was cool, I'd feel really cut up. For the girls the novelty of writing to a prisoner would eventually wear off, and they'd find a boyfriend who wasn't in jail. There was nothing I could do about that. It wasn't a good state to get into, so I wrote fewer and fewer letters.

We were affected very much by news about the ongoing conflict. When we heard about a successful UVF action, my spirits soared, at least in the early years when I still believed the gun was the only way to sort things out. Everyone was affected when people we knew were killed, or there were IRA atrocities. Rarely was there a death that didn't affect someone. These killings made me feel that my own actions had been right, and that I was very much a prisoner of war. Sometimes the deaths were of men who had not long been released from the compounds. Often they were shot in revenge attacks.

Every year around 11 November we had Commemoration Day. We paraded round the compound with a full colour party. Two minutes' silence was observed, during which flags were lowered and heads bowed. Each compound commander read a statement, and we marched around the exercise area. The soldiers and guards in the watch-towers always took photos of these occasions. Our marching would have passed muster on any parade ground.

We were good not only at marking sombre occasions, but celebrating as well. Christmas may well have accentuated the sense of separation from family, but I also remember prison Christmases in the compounds with some pleasure. Our families made sure we had all the food associated with Christmas. We decorated the huts, and there was always a show. The rule was that you couldn't have a drink until you'd performed. I hated doing a turn, but there was a lot of laughter as men made complete fools of themselves. For Christmas and for the 12 July celebrations we distilled poteen, a lethal spirit that had to be made and stored secretly. While the drinking of alcohol was only allowed twice a year, the making of poteen went on continuously, not least because the prisoner officers would carry out searches on a regular basis and discover our hidden supplies.

A black bin was filled with water, and yeast, sugar, fruit, potatoes, carrots, jam, or anything else that could be broken down, was added. This wash needed to stand for three weeks, but searches often meant we had only one week. The still was made from a boiler that was originally used to make tea. A pipe taken from the showers was fixed to it, and the trough used to cool the alcohol was a fluorescent light-shield with a hole in each end for the pipe to go through. Storing the pure alcohol was a matter of trying to keep one step ahead of the screws. Initially we used jars that we hid in the cavities that were part of the Nissen huts. Later we used Coke cans. We turned the ring on the top of the can, pierced a hole through the metal, emptied out the Coke, and refilled the tin with poteen. We soldered up the hole using soldering irons that had been smuggled into the prison. Then the ring was turned back into place, concealing where the hole had been. The tins were returned to the cases of Coke in the stores.

Occasionally we'd make up a very dilute but frothy wash especially for the prison officers to find. This distracted their attention from the real stuff we were working on. Sometimes when we expected a search we'd hang our blankets across the lines between the huts, supposedly to air them. As one hut was being searched, stuff that we didn't want to be found was passed along to the next hut. Eventually the screws cottoned on to this, so we all had to go to the canteen while the searches were made. Then they brought in sniffer dogs that could detect not just poteen but guns and ammunition.

Poteen was lethal. We could only drink it mixed with fruit juice. On one occasion some of the screws boasted that, as seasoned whisky drinkers, they could down poteen with no ill effects. One of them drank a cup and had to be carried out by his colleagues. He was hidden in a van to sleep it off, so that the Governor wouldn't find out.

The yeast for the poteen was among the many things smuggled into the compounds. One prisoner kept pigeons. These were allowed to take part in races until the screws discovered sachets of yeast attached to the birds' legs on their return to the compound. Sufficient component parts and tools were smuggled in for a prisoner who was an electronics expert to make a radio. This enabled us to communicate with men in other compounds and also with people outside the prison. We also communicated with the other compounds using a form of semaphore. Often the soldiers in the watch-towers watched us through binoculars, trying to decipher our messages.

There were times when tension in the compounds flared into riots and violence. This could be due to events either inside or beyond the prison walls. On some occasions it was due to the shooting of a prison officer. At other times conflict between the UDA and the UVF triggered tension in the cages. Occasionally a prisoner may have lashed out at a screw they felt had over-stepped the line, and the prison officers would want that prisoner removed to the punishment blocks. If the CO refused access and agreement couldn't be reached, then conflict was inevitable. Sometimes an escape attempt had been made, or the screws were concerned that a tunnel was being dug for that purpose. In all these cases visits would be stopped for the duration of the confrontation. The compound COs ceased to cooperate with the prison staff, none of whom were allowed into the cages for the daily head-count and lock-up routine. The stand-off could last for days, during which time no food was delivered. Prisoners couldn't leave the compounds for any reason because they'd be taken immediately to the punishment block. It was during one of these periods that I developed an excruciating toothache that no painkillers could relieve. Because I couldn't leave the cage, two other prisoners fixed a copper wire round a piece of wood. Another prisoner held my head, and the wire was placed around the offending tooth and pulled. The force used almost broke my jaw. The pain was unbearable. The tooth was well embedded. It took a long time before it was sufficiently above the gum for the wire to be fixed under a ridge in the tooth and it was finally drawn out. It bled profusely. A couple of days later, when 'normal' services were resumed, I visited the prison dentist. There must still have been tension around because he threatened to put me on a charge for self-abuse!

Generally speaking, Gusty and the other commanding officers tried to negotiate a settlement to any problem that arose, but occasionally a force of prisoner officers or soldiers would be sent into the cages. We prepared for these invasions by wrapping towels around our arms and legs to protect us against blows, and we slept in our clothes with our boots on, in case the compound was attacked at night. Each of us was assigned to a group. When the Army came in, we had to run to a particular point in the compound. I remember on one occasion coming out of the hut and being confronted by 100 or maybe 200 prison officers in full riot gear, with the Army at the side. We were armed with steel bed-ends and anything else that could be used as a weapon. Years later, after my release, I learnt how sickened with fear the prison officers had been on such occasions. Some of them were new to the job and weren't trained for this kind of work. They knew that men on life sentences had little to lose.

Generally, life in the compounds didn't encourage me to see the screws as the enemy: for the most part they had little to do with our lives. My opinion changed dramatically when I moved to the 'H' Blocks. That move came about partly because of my restless nature, and partly because in 1980 I became a practising Christian.

When I first arrived in the compounds I was still a teenager. I enjoyed the camaraderie of being with 'the boys'. The implications of what I'd done had yet to sink in, and it took a while before the novelty of prison life wore off. Besides, as a prisoner detained during the Secretary of State's Pleasure, with no idea when I was likely to be released, I lived under the illusion that I wouldn't be in for more than five years. This belief made me less selective about the men with whom I chose to spend time. Later, when I realised I could be inside for many more years, I tended to stick with other lifers as a means of emotional protection. It's hard to be with someone who's preparing for release when you know you won't be getting out yourself, and if you build a friendship with such a person, the sense of loss when they go is debilitating.

Growing up in prison from being a teenager to a young man in my early twenties, my only role models were the older prisoners with whom I lived. I watched their reactions, listened to their conversations, heard their stories and became aware of the very different experiences and opinions of those around me. Gradually questions began to come to mind about the state of my life. The enormity of what I'd done and the pain I'd inflicted on my victim's family and upon my own began to sink in.

Questions weren't easy to face. They felt like a betrayal of all I believed. One question inevitably led to another. Soon my old securities were under siege and I began to see what I'd done in a different and painful light. When I started to realise the impact of my actions and imprisonment upon my family, I felt really bad. It became hard to see them during visits. For the first time I recognised my own selfishness. That was difficult, but it was also helpful. The combination of the change in perception about myself and the emerging questions spurred me to reading books about other conflicts. I didn't initially feel safe to ask questions relating to the violence in Northern Ireland, but I could explore issues around conflict by looking at similar situations overseas. As a result I read about the Israeli/Palestinian conflict, the struggle against apartheid in South Africa, and revolutions in South America. I learnt about the American Civil War and the treatment of Native Americans. I was enraged by what white people had done to native peoples in different parts of the world when they'd invaded or 'discovered' their lands. I identified with the suffering, and became alert to the pain people cause while claiming they are fighting for freedom. I became curious about the way human beings demonise their enemies, and then are able to hurt them because they've come to see them as less than human. I began to think about my own experience in the light of what I was reading, and in this way I was, for a while, able to explore the questions that were beginning to impinge upon my consciousness, without feeling I was betraying my community.

Through debates in the study hut about conflicts elsewhere, I saw that other men were also wrestling with questions like my own. I began tentative conversations with them. I enjoyed the heated confrontational group discussion where there was cross-talking and shouting down, and the one who yelled loudest was heard, but I needed a space for talking that would allow me to explore tentative thoughts without being accused of betrayal or being silenced for the stupidity of my words.

I'd come into prison believing that right was on my side. God was a Protestant. Everything was neatly boxed in my thinking. I was both naïve and arrogant. Now I began to wonder where my values and principles had come from. I thought back to what I'd learnt in Sunday School. I'd been taught that God was a jealous God who punished the wicked. What would that God think of my violence? What had that violence achieved? It hadn't brought justice or peace, and I was now becoming aware of the pain it had brought not only to people I hated but also to those I loved.

When I came before my Maker, I was no longer sure that I could claim he was on my side.

Four years into my sentence, I began to want something different than a life dominated by violence and revenge. I also wanted a change from the mundane routine of life in the compounds. I'd moved at different times from one compound to another, usually as a means of meeting new men, and hearing different conversations. I was restless, eager for more knowledge and seeking a reason to live that wasn't centred upon fighting. This realisation came gradually. It culminated in me encountering God in a new way and having a sense of salvation that I still remember as a very real experience, even though today I would not call myself a Christian. The following extracts from a testimony I wrote towards the end of 1980 give some indication of my thoughts at the time:

> It is eleven months now since God first saved me from sin, January 1980. He opened my heart to the gospel of Jesus Christ and gave me eternal life ... This is not a testimony as to how Alistair Little found Christ in prison. Nor is it a testimony as to how a convicted terrorist got religion and turned over a new leaf. It is a testimony of how God revealed Himself to me a sinner and hell-deserving creature, and drew me to Himself,
>
> > Nothing in my hand I bring
> > Simply to thy cross I cling
> > Naked come to thee for dress
> > Helpless look to thee for grace
> > Foul, I to the fountain fly
> > Wash me Saviour or I die.
>
> It is five years since as a lad of seventeen I was arrested, charged and convicted of murder. Being too young to receive a life sentence I was sentenced to be detained during the pleasure of the Secretary of State and sent to HMP Maze ...
>
> The hatred that exists between Roman Catholics and Protestants has nothing whatever to do with the teachings of their churches, and few young people who become involved in the Troubles have any real notion of a religious or political ideal ... I pray that God's people will get down on their knees and pray without ceasing for a revival of true Christianity in this land. For God said that, 'If my people who are called by my name shall humble themselves and con-

91

fess their sins and turn from their wicked ways, then I will hear from heaven and heal their land' ...

In spite of the many activities – handicrafts, education, physical training etc., which special prisoners can participate in, there is still an abundance of time in which prisoners, especially young prisoners like myself, can think and reflect on times past, present and future. Reflecting on my early teens and later years, I soon realised the waste of it all. I had it seemed wasted my young days – the best years of my life. I realised too, that many of the things of life one takes for granted became important to me. Things which I could no longer enjoy or hope to enjoy – walking over green fields in freedom, enjoy- ing the companionship and conversation of my family and friends, planning for such future things as marriage and raising a family – all these things and many more were suddenly denied to me. The way I was thinking showed just how empty my ideals really were. And far from thinking of how best I could help my former cause while in prison, my thoughts were centred on how I could make up for these wasted years. My daily thoughts became self-centred and the only thing I cared about was to be free and to plan how best I could enjoy myself and make up for the years I'd lost out on. After about four years of such thinking I became interested in things outside myself. 'Surely,' I asked myself, 'there must be something better to life than the life I had been living and to the life I was planning on living when I got out. There had to be something better than just existing for one's own good.' Just about this period, several of my fellow prisoners had become Christians. One had been a Christian for five years. While this had been an excuse for the rest of us to have a good laugh, somewhere deep down I knew they were right and that God did exist. I could outwardly laugh at the idea of hardened terrorists, including men serving life sentences, giving their lives over to God, yet I knew there was something true about the whole thing ... The Spirit of God who was working upon the hearts and lives of my fel- low prisoners used their experiences to bring to life His words that I had listened to as a child. Now I wanted to know the answers to it all. One of these Christians, R. G. by name, lived in the same hut as me and, as we had opportunities to talk I began to ask him why he had decided to become a Christian.

Even though his answers were not well set out in definite terms, I continued to speak to him about God and the Bible. I asked him dozens of questions which he was not able to answer, and while I may have wondered at what sort of Christian he was ... the Lord still led me to talk to him and to think hard on the things of God ... As my talks with R. G. continued he was able to go to other Christians and discuss with them many of the questions and problems which I had been putting to him ... The Jesus in whom R. G. believed was now becoming more real to me and in an effort to find out more about him I began to read a little paperback ... which R. G. had given me ... Although simple to read the material of this book was frightening to me and caused me great concern. It was frightening in the fact that God used it to prove to my heart that He did in fact exist and that not only did he exist but that Satan existed as well ... He used this book to show me that he cared for sinners such as me and that He was ready and able to save all that came to Him through faith in Jesus Christ. Frightened at the prospect of spending eternity in hell, I became concerned about my soul's salvation and began to read the New Testament scriptures to see what they had to say on the matter.

Every evening in the secrecy of my cubicle I ... read the words of Christ and His apostles. As I say, I did so in secrecy because I was afraid of what other people would say if they caught me reading the Bible. It is strange how people who have been used to acting and talking tough can be so afraid of the comments of other people. I guess that is because most people are of the opinion that becoming a Christian is a sign of weakness. If only mockers would look at the lives of the early Christians who gave their lives rather than renounce their faith in Christ. If only they knew the suffering that Christians in communist countries go through because of their faith in Christ Jesus ... As I read my way through the gospels and epistles the Spirit of God moved upon me ... Left to my own devices I would no doubt have kept resisting the Spirit and kept putting off the day of decision, but I think that God in His sovereign grace and mercy extended to me His irresistible call, regenerated me and granted unto me saving faith, and the grace for repentance of life ...

My testimony contained all the enthusiasm, intensity and piety of a new convert. It marked a major shift in my perceptions about my past, and what I believed about God. The book R. G. gave me talked about individual responsibility, and demolished my belief that as Protestants we had a special relationship with God. According to the author of the book, John Blanchford, God didn't have favourites. He treated everyone the same way. The book gave lots of scriptural references. I had both it and a Bible hidden behind a newspaper, so that the man in the bunk below me wouldn't see me reading them. I knew only too well the accusation, 'Ah, you've turned to Christianity because you're weak and you can't do your time.' Maybe there was an element of truth in that, a desire for a little comfort, but I also felt that if God was against me, I was in real difficulty. I wanted him to love me, so I got into bargaining with him, thinking that's how God operates: *I've read a couple of chapters of your Word, Lord. That must be a good thing, worth a few brownie points.* It took me a while to realise that's not how faith works.

I tried to stop cursing, which was hard. Every other word at the time would have been 'fuck'. That was partly habit and partly how the harder men talked – with the exception of leaders like Gusty. He didn't like that sort of language. He saw it as unnecessary and inappropriate.

My belief in a God who'd punish me to eternal damnation in hell if I didn't turn to him, disturbs some of my friends today who know about this part of my story. They're more drawn to images of a loving God. My God was not without love, but in my world of violence, where talk and actions were harsh, it took a tough image of God to effect change in my life. As I wrote to a woman friend, E., at the time:

> ... the more I read, E., the more I wanted to know about God because deep down inside of myself I had a fear of God ... I didn't have any trouble in being able to forget about my fear but I was scared this time because I knew that somewhere God was watching what I was doing with my life and that someday I would have to answer for all the things that I had done. That's when I started thinking about Hell. Then I was afraid of going to sleep in case I didn't wake up, but E., I'm really thankful to God that I was afraid cause I knew that I needed JESUS ...

The peace of mind that came with my conversion experience shouldn't be underestimated. I've looked back longingly to it on many occasions since, but there's no going back. I can't unlearn what I now know. Even then I didn't simply accept my new-found faith without question. I wondered about the strength of it, and whether it was simply a crutch to help me through prison life. Would it stand up to the greater challenge of another environment? This question combined with the boredom I felt in the compounds, and the growing realisation that my sentence might last longer than I'd originally thought, prompted me to think about transferring not to another compound, but to the 'H' Blocks in the Maze Prison.

The authenticity of my faith was also questioned by the prison officers. I had never, as an individual, caused trouble to staff while I was in the compounds, but as a Governor wrote in one regular report about me after my conversion:

> We are not in a position to verify whether the process of maturation has led to change in attitude; we cannot verify if his religious experience is genuine, but we do know that he still wishes to be located in the UVF compound.
>
> I would be more convinced of this 'new man' had he dissociated himself from his previous life by leaving the compound situation. It could be said that he has opted for the easy course and in such a situation one has to question his motivation. At this stage more positive evidence of change is needed.

I, too, needed such evidence and finally asked to be moved to the 'H' Blocks. On the surface this seemed a crazy idea. After I was sentenced in 1976, I'd lived in just a blanket and my underpants for some weeks because I refused to wear the prison uniform of what were known as Ordinary Decent Criminals. I'd made a point of applying for 'special category status'. Ever since the Secretary of State for Northern Ireland had announced at the end of 1975 that 'special category status' was to cease, paramilitaries who saw themselves as political prisoners had protested. There'd been riots and hijackings in the weeks following the announcement. The IRA had murdered prison officers in protest. Republican prisoners and a small number of Loyalist prisoners had refused to wear prison uniform and worn only a bed blanket.

The involvement of Loyalist prisoners in the blanket protest caused some problems for Loyalist leaders outside the prison. It looked as though the Loyalist prisoners were supporting the Provisional IRA, although the matter wasn't simply a Republican issue, and they received little support from the wider Unionist community.

In March 1978 the Republican prisoners began a 'dirty protest' in the 'H' Blocks. They refused to wash, clean out their cells and empty their chamber-pots. They tipped the contents of the latter out of their cell doors. The screws had to clear it up.

In March 1981, five years to the day since 'special category status' came into practice, Bobby Sands, Commanding Officer of the Provisional IRA in the Maze, began a hunger strike. He died on 5 May. The next day

I was being taken in a van to the visitor block. There were screws with me. They were laughing about the death of Bobby Sands, rubbing their hands together and joking about when the other hunger strikers would kick the bucket. I was furious.

'Don't you ever fucking talk like that in front of me again! Bobby Sands had more fucking courage than you'll ever have.'

Later that night, as I lay on my bunk, I wondered why I'd stood up for Bobby Sands. We were enemies. If we'd met in the street we'd have tried to kill each other. Yet I couldn't deny the courage of his protest. It was the first time I'd consciously attributed a human quality to my enemy. This recognition of my enemy's humanity was a turning point for me. I felt I wanted to know more about the people I hated. There was little chance of doing that in the compounds.

While the prison authorities allowed it, our COs had face to face meetings with the COs of the Republican cages, but the only contact I had with the Provies was during football matches. As in Crumlin Road Prison, the Loyalist and Republican COs had agreed a 'no-conflict' policy while we were in prison. The Provies' compounds bordered the football pitch, and they'd sit and watch our games. Some conversation went on through the wire, and we exchanged the handicrafts we made. We did a lot of leather-work. They were into making harps. Apart from these brief encounters there was little opportunity for further contact.

Restless with compound life, secure in the belief that if I did what was right, God would look after me, keen to test out my new-found faith, and seeking to know more about my enemy, in October 1981 I signed away my 'special category status' and transferred out of the cages. The move heralded a time when I'd lose my faith, sink to the depths of despair and depend on hate to get me through the hell that was life in the 'H' Blocks.

Chapter 10

My God, my God, why hast thou forsaken me?
Why art thou so far from helping me and from the
words of my roaring?

Psalm 22:1

1981–86

'Get up, Little. The Governor wants to see you.'

'Fuck the Governor!'

I was lying on the wooden slats that were all that remained during the day of my punishment-cell bed. I'd no intention of seeing this Governor. He'd refused to see me when I'd asked to speak to him about getting exercise in the punishment wing. Now there were five screws in my cell. They grabbed me and started ripping off my clothing. I remember screaming and yelling and trying to bite them. I'd got past caring. I knocked two of them down, but another caught a fistful of my hair and hauled me through the wing to the Governor's office. As we went I could hear other prisoners banging on their doors and shouting at the screws to leave me alone. I was thrown down onto the floor in front of the Governor's desk. I refused to talk to him.

'You're just an old donkey, Little. Stubborn as a mule. Get back to your cell.'

'You carried me down here. You can carry me back.'

The screws grabbed my heels and dragged me back to my cell, my head banging against the floor as we went.

I should say at this point that a number of prison officers in the Maze were known as 'Governor'. When assistant governors were in charge, they were also called 'Governor'. It was less of a mouthful. Governors came and went in what seemed to us like the blink of an eye. In this chapter, when I use the title, it can mean one of any number of men. Some of them did their job with integrity, while others wielded their power less well.

The first intimation I had of how bad life in the 'H' Blocks would be came when I arrived from the compounds. I was pushed into a cubicle and told to put on some civilian-style clothes. The screw processing me half-smiled as he said, 'So, Little, things are going to be very different from now on. You're not "special" any more, and we'll be "looking after" you.'

His tone of voice made me wonder what I'd let myself in for. At that stage few men moved voluntarily from the compounds to 'H' Blocks. Some prisoners who'd been ejected from the compounds by the commanding officers had no choice but to go there. Others, like me, who wanted a change of scene at the human level, were sometimes given stick for moving. The numbers in the compounds were slowly decreasing because no more prisoners were sent there after 'special category status' ceased to be granted. Those who voluntarily gave up that status were seen by some as betraying a hard-won battle: Gusty had been instrumental in fighting for and negotiating political status for both Loyalist and Republican prisoners. Practically speaking, the fewer the men in the compounds, the harder it was to argue for that part of the prison to remain in operation. Eventually the Northern Ireland Office closed the cages, but only after the men who were still there negotiated to have their own segregated wing and 'special category status' privileges in the 'H' Blocks. That was a while after I'd moved across.

I spent five years in the 'H' Blocks. It was a frightening, degrading and turbulent time. My memories are jumbled, perhaps reflecting the chaos and trauma of those years. Rarely did I feel safe.

There were decent screws who were friendly, and some who, if nothing more, made sure you received what was rightfully yours. Others were brutal. I hated them as they hated me. Looking back, I think that they, like us, were in some ways victims of a brutalising system. At the time they were simply bastards with the power to make prison life unbearable. In later years, when I was running storytelling workshops bringing people together from all sides of the conflict, a prison officer asked me to call at his house to talk with him because he couldn't sleep. Some of the things he'd been involved with while on duty in the Maze, such as beating prisoners, were keeping him awake. It was then I realised how dehumanising the prison system in the 'H' Blocks was, not only for prisoners, but for staff as well.

When the Secretary of State for Northern Ireland announced the removal of 'special category status' at the end of 1975, his purpose was to de-legitimise those of us who saw ourselves as political prisoners.

Prison officers were instructed to treat those convicted of paramilitary activity as criminals. In the compounds where the last 'special category' prisoners lived, and the screws had little to do with our daily lives, we were protected, by and large, from the tensions that raged in the 'H' Blocks in the years following the Secretary of State's announcement. We didn't experience first-hand the 'blanket' and 'dirty' protests that went on through the latter half of the 1970s, but our compound leaders did get involved in speaking out against what was happening.

By criminalising paramilitary prisoners, the government were also able to force the integration of Loyalist and Republican prisoners. The effect was disastrous. While I was in the compounds a statement signed by the five Loyalist and Republican paramilitary leaders of the cages was smuggled out of Long Kesh with the intention of helping the general public understand the issues. It explored the arguments for and against the segregation we'd been advocating since January 1977. It made a number of obvious, but largely ignored points:

It is unreasonable to suggest that prisoners who have had little or no contact with each other in normal life, and have opposed each other in extreme violence on our streets, can suddenly live in peace and harmony with one another, simply because they find themselves in jail. Separate adolescence, separate places of entertainment, separate ghettos, separate schools and in many cases, separate employment environs – and then out of the blue thrown together in jail!

What do the Government expect or did they anticipate the violence between Loyalist and Republican and salve their consciences by thinking it is only the Irish having a go at one another! If integration is to come about it must be sought by the prisoners themselves, and it must be a gradual process, just like what Mr Mason is trying to do with the politicians. Was it not he who declared the people of Ulster must help themselves and come together? Are prisoners not people?

In Long Kesh we, Republicans and Loyalists, have attempted to bridge the gap by engaging in constructive dialogue without conceding principles, but now the Government no longer permits our representatives to meet and discuss our mutual problems – what does the Government want exactly? In this camp we have a 'no-conflict' policy in operation firmly agreed and reaffirmed from time to time. And for almost 5 years that peace has held despite being firmly tested on several occasions. As a result not one sectarian blow has been struck one upon the other. The prison authorities played no part in making the peace except to accommodate a series of face-to-face meetings. It is the most natural thing in the world for people with different political, cultural and religious philosophies and affiliations to cling together in time of adversity.

From EPIC Research Document No. 1, *The Prison Experience –
A Loyalist Perspective* by Marion Green, p. 25.

The criminalisation and forced integration of political prisoners seriously set back the voluntary dialogue that had quietly been going on between Republican and Loyalist leaders in prison. It also made conversations between rank-and-file prisoners across the dividing line almost impossible. I moved to the 'H' Blocks because I wanted to make tentative steps away from my past violence, and have more engagement with my enemy. The reality of life in the 'H' Blocks meant that in order to survive, my UVF identity had to remain strong simply because forced integration put many of us into positions of danger. If we hadn't been obviously aligned to our own organisation we'd have risked assault from another one, and a man exploring new ways of being was vulnerable to attack not only from his enemy, but also from men from his own side who still espoused violence and saw those moving away from it as guilty of weakness and betrayal.

During my early days in the 'H' Blocks, the conforming wings were made up largely of Loyalist prisoners. There were unwritten rules accepted for the benefit of both Loyalist and Republican prisoners. These ensured that although there were tensions, friction and fighting were generally avoided.

Initially I had a cell of my own, but due to overcrowding I sometimes had to share. My cell door was opened at 7 a.m. each day. After slopping out, showering and shaving, I went to breakfast in the canteen. Then I was locked up again for the head count. After the head count, men were allowed to associate in the canteen or outside, or we could go in and out of each other's cells. We were locked up again for another head count before lunch at noon. Following lunch, we were locked up again until 2 p.m. Then we were let out for exercise in the yard, or social time in the canteen. At 3.30 we were locked up for yet another head count before tea at 4. There was another head count after tea. After that we were let out one final time until 7 or 8, when we were locked up until the next morning.

It took some time for me to adjust to my new way of life. Making friends helped a great deal. I'd become used to the lack of privacy in the compounds and the constant presence of men around me. Here I was on my own much more. Noise was far more intrusive because the prison wings echoed, and at all hours of the day there was the sound of cell doors and security gates clanking open and banging shut, and raised voices startling the silence. I'd exchanged the atmosphere of a prisoner-of-war camp for the highly charged atmosphere of sworn enemies forced to live together in an environment designed to disempower and humiliate them. There were always tensions, if not between Loyalist and Republican prisoners, then with the screws.

The latter could change the daily routine at a moment's notice. I might be waiting to go down to the yard for exercise, only to be told it had been cancelled due to staff shortages, or because a search was in process. These searches happened all the time. The screws were looking for razor blades or Stanley knives – the commonest things to go missing – or for weapons, explosives and bullets. The search team, which always came from another wing, strip-searched everyone. They were verbally abusive. When I was told to 'bend over and spread your cheeks', I'd be vulgar with them to cover my own embarrassment and humiliation. 'Do you get a kick out of this?' I would ask. 'Does it turn you on?' Humiliation seemed to be the name of the game, and small issues could loom large in a place where everyday decisions about our lives were determined by others.

When I first went over to the 'H' Blocks, laundry was changed once a week. We were supposed to send down socks and underwear along with our sheets, shirts and trousers. Unlike our shirts and trousers, socks and underwear didn't have an identifying number on them, so when they came back you didn't necessarily get your own. As a result, many of us preferred to wash socks and underwear by hand, and dry them on the heating bars in our cells. This wasn't permitted in the rules. Some screws turned a blind eye to it, but others would put us on a charge for doing it. Trying to talk things through with these men didn't work, so we gave any screw who made an issue of the matter a really hard time. In fact, if we felt any of our group was being picked on by a screw, we didn't leave it to the individual concerned to sort it out, but ganged up together against that prison officer. For our own survival we had to work together to make sure the bullies among the prison staff knew that there were limits beyond which they couldn't go. The system forced men into pack behaviour.

Even supposedly positive pursuits, like that of education, had the potential to be used against prisoners. In 1982 Loyalist prisoners collectively went on protest. At the time some of us were completing courses.

I'd been studying History, English and Religious Education. When the exams came up one of the Governors called me in to say that I couldn't do them unless I came off the protest. Our education was used as a blackmail tool, so we said, 'Stick it!' Our teachers were furious.

That situation also illustrates another point. However important it was to me as an individual to do the exams, personal attempts to change my own life were subject to collective priorities. If I'd refused to join the group action, I'd have become open to attack from other men in the group, or I'd have been left on my own to deal with abusive screws or Republican prisoners on the look-out for vulnerable Loyalist prisoners.

On a more minor scale, prisoners were allowed to have only three books in their cells at any one time. If I had four, I was charged with having contraband. Hardback books weren't permitted at all because they were regarded as potential weapons. I had a Bible and a biblical commentary that I'd only been able to keep because the censors had ripped off the hard covers.

When I was reading about China as part of my exploration of international conflict, I'd asked my parents to send in Mao Tse Tung's *Little Red Book*. Then I was told I couldn't have it because it was considered dangerous material. However, when my parcel from home came up that night, the *Little Red Book* was in it. Later the screws came in and repeated the prohibition about my book. When I said I'd already received it, they demanded that I hand it over. By that time I'd passed it on to one of the other guys. The screws tore my cell apart trying to find it. I ended up in the punishment block for three days because I wouldn't give it up. They searched the whole wing and there was uproar. Sammy, a prisoner from Portadown, wanted the prisoners to wreck the wing in protest, but our leaders wouldn't allow such extreme action over the issue of a book. Eventually I was able to read the *Little Red Book*. Ironically, after all the mayhem provoked by its presence on the wing, I found it rather boring!

The censors stamped any books that passed inspection. Here too, there were opportunities to wield power against us. Some deliberately stamped over the text so we couldn't read the words, or they ripped out the final pages so we didn't have the ending. It was petty and provocative, but in prison such seemingly small things could blow up into violence because men were struggling to keep some sense of dignity and refused to give in to institutional abuses.

On another occasion, all my letters disappeared. We were allowed to keep only so much mail in our cells. The rest had to be destroyed or put into our 'Property'. When our visitors came we signed out what was in our 'Property' box and they took it home. I signed out a large amount of mail, but my parents never received it. They were told it couldn't be found. When I went to one of the Governors to complain, he said, 'The letters don't belong to you because they have a stamp with Her Majesty's head on it, so they belong to the State.'

I was furious, and I felt so powerless. When I returned to my cell I wrecked it completely. I cut up the mattress and carpet with a razor blade. Feathers flew everywhere. I ended up 'on the boards' in the punishment wing – so called because every day at 6.30 a.m. the screws would remove the bed mattress, leaving the slatted wooden bed frame that stood just a few inches off the concrete floor. If there was a decent screw on duty, he'd let me out for an hour's exercise. Otherwise I was locked up for 24 hours a day, apart from slopping out and going to the toilet.

Breakfast in the punishment wing consisted of a bowl of cornflakes, and two rounds of bread covered in thick globs of cooking margarine. This was rounded off with a cup of tea that was stewed to death because it'd been sitting in the urn for so long. Lunch arrived on a plastic plate divided into sections for the meat and the vegetables. Dessert was lumpy custard and sponge-cake. The evening meal consisted of a cup of tea, soggy chips and food that had been cooked to death. Supper was a cup of tea and a piece of left-over sponge-cake spread with jam to cover the dried-out bits. Apart from the bed and a Bible, there was only a water container and a pot for peeing in these cells. No other books or newspapers. No radio. Nothing. The cells were also freezing cold. During another spell 'on the boards', I remember shivering uncontrollably and calling for the doctor. He came, looked into the cell for no more than a couple of seconds, and said it was fine. In frustration I swore at him, 'Fuck off, you old bastard!'

I ended up charged with another offence against prison discipline. It was because I refused to plead guilty or sign a statement about this that I was then summoned to the Governor's office, as I described at the beginning of this chapter. By that stage I'd become so despairing about my situation that I didn't give a damn what happened.

A lot of the time I was 'on the boards', I lay on the planks in a foetal position covered with my coat – that was something I always grabbed when I knew I was about to be hauled off to the punishment wing – in an attempt to keep warm and shut out the light. Then I'd try to sleep. Often it was too cold for that, but the position felt comforting. I'd pass the time by reading the Bible, or developing games. I'd count the cracks or the half-bricks in the wall. I'd do press-ups and run on the spot. Even so, there was far too much time to dwell on stuff I wanted to forget.

While 'on the boards' we were allowed only one visit a month. We also lost our entitlement to tuck-shop goods. What usually happened when we returned to our normal cell was that other guys on the wing had put some of their tuck aside for us – crisps and chocolate bars – and it would be waiting in a box on our beds. Solitary confinement lasted anything from 3 to 30 days. The longest time I did was 14.

There was another prisoner who frequently ended up 'on the boards'. I remember a time when he did 30 days, came back to the wing for a day, and then went back to the punishment block for another 30 days. He was a really tough guy called Victor. He went to the Governor, regularly asking to go into solitary confinement just to get space to sort out his head. The Governor said that couldn't be done: the punishment wings were for punishment. So Victor went back to his cell and smashed it all up. He packed his gear and waited for the screws to come.

When they saw what he'd done, they said, 'Right, you're going to the punishment block.'

'Thank you,' he said. 'If you'd put me down there when I asked, I wouldn't have had to wreck my cell.'

Few men actively sought out time 'on the boards', but as a result of going on protest in the latter half of 1982, Loyalist prisoners *en masse* ended up in the punishment block or, when that was full, on other wings temporarily taken over for that purpose. The problem leading to our protest had its roots in the days following the end of the Republican hunger strikes and 'dirty protests'. The numbers of Republicans on the mixed wings suddenly increased, so that they soon became the dominant group, and few of them wanted to be with Loyalist prisoners. The relative 'peace' of the conforming wings was shattered by this imbalance of power and increased antagonism. Life for Loyalist prisoners became more dangerous. On one wing, for example, only five of us were Loyalists – three UVF men and two UDA. The rest were Republicans. We had to go to the toilets and showers as a group. While one man showered the others would look out for him. One day we were in the canteen and the other four men were called away for visits. I was the only one left watching television. Two Provies came up, swinging their tea-cups and threatening to throw scalding water at me from the boiler. I stayed where I was. When my CO came back from his visit, the Provies called him over and told him to get me out of the canteen, or 'we're going to do him'.

On another occasion I was sent to a wing with another man where we were the only Loyalists sharing with 28 Republican prisoners. I was friendly at the time with a senior prison officer, a Scotsman called S.. On my way down to the wing he said, 'Alistair, they [the Government] are looking for a dead body, so that they can separate Loyalist and Republicans for safety reasons rather than on political grounds. Watch yourself. There's not a lot we can do for you.'

There wasn't much I could do either, except put a plastic knife below the lock of my cell so that the Republicans couldn't break in. Simple tasks like leaving the cell to slop out, wash, eat and exercise became edged with fear. My fear at that time was expressed in a petition I submitted to the Secretary of State via the Northern Ireland Office in August 1982:

> Sir,
>
> I have seen over the past few months an increase in hostilities towards Loyalist prisoners, from Republicans. I have personally been approached by Republican prisoners and feel that my life is in danger.
>
> I have been informed by A.G. [Assistant Governor + name] that there is no way that he can guarantee my safety ... I am at present being told when to wash, where to go for my association [social time] etc. I have accepted this only because I have no choice as failing to do so would result in my life being under immediate threat from Republican prisoners. This has put me ... under a lot of psychological pressure which is continuing with each passing day, and will go on until someone is killed, and with large numbers of Republicans moving into the blocks it means that as time passes Loyalist prisoners will be most likely the prisoners who will be killed. Republicans are becoming more violent towards me personally and I have been watching out for my own safety but the options I have are limited ... Republicans have stated that they have complete freedom within this prison to kill a Loyalist prisoner at any time they so desire and may take revenge on Loyalist prisoners because of the deaths of the hunger strikers. This would force Loyalists to lock up ... [i.e. to be locked in their cells for safety].

This had happened in the Crumlin Road Prison in 1978. Four Loyalist remand prisoners were taken to the prison hospital suffering from starvation because for fourteen days, fearing attack from Republican prisoners, they'd refused to leave their cells for meals.

I'm not saying that intimidation and violence came only from the Republican prisoners. Loyalists were equally capable of that, given the 'right' circumstances. It's simply that at that time the increasing numerical domination of the wings by Republican prisoners inevitably meant the threat was more against one side than the other. Those Republicans who'd rubbed along with us without too much friction when our numbers were more even, withdrew from us once we became the minority. That was understandable. Group pressure made it hard for any man to do anything that wasn't approved of by the group.

Segregation, such as I'd requested, wasn't a route the authorities wanted to go down. By October 1982 concerns about safety and security had become so bad that many of us were kept locked in our cells for our own safety, unable to eat in the canteen or mix with one another. Our COs decided that collective action should be taken. So began the Loyalist Protest that continued throughout 1983 and into 1984. We smashed up our cells, destroying everything in them. The punishment wing filled up with Loyalists. When there was no more room on that wing, the prison authorities removed the beds from cells in some of the other wings, leaving just the mattresses, and ran these cells as punishment units. The result of this action was that we were now effectively segregated from Republican prisoners – exactly what we wanted! However, it also meant that for what I remember as being about a year or more, we were locked up every other day for 23 hours a day, with no visits, no newspapers, no tuck shop, and no other rights. Every 28 days we were brought before the Governor and asked if were going to conform or not. If we refused to talk or said 'No!' we lost 14 days' remission. That's illegal today, because in effect what the prison authorities were doing was adding to our sentences. For prisoners with set sentences or those coming to the end of their sentence, this was a really difficult time. For people like me who had no fixed sentence, it didn't really matter. There were about 60 of us in that position.

On one occasion I was taken to the Governor. There was a screw standing by his side, and three around me. I stood with my hands in my pockets.

'Take your hands out of your pockets and say "Sir" when you speak to the Governor,' I was told.

I didn't move or speak. One of the screws tried to pull my hands out, so I squared up to him and immediately I was put on a charge. But where could they put me? I was already in the punishment block.

'I don't even call my father, "Sir", so I'm not going to call you that,' I said.

When I was told that they were taking 14 days off my remission, I said,

'Fourteen days? Why don't you just take off 28? Why not give me another six months?'

Their threats didn't mean anything.

Reading my prison records recently, I noticed how all the offences I committed against prison discipline happened between 1982 and 1984. Looking back, I felt so brutalised by the system in the 'H' Blocks that I responded like a trapped and wounded animal. I went on the attack. I hadn't got anything to lose. I was a 'lifer' without a minimum sentence. While some prisoners found me to be a sympathetic listener and a good friend, I didn't give an inch to screws who were heavy-handed.

Through those years my prison reports reflect the conflicting experiences prison officers had of me. At regular intervals reports would be gathered from the Governor, the Assistant Governor, the Chief Officer, the Industrial Officer, the Education Officer and the Medical Officer. My disrespectful attitude to staff is constantly highlighted in these documents, but sometimes the opinions of staff conflicted with each other. In the mid-year reports of 1983 the Assistant Governor commented: 'There has been a marked improvement in his attitude and behaviour ... He would appear now to be making a genuine effort to impress all concerned that he is a changed man ...' But the Governor stated: 'Little's behaviour in recent months has not been as good as has been suggested in this report.'

For some officers I was 'very intelligent'. For others I had 'little intelligence'. Some described me as getting on well with fellow prisoners and mixing with men from both communities, while others thought I had difficulty with prisoners from either side. One officer described me as a 'loner'. Some saw me as 'lazy', others as 'eager to work'. While these judgements inevitably reflect something of the relationship I had with the officer concerned, they also indicate the turmoil I felt in the 'H' Blocks, and the conflict I had between wanting to live as a good Christian while trying to survive the brutality of life in the Blocks.

This struggle is expressed in a petition I submitted to the Secretary of State in July 1983 during the Loyalist Protest. It was my second request within four months to be transferred to the Crumlin Road Prison:

> ... I am at present a N.C.P. [Non-Conforming Prisoner] which I do not wish to be. I do not want to be on any form of protest. The only reason I am an N.C.P. is because I felt I was in danger ... I left the compound side of the Maze to break away from paramilitary involvement altogether. As a Christian I have no desire to be part of any paramilitary organisation ... I came to the H Blocks with the

intention of conforming to prison rules. If I could be sure of my safety I would not be here on this protest …

I'd arrived in the 'H' Blocks looking to continue my journey of discovery and personal transformation. Within a short time I'd become an angry and hate-filled man. Hard as it is to understand, it was hate that enabled me to survive. Hate is a powerful energy, and I needed that kind of energy to get me through. But hate is an exhausting and destructive emotion. My time in the 'H' Blocks was complicated further by migraine headaches, insomnia and outbursts of temper. I was furious with this system that couldn't recognise and support anyone who was trying to move away from violence, and didn't care what happened to people.

That's why Mrs Blackthorn and Marty Rafferty are so important in my story. Marty saw something in me that most of the prison officers couldn't see. Neither could I, for that matter. Marty was a Quaker working in the Visitor Centre of the prison. At one point while I was in the 'H' Blocks there was a big dispute going on about visits being cancelled, and greater restrictions being applied to visits. Some guys on controlled visits had been caught trying to smuggle notes in and out. As a punishment for this, a Perspex screen had been fixed between visitors and prisoners. Marty had come in to hear our complaints. She talked about education and conflict and about trying to get better facilities.

At one point I interrupted her: 'That's a load of fucking bollocks. Know what I mean? Coming in here and talking this shit! You've no idea what's fucking going on.'

Other prisoners tried to quieten me down, saying, 'It's not her fault.'

But I was full of venom. Later I learned that Marty had asked the prison officer who I was. 'That's your man, Little. Do you hear the hatred and bitterness in him? He's a nasty piece of work.'

'That's not what I hear,' replied Marty. 'I hear pain and hurt.'

When I heard this, I was blown away. I wondered what she was talking about. How could she see those things? I didn't want anyone saying stuff like that about me. They were weak things. Pain and hurt? What pain and hurt? It's hatred, that's what it is! Hate is much easier to sustain than to treat with humanity people who are hurting you. On the one hand I was filled with hatred, bitterness and violent thoughts. On the other hand these were the very reactions I wanted to escape. It was deeply confusing.

For much of the time I functioned on the fuel of hatred. I had wanted to live a better life, but coming to the 'H' Blocks had set me right back.

However, at night, when my cell door was closed and the darkness took over, I connected with a different part of myself. I can best illustrate this by describing another encounter I had with Mrs Blackthorn, and its impact on me. I was 'on the boards' at the time she came to see me.

'I'll be fine on my own. You can go,' she said to the screw who'd let her in. 'I've just come to check if you're all right,' she said to me. 'I heard you were in the punishment block. I see you're still getting into trouble.'

'Ach, you know what it's like.'

'I have a story for you, Alistair. Do you remember when you snatched my bag of leaflets at the Community Centre?'

It wasn't a memory I cared to recall.

'Well, I didn't tell you before, that you broke my finger at that time. It healed, but with a buckle in it – a lump. The strange thing is, as I went around all the Army camps in Northern Ireland, that finger helped me explain the gospel to the soldiers. I talked to them about how Christ was broken on the cross for their sins. That didn't make much sense to them, so I used to hold up my crooked finger and say how it'd been broken and twisted for their sakes. I told them it had happened while I was handing out leaflets about what they were doing, and asking people to pray for them. You know, that made some of them cry and some of them angry. But Alistair, I could never bring myself to tell them that it happened on a *Protestant* housing estate.'

When I heard this story I felt huge embarrassment, and then I felt fear. Here was a wee servant of God, and I'd done that to her. I wondered where that put me in relation to God. That night I read my Bible and I told God I was sorry, that I regretted what I'd done to her, and begged for forgiveness. Suddenly I had this deeper insight into myself:

'I'm not what I project. Why am I afraid of myself? Why am I afraid to let anyone see me? I'm always putting out this tough image – *Don't mess with me!* – but here I am crying, pleading with God and saying I'm sorry because I hurt a wee old woman. What a fraud! What a hypocrite! I think I've got guts, but it's nothing compared to the courage of Mrs Blackthorn – standing for what she believes, no matter how hurt she gets. Why do I say I stand for all these political things, when inside there's someone different. I don't want this pain, this violence, this bravado. Why can't I be real? Why can't I be true?'

I can't remember any prisoner who didn't understand the kind of emotional extremes I'm describing. Some guys were far more violent than me. They planned on cutting people's throats. They hid tools to use as weapons. They hurled blocks of carbolic soap and scrubbing brushes at the screws' heads. They threw scalding water at them, and aimed darts into their necks. Then the mufti-squad would arrive in protective gear, and beat the daylights out of prisoners. Locked up in the canteen, we'd watch through the grilles as they laid into someone. Then we'd smash up the TVs, the sinks, the toilets and showers, and the prison officers would lock the doors and leave us to it until the riot squad arrived.

The 'H' Blocks were a place where men felt pushed to the extremes, and inhumanity was to be found not only among the prisoners, but also among those who guarded them. It was felt, for example, that one Governor sent down sex offenders onto the wing just to make the point that we weren't political prisoners. He knew that as soon as the sex offender arrived, the man would be severely beaten and put out of the wing, but he kept sending them down. Some screws kept sex offenders locked up for their own safety, but others didn't. Beating up sex offenders didn't solve the problem. Once they'd recovered from the beating, the Governor sent them back to the wing. As a result, some prisoners forced such men to eat razor blades covered in bread. When the bread dissolved in their stomachs, the razor blade would do its damage. As soon as a man had been forced to eat the razor blades, he pressed the alarm and had to be taken not only to the prison hospital, but also to the X-ray department outside the prison. The razors were surgically removed and the man never came back to the wing. Eventually, because this all involved too much work for the prison officers, the Governor stopped sending sex offenders down to us.

I remember one particular sex offender who'd been sent to the wing. The screws wouldn't remove him so some of the guys decided that the next morning they were going to beat him senseless when he came out of his cell. The same day a Methodist minister came to see me. I'd got to know him in the compounds. Although my faith had fallen apart in the 'H' Blocks, I was still quite friendly with him. While he was with me I told him about what the men planned to do. I had a real dislike of sex offenders, and I found it hard even to eat with them, but I didn't want the man to be beaten up. I think I was at a point when I was trying to find out if my faith was real in any way, and I wanted to salvage something of my humanity.

'The Governor knows what's going to happen,' I said. 'The screws know what's going to happen, but they just don't care.'

It took a while to convince him of this, but in the end he went to see the Governor. The Governor refused to take action.

'I'm telling you what's going to happen to him,' said the minister. 'I've been told he'll be beaten unconscious, possibly killed.'

'Who told you?' asked the Governor.

'I'm not prepared to say, but if I come in tomorrow and anything has happened to the man, I'll go to the media.'

'If you do that you'll be in trouble because you've signed the Official Secrets Act.'

'I don't care what I've signed. Conscience-wise and morally as a Christian minister, I'm obligated to state that I told you and you did nothing.'

That evening the sex offender was transferred out of the wing. The minister's courageous action helped me to think about the journey I was struggling to make, to feel that it was real and worthwhile. Throughout my time in the 'H' Blocks faith was hard to maintain. The feeling that it was a weakness was held far more strongly here than in the compounds. Some prisoners and the general public felt that men who came to faith in prison were just pretending in the hope of getting out earlier. I don't know any prisoner whose release date was influenced by his claim to be a Christian. A lot of critics later felt their position was justified because many men who'd been strong in faith in prison, lost their way when they were released, but pressures change and without support it's hard to maintain a way of life that's counter-cultural.

That was certainly my experience in the 'H' Blocks. I'd found it almost impossible to keep any spiritual values in an environment where survival seemed to demand the very opposite characteristics of those proclaimed by the gospel. One of the reasons I'd moved over to the 'H' Blocks was to test my faith, but my beliefs were naïve. I thought that if I did something to please God, everything would be fine. When the opposite happened, I felt God had let me down or wasn't real, or that I was doing something wrong. When we could, a few of us met in each other's cells to talk about the Bible and what it meant, but we had little formal guidance and training.

Communication of any kind was difficult while we were 'on protest'. That finally came to an end due to lack of success in the early months of 1984. In September 1983 there'd been a mass escape of Republican prisoners from H7. This seemed to reinforce the Government's argument for integration. The knock-on effect for Loyalist prisoners was that all handicraft facilities and equipment were taken out of the prison. Integration was immediately forced upon us, but as soon as prisoners from different communities confronted each other, there were fights and we had to be forcibly separated by the screws. Eventually forced integration was abandoned. Brutality in the Blocks began to ease. Staff moved on. Where prisoners from different sides met, it was on a more voluntary basis. The easing of tension gave more time to reflect rather than to react.

Throughout all the trauma of those years, and my own expressions of violence, verbal or physical, there was a deeper self wrestling with the issues, trying to find a way forward and to do something more than simply survive. It would be some years before his voice became stronger, but it was there. It can be seen in the petitions I wrote to the Secretary of State asking to be moved away from the 'H' Blocks, and in my coming off the Loyalist Protest in 1983 before it officially ended.

I was sent to H6, a mixed wing where there was a sufficient balance between the Loyalists and Republicans for a greater sense of safety to be felt. I was able to settle down. From that time the reports about me were much more positive.

While all this was going on in the 'H' Blocks, there was a group out-side who were actively seeking the release of men like me who'd been sentenced during the Secretary of State's Pleasure. There were 61 SOSPs, as we were called. All of us had been juveniles at the time of the actions for which we'd been brought to trial. As a result none of us had been given a minimum sentence. The mother of one of my co-defendants had set up a Relatives Support Group and for some years they'd been lobby-ing our MPs about the injustice of us not knowing for how long we were likely to be incarcerated. Adults with a fixed life sentence for murder had served shorter sentences than we had. My mother, who was a member of the group, had written not only to local MPs but in 1982 she'd also contacted the Prime Minister. That year David Bleakley, an MP from County Down, had taken up the issue with the Northern Ireland Office. In October the Secretary of State for Northern Ireland replied to him, saying:

[that he did] understand that the indefinite nature of this kind of sentence puts a considerable strain both on the inmate and on his family. However, that is unavoidable so long as life imprisonment, and in appropriate cases detention during pleasure, remain the sentences provided by the law.

All such sentences are reviewed periodically in the Northern Ireland Office in the light of all the relevant factors including, the circumstances of the crime, the prisoner's age and background, and the prison reports. Lord Gowrie who is directly responsible under me for prison matters, is reviewing these cases again at present and

I can assure you that we shall take into careful account the points which you and Mrs Little have made.

Very little must have changed, because Stephen Grimason reported in the *Sunday News* of 13 May 1984:

> Embittered relatives of Ulster's 'lost' prisoners are to take on the Northern Ireland Office.
>
> They claim young inmates detained at the Secretary of State's pleasure for murder have been lost in the red tape of an unjust system.
>
> 'We are not condoning what these young people did but what the NIO is doing on them now is a scandal,' said ... [the] secretary of the newly formed Detained SOSP Parents Association.

The mother of one of my co-defendants pointed out that the periodical reviews of those serving indeterminate sentences took prison reports into account. While we were in the compounds these reports couldn't be anything but inadequate, even where prisoners were co-operating with the system. The prison staff had very little contact with us, since each paramilitary organisation ran its own compounds.

By the time the *Sunday News* reported the situation, 30 members of the Parents' Association had met Assembly members at Stormont and enlisted the support of the DUP deputy leader, Peter Robinson and the Official Unionist, John Carson. Our parents were also trying to organise a meeting with the Prison Minister, Nicholas Scott.

As time passed there was general agreement across the communities that an injustice was being perpetrated here. Among the newspaper cuttings my Mum passed on to me after I came out of prison, there is one undated piece with the title, 'The killers who wait'. It reports that by that stage,

> Ken Magennis, the Official Unionist MP for Fermanagh/South Tyrone, succeeded in bringing the issue unto the floor of the House of Commons.
>
> He told shocked MPs of Ulster's two standards of justice – indefinite sentences for children and definite sentences for adults.
>
> The system was creating '60 Rudolph Hesses,' he claimed.
>
> This brought little positive response from Prisons Minister Nicholas Scott, although he stressed that each individual case was reviewed as it came up.

Harold McCusker, MP for Upper Bann, wrote to my Mum on 18 January 1985 in response to a letter she'd sent to him. He tells her that,

> As you know considerable efforts have been made over the past months on behalf of this category of prisoner and the Government appears to be responding sympathetically in public for the first time (they always did express concern in private).
>
> I shall write again to Nicholas Scott MP, the Prisons Minister, and I will let you have his reply as soon as possible ...

Eventually our parents' persistent campaigning finally paid off. In the House of Commons on 4 April 1985, Sir John Biggs-Davison raised the issue of the 61 men detained during the Secretary of State's pleasure, asking the Secretary of State to review their position. He was told:

> We are engaged now in the procedure of reviewing all those serving indeterminate sentences, as the appropriate time in their sentence is reached. The prisoners have the chance to put in written representations, and their cases are eventually discussed by a life sentence review board before being considered by Ministers. Already under that procedure 10 young prisoners have had dates fixed for their release, as well as three life sentence prisoners. That procedure will continue.
>
> My hon. friend has put his finger on a very important matter. In coming to these decisions, the possibility of re-offence, and thus the safety of the public, has to be at the forefront of our minds.

In response to this, Mr Hume of the SDLP said:

> The Minister is no doubt aware that the process that he mentioned for the setting of release dates for young prisoners held at the pleasure of the Secretary of State has been welcomed by representatives of all sides of the community. In the light of that, will he do his best to speed up the process?

The reply was cautious:

> We have to consider each of the cases very carefully on its merits, bearing in mind the time that the person has served, the degree of involvement in the original crime, and the behaviour of the prisoner

while in prison. The final, and in many ways the paramount, consideration has to be the likelihood of re-offence.

I wonder now how much longer I might have spent in prison if it hadn't been for the actions of my mother, the other relatives, and the MPs who supported them.

Looking at a press interview given by the Relatives Support Group around that time, I'm struck by a comment from Michael Warden, the Director of the Northern Ireland Association for the Care and Resettlement of Offenders (NIACRO). He said about those of us who'd been sent to prison as juveniles:

> It's inevitable that these people will encounter problems when released. They've lost the important and formative years of their lives.

That was an understatement. When I was released back into the community, I fully expected simply to go home and get on with the rest of my life. I'd barely been home for any time at all when disaster struck, and in a way I could never have imagined possible.

Chapter 11

There is nothing like returning to a place that remains unchanged to find the ways in which you yourself have altered.

Nelson Mandela

1986–88

I was playing football in the exercise yard when the Governor sent for me.

'How do you feel about getting out for a couple of days?'

'What do you want? Stop messing about with me.'

'No, I'm serious. You've been cleared for two days' parole.'

After almost ten years of imprisonment and a sentence that gave me no idea of how long I'd be locked up, this news knocked me for six. I returned to the yard, telling a friend from Portadown in passing that I was getting parole. Within minutes of rejoining the game, I was caught up in a fight. I was tackling one of the Republican prisoners and it got out of hand. Other prisoners broke us up. It was purely nerves on my part. I couldn't take in the sudden change in my position. When the fight blew up, the screw in the yard was going to press the alarm button, but my friend told him that I'd just been given parole. Thankfully, the officer had some understanding of the impact of that news, and held off raising the alarm. If he hadn't, I'd have lost my parole within minutes of learning about it.

I suspect that the possibility of release was more the result of politics than personal change. Although the prison reports indicate a significant and positive shift in my behaviour, the officers were unclear how deep the change actually went. Their recommendations urged caution in terms of a release date. Their uncertainty was perhaps understandable. I was wary about revealing to anyone how my thoughts and feelings had altered through the years of my imprisonment. I'm only glad that as a result of the campaigning spearheaded by the Detainees SOSP Parents Association it became politically expedient for the Northern Ireland Office to review our cases and to release those it considered appropriate.

The prospect of getting out, even for just a couple of days, filled me with more excitement than fear. At that stage I thought naively that there'd be nothing I couldn't change or overcome when I was released and back in control of my own life. I'd survived a lot in the Maze, so I felt there were no difficulties that could defeat me, no unknowns I couldn't get through. I had no sense that I might have problems getting employment, managing financially or developing relationships. My 'blindness' in this regard was shared by many prisoners. Perhaps it was accentuated in men like me who'd been sent to prison before they'd left home and learnt to stand financially on their own two feet. Inside the prison it was easy to lose sight of what life outside was like. Blocking out any thought of what went on beyond the walls of the Maze was a form of self-defence that enabled long-term prisoners to get through their sentences. We weren't responsible for providing food or shelter for ourselves. When we needed extra things, our families or friends sorted that out. I, for one, had little idea until I came out of prison just what that cost my parents. As far as I was concerned, they had their liberty. I didn't have mine. For that same reason many families didn't tell us how tough life was for them outside. They knew we couldn't do anything about it except worry. That's why they often kept silent about struggles back home.

All in all, I was completely unprepared for life beyond the Maze.

A friend picked me up from the prison. The first thing I did was to make him stop at a shop to buy an ice lolly – a huge cider-flavoured one that tasted fantastic. I gave him 50p to pay for it. He hesitated before going in to get it. When he came back I asked him why he'd paused.

'Alistair, 50p wouldn't buy you the stick.'

Already I was out my depth. For the next couple of days I lived on my nerves. There was so much to take in. I couldn't get over the colours. Prison is a very grey place. Outside, my senses were bombarded from every direction. In ten years fashions and styles had changed dramatically. Of course, we'd seen those changes on television, but it wasn't the same as experiencing them 'in the flesh'.

As we passed certain places on the way home, memories flooded back that I'd completely forgotten about. Seeing my old primary school reminded me of a time and a boy that I hardly recognised.

When I arrived home, the rooms felt claustrophobic. I'd only been a teenager the last time I'd seen them. It was like the feeling that friends today experience when they return after many years to their childhood haunts: all the places they remember being on a giant scale, now seem small. In prison many of the rooms were huge, catering as they did for large numbers of men. Even my cell, which was never cluttered because I was allowed to have so little in it, came to feel the right size.

During that first couple of days on parole, I couldn't sit still for longer than five minutes. I had to be up and about. There were laughter and tears and joy when I met my parents. Mum pulled out an old photograph album of when we'd all been together as a family. Looking at it made me cry. Mum thought she'd done something wrong.

'No, no, it's just everything happening at once,' I said. 'I can't take it in.'

But there was more to my reaction than that: the photos represented a time when everything had been all right, and I suddenly knew that it never would be again.

That night I couldn't settle. I remember walking the estate in the early hours of the morning, my mind racing. I had complete sensory overload.

The next morning my parents gave me some money and I went into the town centre. Handling cash felt very strange. The first thing I did was to go and buy a couple of books for other guys on the wing, and then to see the families of two prisoners. One of them, on the basis of letters he'd received, was anxious about his home situation, so I went to check it out for him. Those actions for fellow prisoners felt the most important things I did during that first parole. I knew what it would mean to them. It was hard for my parents. They thought I'd spend all my time with them, but I simply couldn't be still.

On the one hand, I felt really excited to be out. On the other, I couldn't wait to get back into prison. It seems a crazy thing to say after everything that had happened in the Maze, but the fact was, I knew the way of life in prison. I knew the rules and the environment. It was contained. It may have been brutal, but I'd learnt to survive. 'Outside' there was far too much to process and I didn't know what to do with myself. I felt like I had 'ex-prisoner' tattooed on my forehead, and that everyone was looking at me.

Neighbours came in and said it was good to see me, but I found conversation difficult because I lacked social skills. I didn't really know anyone, at least not in the way I knew my friends in prison. I was bored by the chat about the weather, cars, house and family. It seemed so trivial compared to what I discussed with mates in the Maze. It lacked intensity and purpose. It was, of course, just normal talk, but for much of the last 20 years, I'd lived an abnormal life caught up in conflict outside and inside prison. I was on my guard the whole time. I trusted hardly anyone.

For ten years other people had determined the pattern of my days.

Now I could make choices for myself. I found that really hard. I based my decisions on what others wanted. Having options felt overwhelming.

Mum wanted to make my favourite food, but I couldn't think what that was, so she produced what we called 'fancy pancakes' – savoury pancakes that we'd loved as kids – and chocolate cake. The food ran straight through me because it was so rich, and because I was running on my adrenalin. I didn't feel able to sit and eat. Stopping for meals felt like a waste of time. I found that I desperately wanted to be somewhere and then, when I got there, I didn't know why I'd come and I was bored within five minutes. People kept saying to me, 'You're running everywhere. Slow down.' But I couldn't.

After two days, it was an immense relief to get back inside. Lots of the guys were asking questions about what was happening in the outside world. Others held back because they were on long sentences and needed to protect themselves by not thinking about what was beyond their immediate reach. I understood where they were coming from. Now, however, I found myself in something of a limbo state. The period between that first parole and finally joining the pre-release scheme seemed interminable. Life in prison went on as usual, but psychologically I wasn't the same man any more. I'd been given a flavour of life beyond prison. Not only had I allowed myself to think about what freedom would be like, I'd experienced it for a couple of days. I'd breached the distance from life beyond the prison walls that I'd created in order to get by in prison. My mind drifted frequently to the outside world, and anxiety filtered through those thoughts. I'd had a taster of being free and it was frightening. I'd felt out of my depth. I didn't know the rules or the language. The world had moved on from the one I'd left as a 17-year-old.

Eventually I was transferred to the Crumlin Road Prison to the pre-release unit in the Annexe. There I had my own cell with a three-channelled black-and-white television. There was a pool table in the unit and a small kitchen area. The working-out scheme lasted a year. For the first three months, beginning in April 1986, I was given day paroles. Usually I met with a welfare officer and then either went home or walked around the streets of Belfast, meeting with friends or trying to get my bearings before reporting back in the late afternoon.

I'd been sent to prison in the 1970s when violence in Northern Ireland had reached unprecedented levels. During the early 1980s UVF activity had decreased but the Anglo-Irish Agreement of 1985 had stirred the Unionist community to action again. Within a week of it being signed, the UVF and the UDA came together to form an umbrella group, the Ulster

Loyalist Front (ULF). It would take about six years before the two groups acted together with any real effect. Behind the united front there were major divisions. Nevertheless, they organised a mass rally in Belfast city centre. Many of the 5000 people who participated were kitted out in Army-style clothing and they marched down Royal Avenue in military formation. A couple of weeks later, 100,000 people took part in an anti-Agreement rally in Belfast.

The Anglo-Irish Agreement provoked an escalation in violence between the UVF and the IRA. In Belfast the homes of high-risk targets had become fortified. Leaders within the paramilitary organisations had such things as cameras on their homes and impenetrable steel doors inside and out. In 1987 this prompted a shift in UVF strategy. The organisation moved its focus from northern Belfast to rural areas, and particularly Mid-Ulster, because it was known that RUC intelligence concerning this area was less informed than in other places. (I suspect this change of focus was partly responsible for what happened to me as I came to the end of the working-out scheme. But I'm jumping ahead of myself.)

Whereas the life of the boy I'd been before imprisonment had centred on the conflict and my involvement in it, my adult self, in what I thought was my final year in prison, focused on getting my life back to 'normal', but that was far harder than I'd expected. Many of the boys I'd known before I went to prison had grown up and moved out of Lurgan, or their lives had developed in ways that my own hadn't been able to. Girls I'd known were now married with kids. Their concerns were far removed from where I was. After living in an all-male domain for so long, relating to women was difficult anyway. I found it much easier to relate to younger women and teenagers than those of my own age. In my heart and mind I was in many ways a teenager. I remember on my first parole a girl who was a friend saying, 'Alistair, you can't keep falling in love with every girl you see.'

When I did go out with a girl, I was indecisive about where to go and what we'd eat. I always did what the girl wanted.

I didn't want to be settled like my peers. There was so much life that I had to catch up on, things that I hadn't been able to do, time and experiences that I wanted to make up. Learning to re-engage with the world was a traumatic process.

This was complicated further when my Dad had a heart attack. I was given some compassionate leave. The part of me that had some sense of how my actions had impacted on my family wondered to what extent I was responsible for his illness.

120

During the second three-month period of working-out, prisoners were expected to have a job. We left the prison in the morning and returned after work at night. Because I'd become very involved in fitness training while I was in prison, I was taken on by the YMCA gym in Belfast, teaching people how to use the equipment and planning work-outs for them. I also worked at a place called The Mill.

The Mill was a converted factory in the Crumlin Road area that was used by various businesses. I was there with another prisoner. Both of us had anxieties about working in that place. It wasn't in a safe area. There'd been many murders in the Crumlin Road. We worked alongside Republicans. One day someone in the workshop passed a comment about us coming from the prison and working with him. I don't remember his exact words, but they left me feeling distinctly unsafe. The next day I didn't go to work. I walked about for an hour or so and then went back to the prison. I told the officers that I wouldn't go back to The Mill because I felt I was in danger. I was told I'd breached the pre-release rules because I hadn't gone to work and was put on a charge. I was confined to the prison for a couple of weeks. The prisoner I'd been working with backed me up but other prisoners who lived in Belfast thought I was making a mountain out of a molehill. They didn't understand that my anxiety had been fuelled by my lack of familiarity with the city. A couple of times I'd strayed into the Republican Markets area and been scared. I recognise now that the paranoia I, like many prisoners, felt outside the prison also influenced my fear.

Thankfully, I was able to go home for weekends, and with the help of the Northern Ireland Association for the Care and Resettlement of Offenders (NIACRO), I found a job in a Lurgan woodwork shop. In the final three months I lived at home, only returning once every week or two weeks to sign in at the prison.

Even in my own town things didn't run smoothly. The owner of the carpentry business didn't know how to talk to ex-prisoners. He expected to say what he liked to us, and that we wouldn't answer back because we didn't want to get into trouble. While we didn't want to jeopardise our release date, we weren't prepared to be verbally abused. One day I went to his office to complain about how he'd just spoken to us. I still had my screwdriver in my hand. As we talked I must have been tapping it nervously on my palm. The man felt threatened and reported me to the prison Governor. I've always remembered from that time how easy it is for human beings to misinterpret the unspoken as well as the spoken messages that others give. My fiddling with the screwdriver was an expression of nerves. My boss saw it as a threat.

Inevitably, because of my history and his position, his perception of the encounter was the one the authorities believed. I was severely reprimanded. NIACRO were unhappy with what they saw as my unacceptable behaviour. I was told there wasn't enough work to keep me on, so I had to go back to prison for two weeks – a prisoner could only live at home if he had work. At the end of that time I returned to Lurgan, having agreed to do voluntary work at The Haven in Portadown. This was a centre that dealt with drug and alcohol abuse. I was there for about three or four weeks before getting a job as a care assistant in a nursing home in Lurgan.

It's worth noting at this point that while I was on the working-out scheme, not only was there an increase in sectarian violence, but during the spring and summer of 1986, relations between Protestants and the police underwent a major change. Following the Anglo-Irish Agreement the RUC had to implement policies that put them even more at odds with their own community. There was an upsurge in Loyalist violence against the police. The UVF planned and executed several attacks on the homes of policemen, and they felt that their campaign was effective. A large number of RUC reservists resigned in protest at having to uphold policies with which they didn't agree. Some went as far as stripping off their uniforms in public. Nevertheless the gap widened between the RUC and others in the wider Unionist community.

It's against this backdrop that, as the new year unfolded, I was expecting to receive my licence and finally have my liberty. What actually happened was totally unexpected. This is how the journalist, Jim McDowell, reported what happened in the *Sunday World* on 22 February 1987:

FLUNG BACK IN JAIL!
Early release lifers refused to tout for UVF

Two Loyalists on the verge of freedom after being sentenced to life for a murder 11 years ago, are still in jail because they say they refused to infiltrate the UVF.

The lifers, sentenced to be held at the Secretary of State's Pleasure for the shooting of a Catholic had been back in civvy street for almost the past year under a special SOSP pre-release programme.

And the pair, Alastair Lyttle [sic] and [name removed], both from Lurgan, were due to be freed under licence next weekend.

But when they reported to the Crumlin Road prison for one of their weekly check-ins nine days ago, they were shunted back behind bars again.

Now, the Progressive Unionist Party leader in Belfast, Alderman Hugh Smyth, is claiming the two were victimised.

He says the RUC tried to recruit the pair, one of whom is said to be a practising Christian, as touts and informers.

'They were offered a substantial sum of money, and a new life if they infiltrated the UVF and reported back to the police,' City Councillor Smyth said.

However, he reported that the pair had made legal affidavits, lodged them with their local MP, Official Unionist Harold McCusker, a Lurgan JP, and a local solicitor.

Now the PUP are campaigning for a new deal for the pair. But the Northern Ireland Office is arguing that both men, during their pre-release period of limited freedom proved 'unsuitable for early release' under the SOSP regulations.

A Stormont spokesman said it was not policy to go into details.

Cover-up
But angry Belfast Alderman Smyth claimed last night that the men were being victimised.

'The police tried to recruit them as informers during spells at Gough Barracks in Armagh.'

He added: 'Because they wouldn't play ball, they're back behind bars. It is reprehensible that people should be treated in this way,' said Alderman Smyth.

The report isn't entirely accurate. The prisoner rearrested at the same time was 'shunted back' into prison when he went to sign in at the Crumlin Road Prison. I was woken at 5 a.m. in the morning at my parents' home, rearrested and taken, not back to prison, but to Gough Barracks. There I was questioned for two days about what I'd been doing since I'd returned home from prison. Who had I been seeing? Where had I been? I refused to answer any questions. At one point there were six officers in the room, some being friendly and others putting on the pressure. Eventually they offered me a blank cheque if I were to become an informer. They particularly wanted information on two people I'd known since my childhood. They said that once I'd given them what they wanted, they would give me safe passage to anywhere in the world, with or without a girlfriend. They wanted me to carry out bank raids as a

123

means of getting back into UVF activity. They said I could keep whatever I took. When I refused to co-operate they became threatening. They would, they said, keep arresting me so that the IRA would think I was active again and want to kill me, or they'd send me back to prison.

Informers weren't a new phenomenon. In 1976 their testimony helped to convict more than 20 UVF activists in East Antrim. The use of informers was developed by the RUC in the late 1970s and early 1980s into the Supergrass system. The system meant that paramilitaries could be held simply on the uncorroborated evidence of informers. The latter betrayed former comrades in order to avoid prosecution or to have their sentences sharply reduced. While the Supergrass system put great strain on the welfare resources of the UVF and disrupted command structures, it didn't produce the results wanted and expected by the security forces – that is, the destruction of paramilitary organisations. By the end of 1984 the judiciary were under great pressure to abandon the system: in court the evidence of supergrasses was often found to be unreliable. Nevertheless, as a result of the trials that resulted through the system, the names and addresses of paramilitary men became publicly available. At the time this might have been seen to be to the advantage of Republican organisations. It was thought that Loyalist paramilitary organisations could pick up such details from sympathetic members of the security forces, and that until the Supergrass trials, Republican organisations didn't have access to this information.

Subsequently it's become evident that Republican paramilitaries also received information from security force agents, begging the question as to who was working for whom? Who was setting the agenda? Who was really behind some of the things that went on during the conflict? To what extent did the security forces ever play one paramilitary organisation off against another or use questionable methods to further their own purpose? We talk today about 'Noble Cause Corruption'. It's another way of saying the end justifies the means.

At the time when I was taken into Gough Barracks, the use of informers was much less in the public eye. Today there have been high-profile cases about the issue of informers that have made it clear that the situation was much more complex and murky than most people wanted to believe. I can see why the police picked up men like me. I was utterly vulnerable. As a man working out or on licence, I could be rearrested at any time without any reason needing to be given. I was in a state of transition – always an unsettling space to be – in an unfamiliar world where I was seen by many as undeserving of any human rights. I was the scum of the earth in their eyes, but I had no intention of joining the ranks of informers. I kept silent. On one occasion, I raised my middle finger to the men trying to pressure me into carrying out their wishes.

'What's that?' one of them asked. 'Is it £1000 you're asking for?'

'No, it's just him giving us the finger,' said another of the men.

Another time, one of the men put his hand on my shoulder and I shrugged it off forcefully.

'Oooh, muscles an' all, there! Is that a threatening move?' he said, trying to goad me.

Another picked off a piece of dust from my sleeve and pretended to blow it away.

'We had a man in here just like you. He thought he was tough. He took some dust off the officer and blew it away as if to say we'd be blown away soon, but it was him that was blown away.'

'Him' was an IRA man shot dead in his car coming across the border into the Province.

I was held for two or three days at the Barracks. Video cameras and audio tapes recorded everything. Towards the end of that time I developed a severe migraine. A doctor came and gave me a prescription for Syndol – the tablets I used to treat the frequent bad headaches I was getting. The police refused to give me the medication unless they got what they wanted, so I went without.

During this time my parents were beside themselves with worry. At first they had no idea where I'd been taken. One of the staff nurses at the nursing home had a friend working at Gough Barracks. She knew I'd been arrested but she didn't say anything at work.

Finally I was told to get ready to leave, and that I was going back to prison, but when I came out of the barracks my sister was waiting to pick me up. We went immediately to a Justice of the Peace, a solicitor and my MP. I wrote a witnessed affidavit about what had happened, and what the police had threatened to do because I hadn't complied with their wishes.

On 13 February, when I went to sign in as usual in the Crumlin Road Prison, I was taken to the Annexe 'behind the wire' and was checked every 15 minutes. An hour after my detention, the Assistant Governor informed me that my release date had been withdrawn and that I would be kept in the segregation unit 'for my own safety'. They continued to observe me every quarter of an hour. Although I was in the segregation unit I wasn't on punishment and so, within the hour, prison welfare, committal visits and parcels had been organised. The Chair of the Board of Visitors gave authority to extend the period of removal from association.

I should have been examined by a prison doctor but this didn't happen. On 16 February I was transferred back to the 'H' Blocks. As had been threatened in Gough Barracks, I'd been put back behind bars.

I was utterly devastated by this injustice. My family leapt into action immediately. The JP with whom I'd signed the affidavit followed up my case. Local MPs became involved. Back in the 'H' Blocks I became friendly with an IRA guy called Shaun Paul Docherty. He put me in touch with a couple of members of the House of Lords. I wrote to them about my situation. They replied saying they'd follow up my case. After a while they wrote again to say they were withdrawing because they'd met with senior police officers and learnt that I'd become re-involved in terrorist activity.

To draw attention to my case, I stopped eating food. I drank only tea and coffee. I said I didn't feel hungry. I made it clear I was not on a hunger strike. If I'd been made to say I was on a hunger strike, then the prison could abdicate responsibility for me. They split me up from a long-standing and influential Lurgan friend on the wing in the hope that isolating me would stop me following my present course, but it didn't. Ten days after I'd stopped eating, the Governor interviewed me. In his report he noted: 'Obviously Little is annoyed at being recalled, and this comes through in his interview – this would explain the wretched physical appearance of this individual.'

I started eating again only when asked to do so by the MPs who were pursuing my case. They said that while they understood why I wasn't eating, it was damaging the action they were taking on my behalf. They promised not to let the matter drop.

From what I understood later, they went to the Northern Ireland Office (NIO) to get the details of why I'd been arrested and put back in prison. The NIO said they'd received information that I was active again from a senior police officer in Lurgan. The two MPs, Ken McGuinness and Harold McCusker, went to Lurgan Police Station for the evidence that I'd been reactivated. The superintendent said he hadn't given any. He knew nothing about me being recalled to prison. In fact, he wasn't even aware that I'd been released. He made checks with other local police stations and found that they had no reports on me, nor had my name come up at any point recently. He wrote and stamped a letter confirming this position and stating that my recall to prison was entirely for the Prison Service. When the Under Secretary of State at the NIO saw the letter, he was embarrassed and said he'd look into it. McCusker threatened to pass the case on to the BBC because they'd expressed an interest in the story, but the NIO suggested that to do so could harm my prospects of being released again. They said there must have been a misunderstanding, and they'd get it sorted out. They didn't deny that I'd been taken to Gough Barracks for questioning, but the video and audio tapes of that time mysteriously went missing, despite being legal evidence.

I petitioned the Secretary of State to ask what was going on, what was the 'information received' that had led him to revoke my licence, why I had been put in solitary confinement, who I was being protected from, and why I hadn't been examined by a doctor, as prison policy demanded. No satisfactory answers were forthcoming. Writing in the report accompanying my second petition, the Governor said:

> Little is obviously not happy with his previous reply, however I am of the opinion that he is well aware as to why his recall was necessary. I can see this being a long lasting case. He is quite right when he suggests he has been made an example of. For far too long, prisoners like Little feel that having been given a provisional release date, they are fireproof. This disproves that theory.
>
> Because of security implications it will be difficult to give this prisoner an answer that will satisfy him.
>
> 'Acting on information received' has always been an emotive answer to give to a prisoner. It can give the prisoner more opportunity to question our methods ...

In reality, other than my refusal to become an informer, I had no idea why I'd been recalled.

Three or four months later I was put back on the working-out scheme in the Crumlin Road Prison. I learnt from Marty – the Quaker woman who'd become so important to my experience in the Maze – that after hearing what had happened to me, she joined those campaigning for my release. She made enquiries that brought her to the attention of the policemen involved in my rearrest. She discovered that her mail to and from the House of Lords was being monitored. Returning from a few days away on holiday, she had the distinct feeling that her home had been broken into, although there was no sign of a forced entry, and nothing had been stolen. During further enquiries, a reliable source informed Marty it was likely that her phone had been tapped.

While I was on the working-out scheme for the second time, two people came from the NIO on the pretext of looking at the scheme, but after their visit I learnt from a prison officer that they'd come specifically to see me. When they established who I was, they suggested to me that I shouldn't cause any trouble or go to the press when I was finally released. By that time I was filled with hatred and bitterness towards the establishment, the police system and any form of state authority. I'd been re-arrested and sent back to prison for refusing to take up the activities for which I'd been sent to prison in the first place. The policemen interrogating me in Gough Barracks thought it was acceptable for me to become re-involved in paramilitary activity when that suited police purposes, but considered it illegitimate when I'd gone down that road because it seemed to me to be the only way of protecting my own community. I couldn't get my head around that. Being scooped out of my home and having to spend almost another year in prison, as well as re-doing the working-out scheme, had left me psychologically in a terrible place. Once again I received flak from other prisoners. Some felt I was jeopardising their own release process by making a fuss. Others thought I must have done something to receive the attention I had. All prisoners took the issue seriously because they knew it could happen to any of us. We wondered who might already have become informers. Who could be trusted? When the UVF leadership realised what was going on, they were very supportive of me, but the experience left me in a really dark state of mind. What remained of my faith in the last years of my sentence had all but gone. I felt abandoned by God.

Eventually I'd look back on that time as a good thing because after it happened, I questioned everything. That was very positive. I was able to accept things that previously wouldn't have been possible. Republican prisoners I'd come to know had talked for years about this kind of thing going on and I'd dismissed it as IRA propaganda. Now from first-hand experience I knew it to be true. Other Loyalists told me to keep quiet about it because it didn't make the police look good.

'So we let them treat us like shit?' I replied. 'I don't think so!'

When I had the opportunity, I spoke to anyone and everyone about what had happened. Marty was told 'off the record' that my rearrest had been the work of a Special Branch unit operating outside its remit. I wonder. Part of me suspects that the 'leak' was deliberate. I was closer than anyone else to two men about whom information was wanted, and for that reason, I wouldn't be surprised if the NIO authorised what happened – but as is often the case in such situations, vital evidence goes missing, people deny responsibility or profess ignorance, and getting at the truth is all but impossible.

My licence finally came through on 17 February 1988. I was released

15 days later. The licence, given by the then Secretary of State for Northern Ireland, Tom King, states that:

> A person detained during the pleasure of the Secretary of State under Section 73 of the Children and Young Persons Act (Northern Ireland) 1968 who is released on licence is liable, under the provisions of Section 73(5) of that Act, to have the licence revoked or varied by the Secretary of State at any time. Where the licence is revoked, the person shall be arrested and taken to such a place as the Secretary of State may direct to resume his sentence.

Such an arrest could happen any time and in any place without the need for a warrant. My rearrest, for no reason other than that I'd refused to become an informer for the State, taught me how precarious my position was as a person released on licence. I learnt that lesson as I prepared to leave prison for good, but the early years following my final release also showed me just how vulnerable I was, and in more ways than one.

Chapter 12

Your pain is the breaking of the shell that encloses your understanding.

Kahlil Gibran

1988–97

I'm in heaven. That's how it feels. I'm standing on the fells high above Grasmere in the Lake District. Apart from odd occasions in my early teens when the police or Army took us out for days to the Mountains of Mourne, I can't ever remember being steeped in such beauty. I can see for miles around. So much diversity and all of it connected with everything else! For someone who comes from a place of fragmentation and destruction, that sense of interdependence is mind-blowing. What's more, I feel so small and unimportant, and that's fantastic. Ever since my release from prison I've lived with the sense that everyone knows I'm an ex-prisoner. I feel I stand out like a sore thumb. I'm scared of who I'll meet anywhere I go. I'm always looking over my shoulder, half-expecting to be the victim of an IRA revenge attack. One way or another, since I was first caught up in the conflict and experienced the power and powerlessness that comes with the use and abuse of violence, I've felt like someone at the centre of the universe. I've been a focus of attention, largely for ill, though with the ignorance of youth, I couldn't see that. Standing here, I'm humbled: on the hills I'm totally insignificant, and it's utterly liberating.

I'll always remember this experience. Marty made it possible for me. She knew how knocked sideways I'd been by my rearrest and imprisonment. She fixed up for me to come here with my girlfriend. Other people paid the expenses. I'm staggered by that. What moves people to do such things for other human beings ... for me? I can't get over the fact that I'm here because someone sat down and thought about me and what I needed, spoke my name and linked it to this place. We're staying in a Quaker Centre. This is the first time I've been away as an adult and am free to do what I want. I'm surrounded by people who love the natural world. There's no sense of conflict here. It's deeply healing for me.

Healing and saddening: I realise what I've missed all these years. What I threw away. Suddenly I'm conscious of my time in prison and of those who, because they've been killed or broken in the conflict, can't delight in what I'm now experiencing. Standing surrounded by all this beauty, I realise that wherever I go, I'll never be free of my past.

Our holiday ends all too soon. On the journey home a ferry strike gives us a couple of unexpected extra days by the coast. My girlfriend frets about getting back to work. I'm simply excited by the adventure of it all. I love the unpredictable. I struggle with mundane existence.

My need for something more than the ordinary doesn't make settling into normal life easy. During my second working-out time I was given a job in Boxmore. Boxmore was the factory where my Dad worked for many years. It made papier-mâché goods like egg-cartons and disposable hospital urinals and bedpans. I was on the production line. I found the work mind-numbingly boring. Some guys had been on the same line for 27 years. I couldn't get my mind round that. How could they keep going? Someone said that they did it because they had families to look after. That made me realise how much respect they deserved for doing something awful day in and day out for the sake of the people they cared for. That's why my Dad had worked at Boxmore for so long. It was a job far removed from the Army fitness instructor and talented goal-keeper he'd once been. Mum and Dad made lots of sacrifices for the sake of their children, and for me in particular. My arrest and imprisonment turned their lives upside down.

At one level Mum was glad I'd been caught because she knew I wouldn't be able to do any more damage, but she also felt guilty. She wondered whether, if she'd been stricter, she could have prevented me from getting involved and doing what I did. If she'd sent me to Australia with my sister and her husband, perhaps all of this could have been avoided. Hindsight can be agonising.

When I was in prison, there were people who knew what Mum and Dad were going through and supported them as best they could. My Mum remembers an old woman on the estate who used to look out of her window and watch us children playing in the street. One day she noticed I wasn't around any more and asked after me. When she heard I was in the Long Kesh compounds, she made a cake for me and gave Mum £5. News of my imprisonment had the opposite effect on others. Acquaintances crossed the street to avoid talking to my parents. Neighbours who saw them struggling with shopping no longer stopped to give them a lift home. Women who stood on street corners gossiped as Mum walked by, knowing she could hear them talking about us. My family lived on a daily basis with the stigma of my violence.

Mum eventually only mixed with other women whose sons or husbands were inside, but even that had its tensions. I didn't tell my parents much about my life in prison. I felt the less they knew, the less reason anyone would have for hurting them. I didn't want to worry them and it had become my habit to keep things to myself. A friend who was in prison with me was the complete opposite. As a result of what we'd done, our mums had more to do with each other. Mine often learnt from his what was happening to me. Until she realised I was trying to protect her, it made her angry and upset that I didn't talk to her as my friend talked to his mum.

Sometimes when Mum came to visit, she found my visits had been cancelled, either because I was 'on the boards', or because there was trouble in the 'H' Blocks. It was a long haul for her, usually carrying heavy packages, to get to the Maze. To be turned away on arrival must sometimes have felt heart-breaking. Often the parcels she brought contained things I'd asked her to buy for me – a new pair of jeans, a book, extra food. Occasionally she came without the items I'd requested.

'Ach, I didn't have time to get them,' she'd say. I'd be cross because I had no chance of getting them and she was free to go to the shops. After my release I learnt that when she came empty-handed it was a lack of money, not time, that was the cause. She scrimped and saved to meet my needs. Dad put in extra shifts to earn more. Each week they put by a little money for me so I'd have cash in the bank when I came out and was finding my feet. They never mentioned the hardship, and all I could do when Mum didn't bring me what I wanted, was complain. When my sister told me all this, I cried. I felt so small and selfish.

Unlike my Dad, I wasn't selfless, at least not if that meant accepting a mind-numbingly boring job for the sake of others. Anyway, I had no ties and no incentive to settle for such work. After years in the Maze, I couldn't accept that this was all there was to freedom. There had to be more to life. In prison I'd imagined that when I got out, I'd travel all over the place. I didn't think about having to earn a living. When I first came out, there were collections made for me by people who supported the UVF. Someone gave me an envelope with £300 in it. I didn't want to accept it because I wanted to move away from the life I'd lived before prison, but without it I couldn't have got by. Those donations dwindled quickly, as did the bank balance my parents had built up for me. The real world was different from the idealised one I'd constructed before my release. I felt trapped and powerless doing work I hated.

I'm sure other people experience this as well, but for an ex-prisoner there's an added dimension. Those feelings triggered me straight back into the trauma of my time in prison. The emotions they provoked were as real as if I was actually back in the 'H' Blocks. One night-shift, my frustration burst out and I began beating the production line with a steel rod. It was a sackable offence. Turning round, I saw the foreman watching me. He'd been the one who got me the job.

'I can't stick this,' I explained. Thankfully, he understood, and I was paid off rather than sacked. His generosity of spirit enabled me to claim benefits while I looked for other work. That wasn't easy. When I applied for jobs, I had to disclose my background. At interviews the questions were always around my time in prison and my involvement in the conflict, rarely about my ability to do the job in hand. Often I'd hear nothing more. Fortunately, after a while I was able to get back my old job as a care assistant in the nursing home. I remained there for the next four or five years.

I suspect my need for the unexpected was one of the reasons I became involved in working with people. Human beings are rarely the same from one day to the next. You never quite know what will happen with them.

I was the only male member of staff in the care home, and it was an eye-opening experience. I found the conversations of some female colleagues not only trivial but bitchy. I couldn't understand how they could talk behind each other's backs, and then carry on as though nothing was wrong when the person they'd been complaining about was with them. Men do that too, but in prison we didn't. If you didn't like someone, you didn't bother with them. There were no niceties.

A steep learning curve for me was being around women who were more intelligent than me in terms of their knowledge and skills in that environment. They knew how to keep people out of pain, and to care for them when they were sick or immobile. I didn't. They were more qualified than I was. That was good for me because I came from a world where I thought that everything I knew and put my energy into, was the most important thing in life. Now I was learning this wasn't the case. It was good to be around women after an all-male environment where, instead of overwhelming any opposition with fast and loud debate in order to win an argument, another approach was needed. The way we'd debated in prison was fine in that setting, but it was out of place in the care home. My way wasn't how they spoke or discussed different opinions. Colleagues would tell me to calm down when my passion for a subject

133

changed my demeanour and I became louder and more forceful in my speech. They experienced me as aggressive and intimidating. That scared me because it wasn't how I wanted to be. It took me back to a time when I'd enjoyed intimidating others, didn't care about them, and used violence to get my way because winning was all that mattered. I didn't want to go back there.

Other men would ask me how I managed to stick working with a group of women. In our macho culture they felt superior to women, but I was learning something different, and that was a gift. It helped me to develop my social skills and gave me insight. It also made me vulnerable.

I'd never had a real relationship with a girl before I went to prison. I'd snogged a few, but it was never anything serious. At that age I'd have fallen in love with any girl who showed me attention! I'd tell her I loved her, but I didn't know what that meant. In prison sexual relationships for us heterosexual hard guys could only exist as fantasy. We dealt with our urges as best we could. Lack of privacy made that difficult and sometimes embarrassing, but we were all in the same boat and used crude humour to help us get by. Out in the world again, I was ignorant when it came to the language of attraction and seduction. I was afraid of reading the signs wrongly or giving an inappropriate response. It was like walking through a minefield, even down to something as simple as how you addressed a woman. In prison, whenever we talked about each other's womenfolk, we always called them respectfully by name. One evening after my release, I was with a girl when a friend I hadn't seen since my youth came over and said, 'What about you, Skittle? How are you doing?'

Then, turning to my girlfriend, he said, 'All right, girl?'

I was furious because the way he addressed her felt so derogatory after what I was used to. I wanted to respond. I'm glad I didn't. When I talked about it later with someone, they said it meant nothing. The guy was just being friendly. This is a silly example, but it illustrates how exhausting it was for me in the early days because I didn't know what was appropriate or whether I needed to stand up for someone or not.

Despite my lack of knowledge when it came to women, I didn't have any difficulty making up for lost time. While some women might have been repelled by my history, others seemed attracted by it. In certain groups I was seen as something of a hero because I'd been prepared to act and not just talk about fighting back. Single or married, women came in and out of my life in those early months like there was no tomorrow. If they were willing, then I wasn't going to say 'no'. I went with many girls but had few relationships. When any problems arose, I walked away.

That was one of the 'advantages', as I saw it, of being at liberty. In prison you have to face the difficulties and deal with them in some way. Outside, if I had a problem I didn't have to stick around. At one level that felt good, but it wasn't healthy. After a while it also wasn't what I wanted.

I remember around this time visiting a married friend with yet another girl on my arm. My friend spoke with some envy. 'You've got it made, Skittle. You can go out when you want to, and have all these girls. I'm married and that's all over now.'

I knew what he meant, but as I left his home I felt acutely aware that something was missing from my life. He had something I lacked: a wife and children who loved him, a place where he belonged. While he was thinking I was the lucky one, I was thinking he was. Sex was all very well, but having so many different experiences that lacked any kind of depth became empty and boring.

That's how it was for me: internal adolescent and adult voices vying constantly for my attention. Emotionally I was a teenager in a man's clothing. I lived a psychologically fragmented existence. Freedom was both an exciting and fearful adventure. I was exhilarated by new experiences, and haunted by old ones.

In the nursing home one of the staff nurses stopped me one day. 'Alistair, can I ask you something?'

'Yes, of course.'

'Are you always like this?'

'Like what?'

'Happy-go-lucky. You don't seem to give a toss or worry about anything.'

That was the wee child in me lapping up the fact that I could make choices and experience so many new things. But I wasn't a child. I was a 31-year-old ex-prisoner struggling to find my place in a bewildering new world, and living with a legacy that meant I was rarely free of anxiety.

Whenever I went out I needed to know where I was going, how long I'd be out and who would be there. When I went with family and friends to a pub or restaurant, I always made sure I was never the first to walk in: I didn't want to be the one drawing the attention of people already there. I looked for a seat at the back of the room where I could sit with my back to the wall and see whoever was coming and going. I checked out the toilets and exits.

If I came across ex-Republican prisoners, I'd immediately leave wherever I met them. UVF and IRA killings were on the increase. We knew of many men who'd been shot after they came out of prison.

Capture, trial and imprisonment meant my identity was no longer secret. On one occasion after my release, I was walking on the beach in Newcastle (Northern Ireland) and met two IRA ex-prisoners. I knew one of them and we nodded at each other. I returned immediately to my car just in case they rang their leaders and told them where they could find me.

Another time I went to a restaurant and two prison officers were there with their partners. Within ten minutes of my arrival they'd gone. I felt some satisfaction about this at the time, but their leaving may not have been to do with the fact that they were scared of me. It could equally have been that they saw me as a potential target for a revenge attack and didn't want to be in the vicinity when that happened.

It was this kind of fear that caused problems for me in the nursing home. Initially only members of staff I trusted knew about my background, but then one of the other nurses, acting without permission, read my notes. She'd just bought a new car that was exactly the same make and colour as mine. She wasn't in work the next day. When she returned the day after, her car was completely different. She was afraid that someone might mistake her for me in an identical car, so she'd taken a day off to go and change it. The word spread and, fearful of revenge attacks, other colleagues suddenly refused to travel with me to training days. This was difficult but I understood their anxiety. The escalation of violence put everyone on edge.

Paranoia was a common experience for prisoners after release. It took many forms, from the simple belief that everywhere I went, people would know I was an ex-prisoner, to the ever-present fear of being killed in a revenge attack. I was anxious about any kind of routine in my day. After all, I knew the score. I'd spent many days in my teens watching different potential targets, noting where they were and when, and pin-pointing regular patterns in their daily lives.

Fear of attack disturbed my nights. I woke at the least sound and would check out the windows and make sure all the doors were locked.

I felt very lonely. I experienced lots of headaches and stomach upsets that were all related to tension. People commented about me never being able to sit in peace. At home there was an extra room with a seat and a TV set in it. In the early days I'd sit in there for hours on my own. Mum would come up from the living-room and wonder if there was anything wrong, and why I didn't want to be with them, but I was jealous of the space and the freedom to watch what I wanted. I hated other people talking while I was watching a programme. On my own I could think more easily. Communication, even with my parents, was hard. I had a low tolerance for small talk, and I wasn't at ease with the rules of social engagement outside prison. All these years later, I still find some of that difficult.

Another problem from going into prison as a boy and emerging as a man, was handling money. I hadn't done much of that as a teenager. Now, I became acutely embarrassed about counting out change to pay for things I was buying. I felt it drew too much attention to me. As a consequence I was always handing notes to the cashier. I'd return home with my pockets bulging with change in coins. Mum would count them out for me and give me notes in exchange.

When I was in any shop, I always kept my hands out of my pockets, just to show that I wasn't stealing anything. I still do that today.

In the early years after prison, the local police often stopped to talk to me if they saw me in the street. I was aware that I was being watched and my movements were being monitored. Later I learnt that it was the duty of the police to log when and where they'd seen me. Even if I'd been keen to become active again in the UVF, the fact that the RUC were keeping tabs on me would have made that hazardous. Not that there was ever any pressure on me from the UVF to re-engage in armed action. Men who'd served life sentences were regarded as having done their bit. We received help from the welfare side of the organisation but that was it.

I could have become involved in the political and welfare branches if I'd wanted to, but prison had changed me. When people tried to talk about the conflict, I didn't want to know. I wanted to leave my past behind me and get on with my life. I was sickened by some of the easy talk from men who hadn't put their words into action. Sometimes people said things because they were trying to impress me.

I met police officers I'd known when I was young. 'What a fine line it was,' they said. 'I could have gone down that [the paramilitary] road myself, but I chose to go into the police.'

It meant nothing. There were also men who'd stood by the riot lines encouraging us boys to get stuck in, and going on about why there weren't more men joining the fight, but when I ended up in prison, these same men turned their backs on my family.

I was a bitter man in many ways during the early years of my release. I'd expected to be interested still in the political issues and in fighting for our rights, but part of me was angry with the Orange Order and the MPs who had talked the talk but hadn't walked the walk. They looked down on people like me who'd dirtied our hands and been part of the fight they'd often alluded to in their speeches. Now I felt only contempt for the likes of Ian Paisley, whose words had been so influential in my own taking up of violent resistance. He'd distanced himself publicly from paramilitary activity and condemned the very men and boys his rhetoric had stirred to action. I felt he'd manipulated ordinary Unionists, and used them for his own ends.

This sense of disillusionment with the political process was widespread at the time among Loyalist paramilitary organisations. After the Anglo-Irish Agreement the UVF left the political struggle to the established Unionist parties, and in the following years my sense of having been let down by the latter was shared generally by the UVF. In the late 1980s and the early 1990s two seemingly contradictory approaches began to dominate UVF thinking. On the one hand, the campaign of terror escalated. In 1989 and 1990 the murders committed by Loyalists didn't match the death toll caused by Republican paramilitaries, but in 1991 the numbers were almost the same, and then Loyalist murders exceeded those of the Republicans.

On the other hand, there was an increasingly strong voice within UVF circles for a non-violent solution to the conflict. As early as 1977 a PUP (the political wing of the UVF) paper had put forward an argument for a form of power-sharing government in the Province. Ten years later the UDA published a document entitled 'Common Sense' that also advocated power-sharing within the context of devolved government. The UVF disparaged the latter but it remains the case that by then both Loyalist organisations were willing to call for political arrangements that were seen as far more moderate than those espoused by the mainstream Unionist political forces of the time.

By the end of the 1980s there was a growing realisation among us that endless violence was exactly that – endless. There had to be another way. The sons of men responsible for pub bombings and shootings in the 1970s were now committing murders for the UVF in the 1980s and 1990s. The generational dimension highlighted how long the conflict had been going on, and many of the older men didn't want history repeating itself through their children and grandchildren. The continued killing and the desire for something different ran in parallel. That's how it often is as communities in conflict seek to disentangle themselves from violence.

This dynamic had echoes in my own experience. I still had a strong sense of being British. I was an Ulsterman. That was my birthright. It didn't change just because the British government, my government, might sell us down the river. People might ask why I wanted to be British when our politicians seemed to be washing their hands of us, but that wasn't the right question because I *was* British. Being betrayed by Parliament didn't alter that fact. Prison had made me aware of the complexities of the situation in Northern Ireland. It had changed my view of the world and of myself. I realised that not everything is as it seems. Digging deeper, I'd found that some of the things I'd been told and believed and held dear weren't exactly as I'd thought. I'd become more analytical and discerning. Change had been painful but positive because I was becoming more true to myself as a human being. I understood why men resorted to violence, but I longed for a different way. Finding that way at a personal level had been both helped and hindered by my prison experience. My good intentions were frequently steam-rollered by negative experiences that made it difficult to be anything less than brutal. It's hard to remain true to a process of change when the odds are stacked against you, not least in the inability of others to allow you to become something different. I'd experienced that first-hand when the police tried to make me join the ranks of informers. A couple of years after my release, I experienced it again when, through no fault of my own, I found myself in court yet again.

I was living with my girlfriend of the time in a terraced house. One day my neighbour yelled abuse at me as I passed her door. I told her to get herself back into her home and not to be bothering me. Further abuse followed and she set her Alsatian dog on me. As it leapt up, I kicked out to protect myself. When it landed, I grabbed it by the scruff of the neck to stop it biting me, and I kicked it a number of times until it retreated back into the house.

'Have you any more dogs you want to set on me?' I said as I walked into my own home. Shortly afterwards another neighbour knocked on the door. She said she'd seen the woman having a go at me and setting her dog on me.

'If she makes an issue of this and you need a witness, let me know,' she said.

Later that evening a policeman called round. He told me that the woman next door had made a complaint about me, saying that I'd verbally abused her, and that she could hear raised voices and furniture flying around my flat. I invited the constable in to show him that our house was in order. I told him what had happened. He was sympathetic. He'd dealt with many complaints from and about my neighbour. He said he'd be recommending that the matter wasn't pursued further.

A few weeks later the same officer returned to issue me with a summons to appear in court on the charge of assault. For some unknown reason, his recommendation had been overruled. I was dumbfounded. After my earlier experience of rearrest, what was happening now was deeply disturbing.

Within a few days I was approached unexpectedly by a professional man who wouldn't normally be associated with supporting paramilitaries, offering to 'sort out' my neighbour.

'No thanks. That's not a path I want to go down. It won't help me.'

Shortly afterwards my neighbour's house was petrol-bombed by Loyalist sympathisers who'd heard what had happened and thought a bit of intimidation might encourage the woman to back off. I went straight to the local paramilitary leaders.

'This isn't what I want. It makes things far worse for me. Tell these kids to back off.'

It was some months before the case came to court. Mum was beside herself with worry. I was highly stressed. The terms of my licence meant that if I was found guilty, even though I was innocent (I had little trust in the legal system by this stage), I would be sent immediately to the Maze without any certainty about how long I'd remain there.

At the trial, to my surprise, the woman's daughter, who hadn't been present at the time of the alleged assault, was called as a witness. Her mother and sister sat with a local minister in the public gallery. The daughter testified that I'd attacked her as well as her mother, and in-dicated her bandaged arm. My solicitor immediately raised the objection that this was new evidence that hadn't been submitted prior to the trial. The daughter was questioned about her injury. She hadn't seen a doctor, despite the fact that such evidence would have been important to her mother's case. The bandage was one she'd applied herself. Under cross-examination the daughter burst into tears and admitted that I hadn't hurt her arm, and that she'd said I had because her mother told her to.

The constable who'd visited me at the time, and who'd recommended that there was no case to answer, repeated his recommendation to the Judge. He said that the evidence the daughter was now giving was the first he'd heard about it, and that nothing had been said on the night when the complaint had been made.

Cutting the trial short, the Judge expressed grave concern that the case had been brought to trial at all. He suggested that the woman and her daughter leave the court immediately lest they be charged with perjury. He also demanded that a file be on his desk by the end of the week detail-ing who'd overruled the constable and why they'd done so despite the lack of substantiating evidence.

I was cleared of the charge. It was a harrowing experience, reminding me that I was a marked man. I was grateful to the constable who'd kept his own integrity in the case. It is actions like his that have helped me to keep my faith in humanity when so much encourages me to lose that faith.

My solicitor suggested later that the policeman responsible for pushing the case forward was a Christian who'd heard about the woman being supported by a local minister and, knowing my history, had taken the woman's part. I'm conscious that the prejudice some policemen and prison officers felt regarding ex-prisoners affected their professional judgement.

The fear for ex-prisoners like me who'd been released on licence was that anyone could make an accusation, and our past would be held against us. We could be arrested without a warrant and put back in prison without anyone having to prove us guilty. I'll always be on licence but today, except where terrorist activity is suspected, I'd have to be found guilty before I could be sent to prison. Back then, I feared being in a place where a fight broke out which didn't involve me at all, but which might lead to me being questioned simply because I was there. What would happen if I'd become involved to help out someone who was being attacked? I would always be seen as the bad guy, even if I was trying to do the right thing.

At that time there was a real sense that the security forces wanted to give ex-prisoners a hard time. I remember on the pre-release programme that some prison officers tried to goad us into reactions that would immediately terminate our place on the working-out scheme. When I was in the Annexe three screws came into my cell one day and, after closing the door, began to verbally abuse me. After a lot of swearing on their part, they said, 'You think you're smart and are getting out now, but you'll not be going anywhere.'

They knew I had a quick temper, but I didn't respond except to say, 'Aye, you're a big man standing there with two men beside you to hold your hand. I wonder what it feels like to be a man who needs two men beside him in order to talk to me.'

As more abuse came my way, I put my hand to my ear. 'What? I can't hear anything but a bag of wind.'

The best thing, of course, would've been to say nothing, but that wasn't me.

There was a real bitterness in some screws about some of us getting out on parole. Thankfully, not all of them were like that.

141

I think if I'd been able to speak with other ex-prisoners in those early months and years after my release, it would have helped me a great deal, but there were few ex-prisoners I knew in Lurgan. When I did get together with other guys, it was such a relief not to have to talk trivia, yet many men were reluctant to discuss the problems of trying to reintegrate into 'normal' life.

Some men adapted to life after prison more easily than others. It might be assumed from this that they were tougher men than those who struggled. This belief prevented many guys from being able to talk about the difficulties they wrestled with, because they didn't want to look inadequate. In reality, how men coped with coming out of prison was influenced by many different factors, of which strength of character was only one. Some returned to far more complicated home situations than others. The legacy of violence with which each man had to deal varied. Despite similarities, everyone's personal history was different.

Today people in my field of work tend to talk about 'Sequential Trauma'. It recognises that post-traumatic stress doesn't simply come from the experience of one traumatic event, but is influenced by what happens to a person before and after a key event, as well as during it. Some people have to deal with ongoing complex and painful circumstances that would floor even the toughest of men.

Many of us found it hard to know if the issues that confused us were to do with our extreme past experience or were just part of normal existence. Because we didn't want to look weak, it was hard to discuss these things with other ex-prisoners. Even if we were aware that all wasn't well, getting on with day-to-day living seemed an easier option than trying to understand what was happening.

In the beginning I lacked the insight to see that something was wrong. I was aware that my parents struggled with my behaviour at home and the way I went through relationships, but as far as I was concerned I was just making up for lost time, and why shouldn't I? I didn't realise that the consequences of living in a stressful environment only kick in when you cease to be in that setting. I knew that the thinking and behaviour I'd adopted to help me through prison were causing me problems now that I was out, and that I was having to learn different patterns, but initially I had little idea of just how out of sync I was. Perhaps if I'd have had more contact with ex-combatants I'd have cottoned on sooner. Unexpected contact with one former prisoner certainly had very positive repercussions for me.

I was driving home one day when a guy I knew stepped into the road and waved me down. I'd known him since I was 14. He was a well-known figure in the UVF, an ex-prisoner that I respected very much.

'What are you doing, Skittle?' he asked.

'I'm just heading home.'

'Good. You can come to church with me!'

'No way! I'm not going there. I'm not even dressed for it.'

He jumped in the car. 'Right, drive home, get changed and then we'll go.'

So we did – only because it was him and he'd asked me. Not because I wanted to. He'd become a Christian and was at the stage when he was keen for others to join him. He knew about me and my background and cared about me. He'd been seen as tough and hard-line. He was known by everyone and was significant, so I felt relaxed about going back to church with him. If a minister had asked me to do that, I'd have told him where to go, but this man was part of my world. He was the last person I'd expect to go to church. If he was finding it helpful, then maybe there was something to it.

We began to go together on a regular basis. We tried different places. Wherever we went, we were aware of people watching us. They knew our backgrounds. Some would welcome us. Others would avoid us, hoping we wouldn't come again. It was disheartening and made us angry.

'Who the fuck do they think they are?' we asked ourselves.

We kept going to church together until my friend died. We ended up in a church in Gilford, near Banbridge. The Free Presbyterian Minister was a young guy called Davey Sinton. He drove to church in his leathers on a motorbike. Some people tut-tutted about that. He and I became great friends. He was a really honest and grounded human being, who acknowledged his own weaknesses and struggles. He would tell me what he thought. If he thought I was making excuses, he'd say so. There was no 'better than thou' attitude in him. He told things like they were simply because he cared about me.

'Alistair, you know you're human, and you know what happens if you don't come to church. You get isolated and lonely and it impacts on your faith and your life – but I'm not going to chase you.'

We back-packed together in Israel, staying in strange places like a B&B run by nuns in East Jerusalem. It had solid walls, cells and cellars, and deep silence. Not the kind of space you'd expect a Free Presbyterian from Northern Ireland to hang out in!

Davey kept his own integrity. He refused to read out political statements from the pulpit from other Free Presbyterians like Ian Paisley. That got him into trouble, but he was a pastoral minister and gave lots of time to people. I spent many hours in his home. People criticised him for that. Mixing with a terrorist! It didn't stop him. We had great debates about everything.

He once said to me, 'Alistair, I have to tell you I've never met anyone like you in my life. The things that you've got me thinking about and questioning! The debates we've had – I just don't know how your mind works.'

Davey made me feel good about myself. He, along with the friend who'd got me back into church, was a stabilising factor in my life during that time. He helped me to reconnect with values I'd been blindly reaching out for. Knowing he was there, even if I didn't always get in touch with him, was a saving grace. It seems strange now that I didn't seek him out when I finally spiralled down into the depths of Post-Traumatic Stress. I guess I didn't see that coming. Why should I have done? After all, I'd taken the great step of getting married. In 1991, I finally had somewhere I belonged and someone who loved me. That's what I wanted.

I used to run around with Valerie's brothers. That's how I met her. She'd been in an accident that had left her in a wheelchair. We talked really easily together. Because of my experience in the nursing home, I asked her questions that others wouldn't ask. Maybe I also understood her because, in our different ways, we were both wounded human beings. That gave us a kinship and led to a relationship. We got on well together. It was good taking care of someone I loved. It felt right. We had some great times, but problems slowly began to emerge.

I'd sustained a back injury at work. When I recovered, I stayed at home to be with Valerie. Then I began to feel bored, so I joined a gym and trained most days between 10 and 3. Occasionally I went to give the odd talk at a meeting. That led to me getting involved in EPIC (Ex-Prisoners Interpretive Centre) on the Shankill Road in Belfast, and the Shankill Trauma Centre. EPIC asked me to help with research they'd undertaken with ex-prisoners and their families. I received petrol money and about £30 a week.

Valerie and I had come together partly because we understood each other's vulnerability and found love and friendship through that but, like many couples, the very things that had drawn us together began to drive us apart because we weren't really aware of what was going on. Valerie needed me to be close. As a result of my prison experience I needed space. I didn't want to be responsible for another mess in my life, so I tried to do what Valerie wanted. My intentions were good, but the result was disastrous. I was aware of people around us waiting for things to go wrong, and I didn't want to fulfil their expectations. I was desperate for our marriage to work. I was trying to live a Christian life. Besides, in December 1995, our beautiful daughter, Amy, was born, and I wanted to be a good dad. Valerie took the day shift with Amy, and I sorted out the nights. I really enjoyed caring for our daughter. Often I was awake any-way: the difficulties between Valerie and me were disturbing my sleep pat-tern, which was never good at the best of times.

In prison I hadn't been concerned always about doing the right thing, or considered the feelings of others with whom I was in conflict. If I walked away now from my marriage, I'd feel I hadn't moved on at all from the man who didn't give a fuck, and who was capable of really wounding others. I feared that if I left Valerie I might return to violence because I hadn't really changed at all. I wanted to show that I'd grown and developed. I didn't want to hurt another person, so I stayed, and we made each other very unhappy. At night, unable to sleep even when Amy no longer woke for a feed, I went into dark psychological places. Valerie. hadn't experienced me like that before. My past was something she'd never wanted to discuss, yet now it was bubbling up inside me.

There were a number of reasons for that. While I experienced the novelty of being out of prison and there were always things to do, the trauma of the past was held at bay. When I gave up work to be at home with Valerie, I had more time on my hands so there was less to distract me from intrusive thoughts. At the same time the work I was doing with other ex-prisoners through EPIC put me in touch with my own prison experience and its legacy.

Much as Valerie and I were trying to do the right thing, we were imprisoning one another and for me that fed into the painful emotions from my time in the Maze. I thought, 'I've survived prison, I can get through this,' but it wasn't good for either of us. I sank lower and lower until I realised that I couldn't stay. Our marriage was over. As I left, my overwhelming feeling was that Amy didn't deserve any of this. She was a toddler. She hadn't asked to be born, or to be caught up in our struggles.

I took my clothes, my CDs and my car. I rented a flat. I didn't revert to violence, at least not against anyone else. Instead, for a month, like a wounded animal, I hid myself away. I closed the curtains of the flat. I went out only to buy food that didn't need preparation – bread, baked beans, fruit – and plenty of beer and vodka. I slept late in the morning, got up, showered and then sat in front of the television.

Nobody knew where I was. My family knew my marriage had broken up. Mum had given me a little money, but they couldn't get in touch with me. EPIC had provided me with a mobile phone. I rarely answered it. Sometimes I drank through the day, but not often. Usually I waited until about 5 p.m. before I started. I rarely became wasted. I drank simply to numb the pain. I thought about suicide, but I didn't act on those thoughts.

I'd tried to live a normal life but it hadn't worked. I knew something wasn't right but I didn't know what. I hit rock bottom. At least from there, if I hung on in, the only way to go was up.

Chapter 13

People often say that this or that person has not yet found himself. But the self is not something one finds, it is something one creates.

Thomas Szasz

1997–2000

'Trauma? That's a load of bollocks.'

'Is it?'

The man I'm speaking to is adamant.

'I did 16 years in prison, and when I came out I continued as if I'd never been away.'

'What about the paranoia you've felt since leaving prison?'

'Och, I don't go there.'

'Don't go where? On the one hand you say there's no such thing as trauma, but then when I talk about certain conversations, you say you don't go there. Go where?'

'Well, I don't want to open up all that stuff.'

'What stuff? You said there's no trauma.'

'Ach, that's all you, twisting my words ...'

During my early work with EPIC, I lost count of the number of times I had similar conversations with ex-prisoners. The reasons many men couldn't recognise or accept that they were suffering as a result of trauma, were varied. One ex-prisoner and colleague, whose history of violence and imprisonment is similar to my own, says:

'When I go and talk about my story with people today, they go, "Wow!" because they see it as so shocking and out of the ordinary. That always takes me by surprise, because for me it was just normal life.'

'Just normal life' is what we expect to get on with, without making a fuss. Some men feared that if they looked too deeply into their experiences, it would be like opening up a can of worms, and take them to psychological and emotional places they didn't want to go.

For other men, our macho culture kicked in. They put on a front, denying that their experiences of violence and prison had affected them in any way. Behind closed doors, their families knew different, but in our community the idea of counselling and therapy was alien. It smacked of weakness. Real men just got on with life – except many of us couldn't. I'd tried to and it hadn't worked.

I was still in the Maze when I first became aware of the impact upon me of my teenage experiences and prison life. Not that I'd have spoken about Post-Traumatic Stress. I just knew things weren't right. That sense intensified after my release, particularly following my unexpected re-arrest and further period of imprisonment. I struggled to find my place in the world, juggling the desire to live normally like other people, along with the wish to make up for lost time and the awareness that the experiences I'd lived through weren't 'normal'. There were some great times, but whatever front I presented to others, inside I was struggling. Initially I could ignore that to a great extent. After almost 13 years in prison, there was so much life to discover and rediscover. Everything was overwhelming and exciting, but then the novelty wore off and the practical realities of earning a living, dealing with the closed doors that confront ex-prisoners in terms of work options and the attitudes of others, and coping with the mundaneness of ordinary life began to expose the deeper pain I felt. The breakdown of my marriage was the final straw and, in the month I hid myself away in the flat, I felt utter despair.

Time slowly brought me out of that dark place. Throughout the years since leaving prison, I've had periods when I've had to withdraw from the outside world. I suspect that will always be the case. I know now that these dark times will run their course and bring me to a point where I want to engage again. During these retreats into myself, I reflect on what's been going on, and I try to gain some understanding. Eventually a part of me kicks into action: I realise that if I don't do something, I'm going to get into such a rut that I won't be able to get myself out of it.

People and events beyond my home also draw me back into wider life. When Valerie and I split up it was EPIC and the Trauma Centre that helped to get me back on my feet. The part-time work with them brought me into contact with many ex-prisoners. It was good to be with men who understood where I was coming from without me having to explain everything.

To begin with this contact provoked in me nostalgia for the 'old days'. I had a desire to reconnect with that past life, yet I also felt I didn't want to go down the route of violence again. I was searching for something but wasn't sure what it was. When tensions in the Province became focused on the annual Orange march through Portadown to the church in Drumcree, I decided to go there to see if political protest was something I wanted to take up again.

Trouble between the security forces and Orangemen at Drumcree first surfaced in 1985 when the traditional route was changed from the Nationalist flashpoint, Obins Street, to the equally Nationalist Garvaghy Road. Violence continued across the Province through the next ten years. Negotiations for peace were almost blown apart when, in October 1993, an IRA bomb went off in a fish shop on the Shankill Road, killing one of the bombers and nine Protestants. Two days later the UVF shot dead a Catholic in Glengormley and, the day after that, the UFF (the Ulster Freedom Fighters – a militant branch of the Ulster Defence Army) shot dead two Catholics in Andersonstown. On 30 October masked UFF gunmen burst into a bar in Greysteel, a village just outside Londonderry, shouting 'Trick or treat', and opened fire on the customers. Six Catholics and one Protestant were killed. As the year drew towards a close, the UVF was, on the one hand, negotiating for peace and, on the other, building up its arms stock just in case the peace negotiations failed. In November the biggest arms seizure to that date was made when customs officers intercepted a secret cargo of weapons bound from Poland to the UVF in Belfast. The operation turned out to be a 'sting' set up by MI5. It didn't stop the violence.

Two days after the murder of a UVF senior battalion commander along with two other men in the Shankill Road, UVF gunmen burst into a bar in the County Down village of Loughinisland and killed six Catholics. Those in the UVF, like David Ervine, who were working to bring the killing to an end, were horrified. The IRA retaliated by murdering three prominent UDA/UFF men. For some paramilitaries there was a belief that through an escalation of the conflict, its end would be brought about: Matching the IRA's violence would push them into seeing the necessity of a ceasefire. Perhaps there was some truth in that. In August 1994 the IRA announced 'a cessation of military operations'. Later that year in Fernhill House in West Belfast, the combined Loyalist Military Command declared its own ceasefire. Gusty Spence read the prepared statement:

> In all sincerity, we offer to the loved ones of all innocent victims over the past twenty-five years abject and true remorse. No words of ours will compensate for the intolerable suffering they have undergone during the conflict.

Let us firmly resolve to respect our differing views of freedom, culture, and aspiration and never again permit our political circumstances to degenerate into bloody warfare.

We are on the threshold of a new and exciting beginning with our battles in the future being political battles, fought on the side of honesty, decency and democracy against the negativity of mistrust, misunderstanding, and malevolence, so that, together, we can bring forth a wholesome society in which our children, and their children, will know the meaning of true peace.

Despite the existence of the ceasefires, the political process didn't progress. The decommissioning of weapons was a major sticking point. Unionists wanted decommissioning before entering further negotiations, but those who were armed didn't want to relinquish their weapons because the success of the peace process was far from certain.

In 1995 there was violence again at Drumcree when the Orangemen were prevented from marching home along the Garvaghy Road. Only when they agreed to do so in silence without the accompaniment of the flute bands, were they allowed to continue. In 1996 the IRA, frustrated by the lack of progress, set off two bombs on the British mainland – one in London's Docklands, killing two men and injuring more than a hundred, and the other in Manchester. By breaking the ceasefire the IRA prevented Sinn Fein, its political wing, from taking up the 17 seats they had won in the May elections to a Peace Forum. It was from this Forum that those who'd become involved in all-party talks would be drawn. By July 1996 frustration in both communities found expression at Drumcree. Catholic residents, furious that Sinn Fein had been excluded from the political process in the Peace Forum, were confronted by Orangemen from all over the Province who felt their way of life was being sold down the river. Portadown, which was seen as the birthplace of Orangeism, became the place where they took their stand.

I was present at the 1996 'stand-off' in Drumcree with a group of friends from the bands. Although no guns were visible, it was a major confrontation. I'd no intention of taking any action, but when I heard the police, who were all lined up in riot gear, shouting abuse about the wives of some of the guys who were there, I felt angry. I started taking photographs of them, one by one, knowing it would unsettle them. Later, after I'd drifted away from the crowd and was thinking about it all, I thought what a stupid thing it was to have done, to take pictures. I realised there was nothing there for me any more. It wasn't where I wanted to be.

Returning to the front line wouldn't provide what I was looking for. In fact, the opposite was true.

At EPIC, Jim Crothers and a team of volunteers were gathering the stories of ex-prisoners like me, and recording our post-prison experiences and concerns. Some prisoners weren't ready at that stage to acknowledge the problems but, through conversation, I became aware of those men who were in a similar place to me and were prepared to talk about it. I found that my difficulties weren't unique. It was an immense relief. Relationship problems, discrimination in the workplace, difficulties in reintegrating in the community, grief about the 'lost' years in prison, and the symptoms of Post-Traumatic Stress Disorder (PTSD) were common among us.

In PTSD three broad categories of symptoms have been defined – hyperarousal, intrusion and constriction. Hyperarousal, or hyper-vigilance, can be summed up simply as the persistent expectation of danger. I knew that only too well. Intrusion is the way in which traumatic experiences are indelibly imprinted in the mind, intruding into consciousness in overwhelming ways and without warning. That too, dominated my days. Constriction is the numbing response of surrender. My experience when my marriage broke down and I hid for a month in my flat was a classic example of such a symptom. Discovering that I was going through recognised reactions to trauma was incredibly helpful. It reassured me that I wasn't going mad, and opened up the possibility that there were ways of treating these disturbing responses, or at least dealing with them better than I had been.

EPIC had contact with groups from other conflict situations that were familiar with the legacy of violence. Exchange programmes were arranged. One of these involved Vietnam War Veterans. I spent a lot of time talking with Tom, an American who spoke movingly of his traumatic experience in Vietnam, and of struggling to fit back into society when he returned home. He identified with my experience and recognised how vulnerable I was. Restlessness, emptiness, the psychological battle with past experience, loneliness among a crowd, feelings of isolation and separateness, anger, suicidal thoughts, spiritual anguish, the fear of allowing others close and the need for lots of space – all these things we held in common. Tom asked Martin Snodden, the Programme Co-ordinator at EPIC, to keep an eye on me. Martin was already doing that. He'd rung me a number of times when I was holed up in the flat, and although I didn't always answer, it made a difference knowing that he'd been thinking about me.

Tom talked about the workshops and therapies that Veterans like him had found beneficial. Conventional talking therapies hadn't worked for many of them. By trial and error they'd discovered tools that helped deal with their symptoms. These could be as simple as wearing an elastic band on the wrist: when intrusive thoughts threatened to overwhelm, they pinged the band against their skin. The sharp pain it gave was enough to break the thought pattern.

I was hungry for understanding. Somehow it brought back purpose to my life, and that was crucial. I didn't feel judged by the 'Vets'. They invited me to go back home with them for three months, but because of my prison record I wasn't allowed into the States.

It was a combination of formal encounters and informal conversations that enabled me to begin to work with my own experience, and to see the wider questions. We recognised the symptoms of PTSD/Sequential Trauma among us, but could we be described as victims? Had we been involved in a war? Answers to these two basic questions had major ramifications in terms of the peace-building process. I was reluctant to describe myself as a victim in the way that an innocent person going about their ordinary daily business is a victim when they're blown up by a bomb in the main street. Although in the back of mind I question the idea that a person who takes no action in a conflict zone is by definition innocent, I think they are different from those of us who choose to take the law into our own hands.

Nevertheless, I couldn't simply see myself as a perpetrator. I'd grown up with bombs destroying my home town, and friends being shot and killed. I'd lived surrounded by violence for which I wasn't responsible, and that had affected me deeply. The child Alistair, whose friend's father was murdered in his home, was surely a victim. Did I cease to be a victim when in response to these experiences, I took up arms and fought back? Many paramilitaries were motivated to take action precisely because of traumatic past experience caused by the other community. They'd lost friends or relatives. They'd been burnt out of their homes. They'd lived on a daily basis with the fear of violence. They felt themselves to be at war, and being at war changed the rules.

If my society wasn't engaged in civil war, then my violence could be regarded as criminal rather than a 'legitimate' response in the context of war. On the streets where I lived it felt like war, and the government and security forces seemed incapable of stopping the IRA. In such circumstances, what is the right thing to do? Take action, or do nothing? It could be argued that those who sat by and did nothing were as responsible for the ongoing conflict as those who fought back. This isn't easy to say, but the reality is that while victims need others to take action in order to help them cease to be victims, the only thing that perpetrators ask of bystanders is that they do nothing.

Sometimes the question of whether or not to act can impose agonising decisions upon us. I remember a conversation with a police officer. He and some other officers knew who'd been responsible for the murder of two of their colleagues, but their evidence wasn't of the type essential to convict the men in a court of law. The officers discussed whether they should 'take out' the Republican paramilitaries they knew were guilty of the killings. It was his deeply committed Christian faith that prevented the officer I was speaking with from going down that path. Shortly afterwards two more policemen were murdered by the same men, and two more families were destroyed. The officer had never been able to forgive himself for not taking the law into his own hands. If he had done, he felt those families would still be intact.

Perhaps like me, he struggled to understand what rules we were working by: those of war or those of peace? Paramilitaries like me were charged and found guilty according to peace-time laws, but the very security forces that were there to keep the peace often operated according to the 'rules' of war. In times of conflict the boundaries become blurred and it isn't always easy to tell the good guys from the bad. How, and by whom are the terms 'good' and 'bad' defined?

If Northern Ireland were to have its own Truth and Reconciliation Commission, as is sometimes debated, the question arises of what it should look at, and who it would include. Some say only paramilitaries. Others say the politicians should be brought forward to tell the truth about their words and actions, along with the churches that fostered sectarianism. I realised, as I discussed these issues, that paramilitaries were often scapegoated as the source of all Northern Ireland's ills, but reality was far more complicated. It's a far easier response to condemn the actions of others than to understand why they happened and to take responsibility for your own actions or lack of action.

I'm often asked if I regret my involvement in the conflict and my use of violence. Some friends would say they've no regrets because regret suggests their actions were wrong, and they don't believe they were. That position is difficult to hear for those who've lost loved ones.

It's also hard for people like me who've spent years in prison as a result of what we've done, to consider the possibility that right wasn't on our side when we took up arms. How can anyone live with that? If I said I regretted what I'd done, understandably I'd be criticised by other para-militaries for undermining the political cause.

As I wrestled with these questions, I began to feel that holding up the political cause could be a way of avoiding personal responsibility for the pain and grief we'd caused individually. I *do* live with regret that I was involved with actions where human life was lost and people were injured or bereaved. At the same time I recognise there were factors and circum-stances that contributed to me becoming involved – the religious and political leaders whose speeches encouraged me to take action, govern-ment policy which put the well-being of my community at risk, institu-tional segregation and sectarianism, and violence on the streets where I lived and grew up. All these things created conflict and motivated people like me to fight our corner. I felt I was doing the right thing at the time, but at a human level it remains possible to say I regret that people suffered as a result of my actions.

While exploring my experience as a paramilitary and as an ex-prisoner, I became involved in workshops where both Loyalist and Republican ex-prisoners were present. I'm grateful to a couple of the Republican prisoners I met, who spoke with me on a one-to-one basis and gave me insight into their world. They took risks in that sharing, but the result was that they helped dispel some of the myths I had about them, and enabled me to humanise my enemy. I could've caused them great harm if I'd told others about what they'd said, but they trusted me not to, and that in turn fostered trust in me.

My work with EPIC became full time in 1998. Ever since I'd first started working there, Martin Snodden had supported and encouraged me. He'd known me since I was a 17-year-old on remand in the Crumlin Road Prison. He saw potential in me that I didn't recognise. With his encour-agement, in 1996/7 I gained a Certificate in Counselling Skills and an-other in Counselling Theory from the Central School of Counselling and Therapy. After gaining a Diploma in Counselling, I went on to add a Certificate in Community Relations from Ulster People's College, and a year after that a Certificate in Mediation from the Mediation Network of Northern Ireland.

Martin's own input into my development was perhaps the most valu-able training I had through those years. He took a calculated risk in putting me into new and difficult situations that he felt I could manage. Without his encouragement I wouldn't have volunteered for such ex-posure, but as a result I discovered skills I didn't know I had, and was able to develop them. International groups, like the Vietnam War

Veterans, frequently came to the Province and visited organisations like EPIC. Martin would invite me to come and share my story with these groups. I wouldn't know who the group was until I arrived. After I'd told my story I answered questions. Martin was always there but he wouldn't intervene unless something came up that was embarrassing for me, or that I said he could answer better. To begin with I worked from notes on bits of paper. I was overwhelmed with anxiety. I couldn't stick to the script and in trying to do so, my storytelling was stilted. I had to learn to speak simply from the heart. Every time I was asked questions I hadn't been asked before, I'd do my best to respond, but then I'd go away and think about them afterwards so that I could do a better job the next time round.

Once I was asked, 'Alistair, can you understand what a family might feel who've lost a loved one?'

'Yes, I can.'

Afterwards, during our usual debriefing session, Martin challenged that response: 'Remember when you said you could understand what a family felt like? But how can you?'

'What d'you mean?'

'I'm interested in how you can understand.'

'Well, their father-in-law was shot. If my father-in-law was shot ...'

'But he wasn't.'

'I know, but if he was ...'

'But he wasn't.'

'I don't understand.'

'Alistair, there are some things you don't know, and you need to say you don't know. You can say, "I can only imagine ...", but you can never know, unless it happens to you.'

I went away and thought about that. To begin with I disagreed. You don't always have to experience something to understand how it feels. Then I realised, there's a difference between 'knowing about' and 'knowing through experience'.

Martin always gave me time to reflect on how a meeting had gone. Then he'd ask me what I thought I'd done well, or what could have been done better. I'd go away and think about our discussion before coming back to talk about what had come to mind. Martin put a lot of time into me, and opened up options I could never have imagined when I first came out of prison.

Prior to working full time for EPIC, I'd split my time between EPIC and the Shankill Trauma Centre. In the latter I did one-to-one counselling with the focus on conflict resolution. I was also involved with group counselling, personal development and going on home visits as part of the befriending service. As I began to think through my own experience and relate that to the formal training I was undergoing, I was struck by the discrepancy that sometimes existed between that experience and what I was being taught on a formal basis. In a way the gap relates to the conversation I mentioned earlier between Martin and me, and can be illustrated by comparing two forms of training that EPIC enabled me to do during my first couple of years of full-time work with them.

One training course was extremely positive. EPIC funded me to go on a Trauma Management Course at the Centre for the Study of Violence and Reconciliation in Johannesburg, South Africa. We spent two weeks there, and then they came to us for two further weeks. The two trainers in South Africa both had personal experience of conflict, and had worked in many conflict zones. We were exploring how to deal with trauma in conflict situations and with victims of torture. All I learnt from them matched my personal experience. It rang true. At the same time I was also studying in Belfast for a Diploma in Counselling, awarded by a university in England. It was here that I encountered an academic elitism that I've struggled with ever since. Maybe the roots of this conflict go back to my teenage years where the education system demanded that we respect authority and do as we were told, while failing utterly to take into account the reality of the violence we were dealing with on the streets. Such experience made me sensitive to theory that didn't seem grounded in fleshed-out human experience. A simple example of this was the assertion by a tutor on one counselling course that it was inappropriate in a counselling session to offer a client a cup of tea because it could be a distraction and become a barrier to progress. The people I was seeing through my work usually had to come and see me in their lunch-breaks. That meant they often went without their meal in order to be with me. From our session they'd have to go straight back to work. In the light of this, the tutor said that offering them a cup of tea might be right, but the counsellor shouldn't have one. I knew that people in my community wouldn't be comfortable eating and drinking if I wasn't joining them, and my abstinence would hinder rather than enable their ability to talk freely. Perhaps what the tutor was teaching was relevant with certain types of people, but it didn't make sense in my context. I felt that the teachers on these academic courses were working with theory, not from hands-on experience in the traumatised working-class communities where I worked. It became crucial to me to apply my developing skills in a human way that moved away from the power structures that blight counselling disciplines as they do any other area of exploration.

Many of my tutors had done their research in the controlled environments of academic institutions, and not on the ground in conflict situations. I often found myself at loggerheads with established thinking. The respect for qualifications over experience is utterly misguided. Often we had to pick up the pieces left behind by so-called experts who would come into our communities, run their courses and then leave, happy to be able to put on their CVs that they'd worked with paramilitary organisations and ex-prisoners, and utterly unaware of the damage they sometimes caused. As a result many grassroots community groups, Republican and Loyalist, began to develop their own way of working.

Workshops in which Loyalist and Republican ex-prisoners were brought together went on without publicity. After the ceasefires, when such meetings became more public, there were those who said they shouldn't be happening, little knowing that they'd been going on for years. Before the ceasefires were announced, these meetings were very risky, and I found the experience deeply unnerving, albeit helpful to me in connecting with the humanity of my enemy.

The element of 'watching our backs' that came with my job at EPIC was illustrated when Davey first came to see me at work. He arrived on his motorbike and parked outside the centre on the Shankill Road. When he asked at reception if I was around, he was quizzed about who he was, but eventually he was told I wasn't available. Wondering where I could be, he left the building and biked down the road to a public phone box, where he rang my mobile number. As we were chatting he noticed that a car was driving up and down the street, slowing down when it passed the phone box. The men in the car were taking particular interest in him. The hairs on the back of his neck prickled. He wondered if he was about to be shot in a drive-by shooting. I could hear the anxiety in his voice. As it turned out, the men in the car were colleagues from EPIC who'd followed Davey to check out who he was, and whether he was dangerous. With bombs and shootings intensifying in the early 1990s, we couldn't be too careful.

While I was with EPIC my work expanded into the role of advocacy. I'd become known in the UVF for sharing my story and listening to and engaging with the stories of other paramilitaries. I'd also spoken about that experience outside the organisation. That began informally through my membership of the church where Davey was the minister. I was asked to give my testimony to a church group. Youth workers at that meeting

157

then invited me to speak to their young people. Marty, my Quaker friend, had also encouraged me to speak at meetings she was involved with organising. I had a go at that, but withdrew when the pressure of everything became too much, and the danger of engaging with my enemy felt too close for comfort.

After the ceasefire was announced by Gusty Spence in 1994, the Dublin Forum for Peace and Reconciliation came into being. It was to be a vehicle for all democratic political parties in the North and South to discuss together the political way forward. At Gusty's invitation I went to one of the meetings in Dublin Castle. The Unionist parties had agreed to boycott the Forum. Gusty asked if I would go along as an independent former Loyalist prisoner to speak about prisoner issues. I was the only Loyalist present on that occasion, and was deeply intimidated by a group of IRA men, but student representatives drew me into their own group, and were very supportive. I was thanked for my contribution by the TDs (MPs in the government of the Irish Republic). F. W. de Klerk from South Africa was present.

When I attended meetings through EPIC, my role was to speak out for Loyalist ex-prisoners, and to make sure our story was heard. I was keen to get in on the discussions and to score points in the arguments. That remained my focus for some time, but new encounters began to challenge that position, and to make me aware of greater complexity. These encounters were with the victims of violence. Because ex-prisoner/UVF voices were missing from workshops that focused on the issues of victims, I was encouraged by EPIC to go to these workshops. My purpose was to share our own experiences, but many people at the meetings felt that paramilitaries like me shouldn't be present. Arriving at one conference in a hotel in Enniskillen, I was recognised by some of the other participants. As I walked towards the entrance I could see them turning to whisper to one another. Before I reached the front door one of the women stopped me. 'You shouldn't be here,' she said.

I was seen as someone who created victims, not a man who was one. Later, during one mealtime, I was asked by the other people on the table to sit somewhere else because they were uncomfortable having me there.

'Why are you here? You shouldn't be. This is for victims, not murderers and terrorists.'

Two women on another table, both Republicans, noticed me moving. 'What's going on?' they asked.

'Ah, it doesn't matter,' I replied.

'No, tell us what happened.'

158

'Just some people were uncomfortable having me sit with them.'

'Well, you sit with us instead.'

Both women were angry at how I'd been treated. I was deeply moved. They'd both lost loved ones through the actions of Loyalist paramilitaries like me. They knew my background, and yet they felt for me. At that stage ceasefires hadn't been declared, yet individuals like these women, who might be expected to reject me utterly, or hurl abuse at me, were prepared to take risks and cross boundaries.

The differing reactions at that conference encapsulate the diversity of response that my presence provoked among victims/survivors. Both reactions were understandable. Organisations working with victims struggled around the issue of involving representatives from ex-prisoner and paramilitary groups. Those running the conference in Enniskillen hadn't sent an invitation to any ex-prisoners groups – Republican or Loyalist – so we'd contacted them, asking why not? Their literature spoke of them seeking to understand *all* perspectives, but their concern about public opinion meant that while we were never prevented from going, they wouldn't let us know directly what was happening and when. Their fear was that funding for their work would cease. The politics got in the way of them being able to carry out the task of building understanding and transforming conflict.

My involvement with victims made me conscious that there was a hierarchy of victims. I bought into that idea to some degree. I didn't call myself a victim. A victim was someone who'd been injured or bereaved through the actions of perpetrators like me. I knew that I'd become a perpetrator in response to being a victim of the conflict, but I wasn't comfortable calling myself a victim.

Those who'd lost more than one member of their family, or were themselves severely disabled as a result of a terrorist attack, or had lost children, were regarded as greater victims than others who'd recovered fully from their injuries or lost only one family member who was elderly. Some representatives of victims' groups, who were on decision-making bodies and not using their power appropriately, went unchallenged because their suffering seemed to put them beyond question in the minds of others. These responses are understandable but unhelpful. Pain is pain. It doesn't help to rate it. That just adds to it, when what we really need is for others to take our pain seriously. No one feels better because they lost only one family member rather than all of them. Their grief at the loss of one is overwhelming. If I hit out as a result of trauma, that doesn't make my pain, or the need to address it, invalid. Leaving people unchallenged simply because they're victims may only create more victims through their inappropriate decisions and actions.

I became particularly conscious of this hierarchy of victims when I was doing the trauma training in South Africa. While we were in Cape Town, our hosts took us to meet government officials. We spoke with Cyril Ramaphosa, a lawyer, politician, activist and businessman who'd played a key role in helping South Africa to move as peacefully as possible from apartheid to democracy, and who'd set up and run the most powerful trade union (the National Union of Mineworkers) in South Africa, which transformed the appalling conditions of the mining industry there. We visited the townships. That was a frightening experience. Our ANC hosts protected us, blocking off certain roads. There were places that we couldn't go because we were white.

'White bastards!' was shouted at us numerous times, but we were able to speak with many men and women about their experiences. We were invited back to one township for an evening, but were advised that it was too dangerous to go. The next day we went to a *shebeen* (drinking den) in the township. Local women came in for the first time because we had women in our group. We heard resentment expressed by many ANC guys who felt betrayed by the new government. They still had open sewers in the street, and tin shacks, no access to education, and limited medical facilities. Across the motorway from the township were the huge houses of white people. How could anyone living with their whole family in a 16-square-metre shack not feel angry, or not find it hard to resist the temptation to turn to crime in order to ease the terrible conditions in which they lived?

One day, sitting in the home of two white South Africans, we talked about these inequalities. Alongside those of us with experience of conflict and dealing with its legacy, there were journalists and photographers. We were a mixed group of whites, blacks and Asians. I started asking questions about the plight of people in the townships. We talked about Nelson Mandela, and the Truth and Reconciliation Commission. We spoke of the human cost of apartheid. It was this latter discussion that prompted me to ask about the suffering of white families who'd lost sons in the violence. The room went very quiet.

'What's the problem?' I asked.

'We don't have this type of conversation,' was the reply. 'Whites just get on with it. They're not allowed to be victims. They were the perpetrators of apartheid.'

'So their suffering can't be recognised or considered valid? Is a mother's grief for a lost child any less because her skin is white, or because she supports an oppressive system?'

I was struck deeply by the realisation that whereas there had rightly been a complete change of government and condemnation of apartheid, the pain suffered by those who'd supported apartheid couldn't be addressed. This suggested there were legitimate and illegitimate victims, innocent ones and guilty ones. I wondered about that. It also seemed to me that unless we understand that perpetrators and their supporters have a story to tell, and as human beings are capable of being traumatised, we'll never find ways of preventing the creation of more perpetrators, or of helping people like me to move away from using violence. That's why I wanted the stories of ex-prisoners to be heard, and why I went into difficult situations in order to tell them, but I found it really hard.

Before attending meetings involving victims' groups, I was racked with anxiety. I worried about how I'd be received, and how I'd cope with the reactions to my presence. To walk into a room knowing that many of the people in it would see me as the face of the organisation responsible for the death of their loved one or the disabilities they lived with, was frightening. Yet, the more I did it, the more I realised I needed to do it, even though it added to, rather than eased my own pain. Being around those who'd lost loved ones, and hearing their stories and the impact of the violence perpetrated against them and their loved ones, made me think about the murder I'd committed, and how that might have destroyed my victim's family. It brought home the consequences of my actions in a very real way. Until that time I'd had an intellectual understanding of the cost of what I'd done, but when you hear first-hand the pain of people before you, who live bereft of a child or a parent or a partner, whether or not you can politically justify what you did means nothing in the face of their human anguish.

Although this was hard, it helped me to acknowledge my own lack of inner peace. Through my work I was trying to regain that, but I realised, listening to men and women sharing their pain, that I'd never regain it. Some might wonder why I didn't walk away from such encounters, since they caused me greater grief, but I felt it would be cowardly to do so. I'd also begun to realise that it's impossible to understand the psychology of conflict, its cost and trauma, without understanding the really human level of experience. I could have said that I grew up surrounded by conflict, that there are many different reasons why I did what I did, and that while I might not be like that now, I can justify what I did then, and get on with my life. But that wouldn't have been the whole story. I wasn't happy just accepting that others saw men like me as monsters and the cause of everything that had gone wrong in Northern Ireland. I wanted them to understand how our society, our churches and politicians were complicit in the mess.

If I was concerned about understanding, then I had to hear the stories of those whose experience was different from my own. Inevitably that demanded I go into places I wouldn't want to be, and have contact with people who'd every reason to hate my guts. I had to face a mother who'd lost her child in a bombing, a wife whose husband had been shot, a son whose parent didn't come home one day, and never would again. No one would willingly choose to have such encounters, nor face the reactions of those people for whom I was the enemy. The words they needed to say to me are not words to be repeated here, but I had to hear them in order to understand. Only with understanding could I make a difference and be an agent for change.

I always returned from such meetings utterly exhausted and often in a very dark psychological space, but I also found that over time my experience with victims' groups began to bring meaning into my life, however difficult the encounters. Somehow the despair and pain I felt was easier to manage as my understanding developed. That encouraged me to continue despite the difficulties. Change and growth is painful. That's why many people choose to remain where they are psychologically, but the answers to questions about ourselves and others often lie in the painful places, the challenging places, the disturbing places, the darkness. I wanted to understand the conflict not just at the level of the head, but at the level of my heart. Intellectual exploration alone can protect you from raw human experience.

One unexpected problem these individual encounters with victims caused for me was that they sometimes put me at odds with my role as a representative of EPIC. My job was to follow through on the organisational agenda, but sometimes that was in conflict with the personal impact of listening to victims. The organisational position was to try to bring some understanding about how the conflict wasn't just about individual reactions, but had political, social, religious and historical dimensions that exerted influences way beyond the behaviour of a minority of individuals. The bigger picture needed to be considered. We had to get to grips with institutional sectarianism, with how the government operated, with the policies and practice of the security forces, with what was happening in our churches and schools. Organisations like mine weren't prepared, quite rightly, to be scapegoated for what had happened and was still happening in Northern Ireland. Sometimes, though, I felt this position could be used as an excuse to avoid facing up to personal responsibility. I tried to convey both perspectives, but I never felt satisfied talking about the conflict in a collective way. It was too easy to stay with the collective. It enabled us to justify and commit acts of violence, immune or indifferent to the human consequences. Sometimes this point of view left me feeling isolated at EPIC. In the early days, before the ceasefires, and before more men were exploring the legacy of violence, I found myself struggling to find my place not only in conferences for victims, but also on home territory.

Before the ceasefires, bridge-building was extremely difficult. Many victims felt that anyone who'd been involved in the conflict as a paramilitary was a scumbag, a drug dealer, a gangster, a man without any sense of right or wrong. I was working to humanise those of us who'd been demonised. This is a necessary part of conflict transformation. Unless we understand the nature of conflict, the motivations and experiences of those involved in it, we can't deal with its legacy. By sharing my experience, I showed listeners that I had a story to tell, that I wasn't without humanity, that I wasn't a monster. The trouble was, at the end of a workshop, participants would go home to news of yet another atrocity which undermined everything we'd been exploring during the day. Then they'd think that all they'd been listening to was bullshit, and that I was just a perpetrator trying to manipulate their vulnerability. Some might view the news differently as a result of the workshop, but often, in the light of further violence, I'd feel my efforts were pointless. I could well understand how it was easier for victims to see all paramilitaries as less than human. Many felt that to think otherwise was to betray the loved one they'd lost.

I remember a workshop where a Republican ex-prisoner had shared his story. He'd had a difficult reception from the Protestant participants, but he'd answered the questions as well as he could, and we'd made progress. That evening the participants saw him on the news taking part in a protest against the police. Next minute my phone was ringing.

'What's the score here?' I was asked. 'Is everything he told us today a bunch of lies?'

The news bulletin made the man appear to be anti-police – he was protesting against them, after all, wasn't he? If that was the case, he must want *his* people to be in power and to control their own areas.

But that wasn't why he was there. He was making a different point. He was drawing attention to the fact that the police work going on was being heralded as inclusive of every community in the Province, but his group had been excluded. He was challenging the claim being made. He had valid political points to make, but those listening simply saw him as anti-police. Only when I'd rung him, clarified what he'd been about and got back in touch with the participants did we begin to make headway again. It was very much a case of two steps forward and one step back, or sometimes one step forward and two steps back.

Working with victims made me wonder about what my own reactions would be if I was in their position. Would I want to meet with the perpetrators of my personal pain? Would I want to understand their position? Sometimes I thought, absolutely not! I could understand when my attempts to understand the pain of the Republican community provoked anger and hostility in my own community. Think of bereaved parents whose son has been murdered by the IRA. If Republicans were suffering, why should they care? 'Serve them right for supporting the IRA. Slap it up 'em. They deserve everything they get.' When people expressed that attitude, I'd ask how they'd feel if they lost someone in their family and the other community said, 'Slap it up 'em. They deserve everything they get.'

Would they feel they deserved that reaction? My question made them uncomfortable. They'd get angry with me because I was muddying the waters. It wasn't a conversation they wanted to have. I lost friends trying to help them see the humanity of the other community.

What kept me going time and again was the grace I experienced from victims who, despite the grief caused by people such as me, offered support. I remember a Republican woman whose home had been broken into by Loyalist gunmen set on shooting her husband. He'd survived. Some time after we'd shared our stories, when a feud between three Loyalist groups, including my own, put my life in danger, this woman rang me up.

'I'm on the phone to you. I don't know what to say, but I've been thinking about the feud and what that means for you, and I wanted to let you know I'm thinking about you and hoping you're OK.'

I found such expressions of care difficult, embarrassing and painful. I didn't deserve them, and I felt I shouldn't accept them. At the same time, they moved me deeply and were profoundly inspiring.

For me, the paradox in becoming involved in peace-building was that it heightened conflict within me. It's much easier to live in a black-and-white universe than one which recognises shades of grey. Hearing the experience of others, including my enemy, and those who were victims of

164

violence in a way that I hadn't been, confronted me with my own hypocrisy. I've always been quick to react when I feel an injustice has been committed against me, but I've committed injustices against others. I was irate about being portrayed as a monster, but I'd done a monstrous thing that had destroyed not only the person I set out to kill, but also his family and my family. I protested vehemently when my human rights were under threat or denied, but I'd taken those same human rights away from others.

That made me wonder if, when you keep respecting someone's human rights and they continue to damage others, they should forfeit their human rights. It struck me that if by honouring those rights, you enable them to continue abusing the rights of others, you become complicit in their abusive behaviour. That's what the police officer wrestled with who couldn't live with himself after two of his colleagues were murdered by the men his faith and integrity had prevented him from 'taking out'. He felt as responsible for those further deaths at the hands of the IRA men, as if he'd shot his colleagues himself. For him, doing the 'right' thing brought greater evil. He didn't know how to live with this contradiction.

The more I listened to the stories of other men and women whose experience differed from my own, the more the complexity of the conflict struck me and the more questions there were to think about. I felt like I was on an emotional rollercoaster, exposing myself to the challenge of the stories and attitudes of Republican ex-prisoners and of victims from both sides of the community, sharing my own story in sometimes hostile environments, wrestling with the questions that these experiences provoked. It was a terrifying time in many ways.

Throughout this turmoil I continued reading widely about other conflict zones. I watched the unfolding of the Truth and Reconciliation Commission in South Africa. I read personal accounts of conflicts in South America. I noted that in Israel there didn't seem to be active paramilitary groups. That appeared to be because Israelis felt their government was doing everything necessary to protect them. In the light of that, I wondered whether paramilitary groups were in part the result of sections of the population feeling that their voice was going unheard, and that violence was the only way to get the attention of those in power. I studied the use and abuse of power, and I tried to understand what I was reading in relation to my own experience. That experience reinforced my natural inclination to the human, rather than the political level of operation. Personal stories rather than political rhetoric were far more influential in my own journey.

In 1999 the opportunity arose for me to develop storytelling as a key part of my work. Marty Rafferty had continued to keep in touch with me, even when I'd stepped back from speaking at conferences and workshops she was involved in running. Marty was involved with an organisation called Kairos. That particular year they invited Michael Lapsley, an Anglican priest and monk in the Society of the Sacred Mission (SSM), who was based in South Africa, to run one of his Healing of Memories workshops. Michael had been an outspoken critic of apartheid. In 1976 he was exiled by the South African government and went to live in Zimbabwe. He joined the ANC and became one of their Chaplains. During that time he discovered that he was on a South African Government hit list. In April 1990 he received a letter bomb that blew off both his hands, took out one of his eyes, and shattered his eardrums. After he'd recovered from his injuries and learnt to deal with his disabilities, Michael became involved in helping the new post-apartheid South Africa deal with the legacy of apartheid. He set up the Institute for Healing Memories in Cape Town and developed a workshop in which people from different sides of a conflict could come together to tell their stories in a safe, non-judgemental environment. The workshop used colouring and clay exercises as well as word-based tools to help participants share their experience.

I was fascinated by this. I knew only too well how certain stories can be used to fuel hatred and division, but Michael had developed a story-telling process that helped people to deal with the legacy of conflict in a way that fostered peace-building and enabled positive transformation. I attended a couple of his workshops as a participant. I was then invited by Michael to do the facilitator training for the workshop. I was blown away by that. It seemed unbelievable to me that I could receive affirmation of such a kind from someone who was, in my eyes, a victim. Here was a man with no hands, teaching me that you can't shake hands with a clenched fist, and providing the helping hand I needed to continue on my own journey.

After the training workshop I facilitated further workshops with Michael. I was convinced that this structured storytelling process, when adapted to the context of Northern Ireland, could be a powerful healing tool, bringing together people from different sides of that conflict who were ready to hear the story of the 'other'. Through EPIC I'd met Linda Britton. She was a therapist who shared my interest in the use of story-telling and providing a process where the safety of participants was paramount. She had a great way of being. I valued her support and insights, her attention to detail and her carefulness around traumatised people. Together we took on the Healing of Memories Process and began to develop it. We booked venues where security force members, the victims of bombings and shootings, and Loyalist and Republican ex-prisoners could come together to share their stories. We put a lot of work into making sure that those who came were ready to hear the stories of those they considered their enemy. We met with potential participants to explain the process so that, with us, they could determine whether this was the right next step for them.

There was a hiatus in this work when my own life was threatened. A feud had blown up between the UVF and another Loyalist paramilitary group. On New Year's Eve at the end of 1999 Mum phoned while I was in my car to say that the Lurgan police had called at their house and were looking for me. I rang them. They wouldn't say what the problem was, except that it was a security issue and could I come to the station? When I arrived they told me that a warning had been received via the Samaritans saying that I was on a hit list. It was deeply unnerving. I moved from my flat immediately and spent the first six months of the new millennium moving from safe house to safe house in Belfast.

When I rang a friend to tell him about the threat, his first response was to say, 'What have you done? How did you get yourself into that?'

I was staggered. 'What are you talking about? I've done nothing. I've spoken to no one. The only way I can make sense of this is that I'm known to work for EPIC. I've been interviewed by the media. I've spoken out against the drugs culture of some groups, and about the need to find ways other than those of violence to deal with our differences. I work with Republicans in conflict transformation. Apart from that, I've done nothing.'

I was angry. My friend realised he'd overstepped the mark and tried to rectify his mistake. In our situation you didn't have to do anything wrong to become a target. At one level, internal feuds were much more danger-ous than the conflict between Loyalists and Republicans. In the latter, my enemy lived in another area. With internal feuds, the enemy was within my community. He could be my neighbour. He walked down the streets I walked down. Sometimes he could even be in the same family where loyalties were split between different Loyalist organisations. That wasn't the case for me, but I was no longer safe in places where previously I might have felt safe. My fear wasn't misplaced. Another man on the hit list was shot dead. As it turned out, the UVF was the stronger of the groups involved in the feud. With their negotiation from a position of strength, the threat to my life was removed. The experience heightened my already high sensitivity to danger, and confirmed my feeling that I would never be truly free from the legacy of the conflict in Northern Ireland.

Shortly after this disturbing time, I was invited to speak at a meeting in Belfast City Hall that was part of the 'Way of Peace 2000'. This three-day event was organised by The World Community for Christian Meditation. The Dalai Lama had been invited to spend three days in the Province, crossing the physical expressions of our divided communities – the streets closed off by high walls and gates – planting trees on both sides of the community divide, spending time with victims, politicians, religious groups and, in my case, listening to the story of a perpetrator as well.

About 500 people had gathered in the City Hall. I came down from Newcastle, where I'd been facilitating a Restorative Justice workshop for Alternatives. Alternatives was an organisation on the Shankill Road committed to restorative justice, and I'd become involved in doing some work for them. As I made my way down from Newcastle I felt sick with anxiety. My black T-shirt expressed the darkness of my mood. I was scared.

On the platform with the Dalai Lama, his translator and the chairman facilitating the meeting were men and women who'd been victims of terrorist attacks in Northern Ireland. I was the only paramilitary on stage. They'd tried to get a Republican, but no one would do it. After a brief time of meditation, Johnston McMaster, the chairman, began to speak:

'Holiness, ladies and gentlemen, in a moment we will listen to testimonies from people who in different ways have been affected by the violence of the last 30 years, and so I ask you to listen with empathy, to be personally and collectively present to personal narratives of pain ...'

The victims present then told their stories. I remember Mary Hannon-Fletcher speaking. In 1975, when returning from seeing *Godfather II* with her boyfriend, she was gunned down in a drive-by shooting, with the result that she's been confined to a wheelchair ever since. She finished off telling her story with these words:

'I think that no other family should have to suffer like that. I don't think it's acceptable. I don't think anybody has the right to take another life or to harm someone, and I think that that would be my greatest prayer. And we need decent, honest people to help us get peace, and that's what I want to say.'

As people shared their stories, you could have heard a pin drop. Every so often the Dalai Lama would lean back towards his translator, who'd clarify whatever had just been said, whispering in his ear. The man next to me, a minister and the son of a policeman, didn't look at me. We'd met on previous occasions at conferences and workshops but there'd been little interaction between us, or desire for that.

Eventually it was my turn. I kept my eyes focused on the stage in front of me as I tried to think about what I was saying. Every so often I glanced up at those around me.

'My first contact with the conflict in Northern Ireland was when I was 14 years old,' I began. 'My home town had been destroyed twice by IRA bombs. A number of men – fellas who I went to school with – had fathers who'd been killed who were members of the UDR, and there was a sense, growing up, of losing all that was dear to you. I joined the paramilitaries at the age of 14, and at 17 I went to prison and served 13 years.

'During the Hunger Strikes, when Bobby Sands died ... there was always significant events in your life that are a catalyst for change. I had already begun a journey, for about two years, of reflecting upon the use of violence, upon my role within the conflict – constantly feeling guilty about the pain and hurt that I'd caused my family. Both my parents who had aged maybe ten years in a matter of years – but when Bobby Sands died, I can remember going on a visit with three prison officers in the back of a van, who were laughing at the death of Bobby Sands and said that they couldn't wait until the rest of them died.

'And I can remember being angry at that. I can remember attacking them verbally for what they had said. I can remember coming back from the visit and lying on my bed in the cell that night, wondering why I was defending Bobby Sands. I despised everything he stood for politically, and certainly, if I'd had the opportunity, I'd have tried to kill him and he'd have tried to kill me. I felt I was betraying who I was because I was defending him, but I realised that although I despised him and he was my enemy, I'd seen a certain courage in the fact that someone was prepared to die for something they believed. I realised that I'd seen him as a human being for the first time; that I was actually prepared to accept that my enemy were human beings. Until that time I had them demonised.

'And it's easy to commit acts of violence against people you've demonised. You don't consider their pain. You don't consider their families. You don't consider the damage you're doing to yourself. On my release from prison I was determined to try and live my life and to commit something to the community ... and it was almost a vocation that I had to get involved in something in the community ... I suppose, in my own thinking, in order to redeem myself.

'I'm still involved in the community. I'm a counsellor. I work with prisoners and their families and their children, and also with other people in the community and cross-community.

'But there is no sense of having redeemed myself. There's no inner peace. I am unable to find that inner peace. And I think that that's the price you pay for being involved in violence, in the conflict.

'I'd just like to finish with a brief reading of something that sums up my feelings. It's thoughts on war from Deng Ming Tao, a Taoist monk who lived several thousand years before Christ:

> If you hold a real weapon in your hand, you will feel its character strongly. It begs to be used. It is fearsome. Its only purpose is death, and its power is not just in the material from which it is made, but also from the intention of its makers.
>
> When death, pain and destruction are visited upon what you hold to be most sacred the spiritual price is devastating. What hurts more than one's own suffering is bearing witness to the suffering of others. The regret of seeing human beings at their worst and the sheer pain of not being able to help the victims, can never be redeemed. If you go personally to war, you cross the line yourself. You sacrifice ideals for survival and the fury of killing. That alters you forever.'

Those words cut deep. I felt tears welling up inside and struggled to hold my voice. For a few moments I couldn't continue as I tried to hold myself together. The man next to me reached out and put his hand on my shoulder. I could see he was visibly moved. I looked across at Mary. There were tears in her eyes, and she was smiling encouragement across to me. I read the final words of the quote:

'"That is why no-one rushes to be a soldier. Think before you want to change so unalterably. The stakes are not merely one's life, but one's very humanity." Thank you.'

There was a silence after I'd finished, then people clapped. I looked across at the Dalai Lama. He seemed touched by my words. Eventually he spoke in response to all our stories. As he drew his comments to a close, he looked at me very intently, saying in broken English, 'Inspite difficult, painful experience ... your attitude is something of very, very positive ... I feel hope.'

Chapter 14

You will learn something more in woods than in books.

St Bernard

2000–2006

The fire is burning brightly. Its flames are a comforting sight: they help keep the wild animals at bay. One night lions came into our camp, but they didn't venture out of the shadows into the firelight. We discovered their paw-prints in the morning. Last night we heard them roaring not too far away. Tonight I'm on guard with a Republican ex-prisoner, an irony that isn't lost on either of us. I'm supposed to be keeping watch on my own: it's all part of the experience of being in the bush, and making discoveries about who we are when everything familiar to us has been stripped away. That's the purpose of this wilderness trek. When we have to rely for survival on someone who once wouldn't have thought twice about killing us, it challenges our perspective and helps break open the boxes in which we've put others. It gives us the chance to see and experience their humanity instead.

In a day or so, I'll get the hang of solo guard duty, but tonight I needed a bit of moral support. So Ron and I are sitting close to the fire, keeping watch while everyone else sleeps on the ground around the burning logs. Above us the wide black velvet of an African sky glints with diamond-bright stars, and around us all the noises of the bush keep our heads turning this way and that, alert for signs of danger. We talk quietly as we strain to see into the shadows. Suddenly we hear a buzzing noise close at hand and out of the darkness, two huge creatures fly at us.

'Bats! Bats!' we yell, as they hit against our bodies. We leap in panic from the ground – vertical take-off! Our mugs of coffee go flying and everyone else is suddenly awake, wondering what the hell is happening. Our South African guides get a grip on the situation very quickly. They're smiling broadly as they point out the giant moths we've mistaken for bats. There's a lot of laughter and rude comments from those dragged so

171

abruptly from sleep. Feeling very sheepish – how we needed those moths to be vampire bats at the very least! – we take up our post again and everyone else settles down to try and catch a bit more sleep before the dawn drags them, aching, into another day.

It's a far cry from the platform in Belfast City Hall where I told my story in front of the Dalai Lama. Yet the two experiences aren't unconnected. Unbeknown to me at the time, if I hadn't accepted the invitation to speak, as I very nearly didn't, some of the opportunities that have subsequently come my way might never have happened. The meeting with the Dalai Lama was filmed. Since that time I've received enquiries from programme-makers who've seen the footage, and want to know more about the work I do, and the story I have to tell. While I've been working on this book I've been in discussions with an American documentary-maker who wants to film us running one of the Wilderness Treks that have become a part of my work since that first trek when a couple of moths reminded me that I wasn't as tough as I thought!

It fascinates me how one decision can set the direction of our future, without us having any idea at the time how influential it will be. Often that influence is the result of factors over which we have no control: if the World Community for Christian Meditation hadn't filmed the event, and other people hadn't had access to that footage, projects I'm involved with now wouldn't be happening. Yet at the time, when the presentations on the platform were finished, I wanted nothing more than to be away from the place. I felt utterly drained.

As I was preparing to leave, the Dalai Lama made a specific request to talk with me alone. In a small room he spoke words of affirmation about the journey I'd made, and the difficulty of that. He spoke of change and the future. He'd seen my darkness. He'd heard where I was – struggling with my identity as a perpetrator, more able to see the negatives than the positives in myself – and he wanted to give me hope. We spoke for about 15 minutes before he was whisked away.

The meeting both moved and disturbed me. It was moving to experience the Dalai Lama's compassion and care. It was disturbing because I had difficulty with other forms of *Christian* expression. The Dalai Lama was from a different religion altogether and one where the chanting and meditation felt deeply alien to me. Subsequently, as I've experienced different faiths and cultures, I'm struck by the fact that the point of connection between people always comes at the human level of the heart. When there is a relationship of trust, difference need not be a source of division but can be a cause for celebration.

Back in the Hall, members of the audience came up to thank me for my words. 'You spoke well. That took courage.'

As always, I was embarrassed by the attention. Two Republican lads from the Ardoyne or Ballymurphy stepped in front of me. I tensed up, expecting abuse.

'Fair play to you. That must have took guts. Just wanted to shake your hand.'

Some women present were more emotional, touching my arm, rubbing my hands as they held them, being intimate in a way that was uncomfortable, coming as it did from strangers. They spoke in quiet, calm voices that disturbed me. A couple of men noticed my discomfort and came over.

'You look as though you need rescuing!' they joked, guiding me away from all the people who were trying to talk to me. Grateful to them, I made my escape.

As 2000 became 2001, the emphasis at EPIC changed. The organisation began to focus more on human-rights issues in relation to ex-prisoners and their families. My own interest was in dealing with trauma and counselling at a basic human level, and developing the use of storytelling as part of a healing process. Martin had left EPIC to start up the Conflict Resource Trauma Centre (CRTC). He wanted me to join him there but I fell ill and was in hospital for a month with a stomach problem. The post couldn't be held open. Instead I went to work at Alternatives, with its focus on restorative justice, mediation and family counselling. Here, I was able to do a Mediation and Restorative Justice Training Course run by the Thames Valley Police.

I also learnt a great deal from Debbie, one of the team at Alternatives, whose skills and insights gained from her work in restorative justice and mediation opened up my own understanding. She was immensely patient, and expert at dealing with difficult people. She wasn't afraid to speak out.

It was while I was at Alternatives that I became more aware of the resistance many people felt about ex-prisoners being involved in this kind of work, and their belief that we shouldn't be paid for what we did. We'd taken life, so we should suffer for the rest of our own. We didn't deserve to receive benefits, but neither could we be seen to earn a living if that living had some connection with our past history. What we were supposed to live on, goodness knows. I can understand people feeling that I shouldn't benefit financially as a result of my past, yet it's through wrestling with that past that I have the kind of insights and expertise that both victims and perpetrators find helps them deal with their pain in the present day.

Sometimes I feel that others would prefer it if I remained a man of violence. That way I wouldn't challenge their perspective. Mostly, as human beings we find it easier if people stick to the labels we give them. So, paramilitaries are evil in the eyes of many. Many of us did do evil things, though we thought we were right to do them at the time. Yet when the opportunity arose, we debated the issues, changed our thinking, met with 'our enemy' and began to work for peace, even when bombs and guns were still going off and threatening our lives. The decision to move away from conflict and violence began in the prisons with Gusty Spence and men like him. If the men on the ground hadn't wanted to live a different way, the task of politicians would have been so much harder, if not impossible. That's not a popular view. We find it hard to acknowledge 'badness' in 'good' people, and 'goodness' in 'bad' people.

For me, prison was a brutal place, horrific at times, but I also have to acknowledge that it was a beneficial experience. I learnt a great deal. That was largely due to other prisoners and the amount of time there was to read and reflect, rather than because the system was a good one. The reason I went to prison was something that shouldn't have happened, yet the negative has led to something positive. Wrestling with the legacy of my destruction of other people's lives has given me gifts that today help others who are suffering.

I spent a year with Alternatives before leaving to work freelance. This wasn't an easy decision. There seemed to be so much against me. Funding usually is given to organisations, rather than individuals. I wondered if I'd be able to earn a living working in this way. Yet I knew from experience that while the support of an organisation can be helpful, it can also be limiting. Every organisation has its own agenda that its employees are expected to fulfil. I wanted to develop my own work, with storytelling as a central strand of that work. Through my experience as a participant and then as a facilitator of workshops, my conviction about the importance of preparation was confirmed time and again.

As Northern Ireland moved closer to peace, and particularly after the Good Friday Agreement (1998), all kinds of funding became available from sources like the European Community. There was a growing interest in storytelling. People who'd been along to storytelling workshops noted what went on and thought they could replicate them. The exercises can be easily reproduced, but dealing with the issues and conflicts that sometimes arise through those exercises takes great experience. If the inevitable tough moments aren't handled well, participants leave more damaged than when they arrived. Issues around conflict, truth and justice, prison and prisoners, victims, perpetrators and survivors – all these needed careful attention in workshops. They're highly complex and in the hands of inexperienced people, dangerous. The boundaries have to be clear.

I meet people all the time who've been damaged by badly run workshops. One organisation allowed participants to bring alcohol into the storytelling work. A drink at night is fine, but an inebriated participant among a group of vulnerable people isn't. Another group invited a participant along to tell their story, then when he arrived told him not to share his story because others would find it difficult. The person felt utterly betrayed.

My lack of compromise regarding the safety of participants means that some people don't always find me easy to work with. I don't let things drop if I think they're important. This means that when a charity feels they've learnt what they need to from me, they don't ask me back and their own staff facilitate the workshops instead, often without the same degree of safety. Yet, if you're bringing together enemies, victims and perpetrators, security force members and those who tried to kill them, safety has to be paramount, and preparation, meticulous.

All this fostered a desire in me to work with people I trusted, whose attention to detail and care in running workshops were the same as mine. Going freelance was a big step to take, not least because I was always questioning my abilities. I knew my own skills were developing. I just didn't know the extent of them, and I often found myself in conflict with the so-called experts. It'd been like that ever since I started training in counselling.

On formal courses I felt the hearts of tutors must always sink when they saw me coming because I'd argue until the issue I had with them had been satisfactorily addressed. When I'd completed the two-year counselling diploma I'd undertaken before leaving EPIC, I didn't feel it had equipped me to carry out the work that the qualification entitled me to do. All the way through, while other students had complained privately about how the course was run but kept their heads down and said nothing to those responsible for it, I'd made myself really unpopular complaining about what was going on. There were tensions between tutors that affected the learning processes of the students, how their work was or wasn't marked, and what parts of the course did or didn't get done. It wasn't until one tutor finally had the courage to challenge her colleagues about what was happening in the department, that my questions were vindicated, and the senior academics finally acknowledged that the course hadn't been run as it should've been. My teacher's courage cost her her job. I realised that sometimes it's much easier to stand against an unjust enemy than to stand against an unjust friend. The experience also taught me that because of my background, getting heard by academics might never be easy for me.

After the ceasefires, and then the Good Friday Agreement, it became standard practice for ex-prisoners from both sides of the community to speak at workshops and conferences. For the organisers it was good to be able to tick the box about having ex-paramilitaries/prisoners present. Judging by the reactions of participants, my contributions were well received. They often came up afterwards to say that I'd made them think in a different way. Students on courses relating to peace and reconciliation were enthusiastic about my words. 'This isn't what we hear in lectures,' they said, 'but it really makes sense to us.'

Yet though our experience and expertise might be greater than that of the academics present, we ex-prisoners were never treated on an equal basis. It seemed that the letters they had after their names were of greater importance than the experience we had under our belts. I wanted to challenge this perspective, but it was an uphill battle, and sometimes I just wanted to throw in the towel. There were academics who'd blind us with psychobabble or complicated language, yet I'd expect anyone working in the field to know that a key requirement to peace-building and conflict-transformation is being able to make yourself understood, to find the right language for the people you're with.

Prison had taught me to argue quite vigorously. I'd learnt a great deal from the cut and thrust of debates with prisoners who didn't suffer fools gladly and who, in an argument, won respect not because of who they were, but because they'd been able to make a strong case for whatever point of view they were putting forward. I challenged perspectives that I didn't understand, or that didn't ring true with what I knew from experience, and I expected that whoever I challenged would come back at me to prove their own case. Either way, one or other of us, or both would see that our argument was faulty and respond appropriately, but that wasn't the case when I got into debate with some academics. I remember being at a workshop where an expert was talking about anger management. He said that he could train anyone to deal with their anger so that they never lost their temper again. It was a sweeping statement and one which went against what I knew about human nature, so I questioned his assertion. In response he asked me what I did.

'I'm involved in conflict transformation work,' I replied.

Immediately he asked me if I knew the work of two academics in that field. I didn't.

'What?! You don't know them?! I'd have thought if you were engaged in conflict transformation, you'd know these people.'

I didn't say any more after that. I needed to think about what was going on. His response had nothing to do with answering my question. He'd simply deflected attention away from his assertion, and deliberately put me down in the process. Later the next day, I found myself questioning another point he'd made, and I countered what he'd said with a quote from another expert in the field of conflict transformation who I'd personally worked with at Stanford University in California. Stanford is renowned for its work in peace-building and peace-implementation, and the man I was quoting had been involved in facilitating 16 peace agreements around the world.

'Do you know Steadman and Ross?' I asked.

He didn't, so I gave him the same reaction he'd given me the day before: 'What?! You don't know them?! I'd have thought if you were engaged in conflict transformation, you'd know these people.'

I'm committed to working for mutual understanding. That sometimes means if someone tries to play power-games, or doesn't keep to the working agreement that we've put together at the beginning of any process, I'll make sure they experience being on the receiving end of the destructive responses they've inflicted on others, and point out what I'm doing if that becomes necessary.

Of course, as in every other area of my experience, I was full of contradictory responses as I tried to address the elitist realm of trauma academia. Often I felt inexperienced and inadequate. What did I know? I'd go into a room feeling intimidated by those who had PhDs, but as the day wore on I realised that far too often their theories didn't match the reality of those living through traumatic experiences. That made me aware that I did in fact know a great deal. It encouraged me to talk from the heart and to trust my intuition, which was rooted in experience. That's what was valued by the people who listened to my story and responded to my work.

Then, at a number of conferences when I spoke out about such things, one or two academics would make a point of supporting what I said. They gave me hope, and also made me think more about my own reactions. I'd decided to engage with academics to challenge their prejudice, but now some of them were forcing me to face my own prejudice. I didn't need to condemn the whole of academia in the field of conflict transformation and trauma just because some were unable to value the wisdom and experience of ex-prisoners and paramilitaries.

When I first met Dr Brandon Hamber, I was critical and suspicious of him. He is Director of INCORE, a United Nations Research Centre for the Study of Conflict at the University of Ulster. My attitude towards him might not have changed had we not been facilitators of the same group on one of the Wilderness Treks. I noticed how he mucked in and connected with people at a very human level. That made such a difference to me. We went on to be involved together in a workshop organised by Swiss Peace on storytelling, demilitarisation, demobilisation and reintegration. Brandon has played an important part in challenging my own prejudice and in working to bring academics together with practitioners like myself.

Among the Vietnam War Veterans I'd met, there were a couple of academics who were very human and genuine. After them I met Byron Bland, an academic at Stanford University. He invited me to an International Peace Building Conference at the University in California to make presentations on the subject of 'Looking at the legacy of violent conflict and peace building' and to run workshops for his students. He wanted to access my experience. We talked about exploring methods to reduce the gap that exists between academics and practitioners involved in peace-building, who have roles in and responsibilities for the communities in which they live and work. Back in Northern Ireland, I also began to meet with academics who shared the same interest. Today we are working together to bridge the gap and build respect between academics and grassroots practitioners.

One close friend and colleague is Dr Wilhelm Verwoerd. When we first met, Wilhelm was the programme manager on the ex-combatants' programme at the Glencree Centre for Peace and Reconciliation in County Wicklow, not far from Dublin. The Centre ran groups for victims and for ex-prisoners from both sides of the divide. Sharing our stories over a pint in a local pub one day, Wilhelm and I discovered a joint love of nature. I told him that being in the natural world was one of the few places where I could experience a sense of peace. He talked about the treks that were run in his native South Africa. At that time I'd been trying to do a wilderness trek in Colorado, but because of my history I couldn't get a visa. My criminal record meant that although I was allowed into the States to do some work at Stanford University, I wasn't permitted to do much else. At Stanford I'd met with a number of Native Americans. I was fascinated to hear about their cleansing ceremonies and the use of sweat lodges in restoring the balance between heart and mind. In the past that was to help warriors returning from battle. Today it's used to help gang members dealing with violence, substance abuse, and the loss of any sense of who they are. I was invited by the men to experience the sweat lodge – an invitation I later learned was a great honour to receive – but my visa restrictions prevented me from being able to accept it.

This wasn't the case in relation to South Africa, and I was fascinated by Wilhelm's descriptions of the wilderness treks that took place there. As we talked, we both felt that bringing men and women from conflict zones on a trek where the group lived very basically and needed to care for one another if all was to go well, could be a powerful tool of transformation. Ian White at Glencree heard about our conversation and was able to secure funding for us to try a pilot trek. We went with a Republican ex-prisoner, Ron, and joined up with some South African participants. Despite the embarrassing incident with the moths that Ron and I thought were bats, the trek was fantastic! We carried our own food and cooking utensils. We had the barest minimum of clothes. We slept in the open. We were led by armed guides who could protect us from the animals if necessary. They also made sure that we left every place where we camped looking as if no one had been there. I felt both steeped in beauty, and scared because of the dangerous animals, snakes and insects. Enjoying the glory of an African sunrise, I felt guilty. I didn't deserve this, and I thought of the people who'd never experience this because of the actions of men like me. I was alive to all the new things in the present moment, yet the pain of the past kept breaking through.

At times we had snakes slithering across our feet. Rhino came into the camp one night, and we had to get up and hide behind trees. One day we walked into a group of rhinos by mistake, and had to back away very carefully. We learnt to 'go to the toilet' only during the day because at night it would be too dangerous to wander off alone into the darkness. We'd take a spade, leave the camp, do what we needed to do and bury the evidence. It was the only time we were on our own. My nerves were wrecked by it because every sound I heard in the grass I thought was something creeping up on me. The vulnerability of being in the bush meant a great deal. It doesn't matter who you are in that place, or what power you have, or about any of the other things you hide behind in your own world. Here, they were stripped away, and we couldn't deny we were scared. The guides and the animals were in control. We felt dependent on others. That was hard. It was challenging and therapeutic. The guides helped us to work with nature, and that opened up conversations around the campfire.

Returning home, I realised the experience had been very healing, so we decided to plan another trek. We knew that it wouldn't be something that everyone was ready for. Again, there had to be careful preparation in selecting the people we thought could benefit from it. We thought about taking ex-combatants, ex-prisoners and victims from both communities. Everyone had been selected, and then the politics erupted. It'd been reported, inaccurately, to a powerful Loyalist group that I'd said there weren't any Loyalists ready enough to go. Rivalries and power-politics in my community meant that Glencree was confronted with the choice of taking the people those in power felt should go, or alienating them by following my advice based on experience. In the end they went with the former. I was asked to withdraw from the process. That hurt me deeply, but it isn't an uncommon experience. Many decisions are made in the light of power-politics, rather than because a particular action has integrity. Groups working in the field of peace-building struggle with internal conflicts like any other organisation.

My relationship with Wilhelm was inevitably damaged by the difficulties around organising the first wilderness trek. Though later I felt my position was vindicated, at the time all my prejudices about well-intentioned academics like him were provoked. It took us a couple of years to work through that upset. I didn't walk away, because I liked Wilhelm very much as a person. I wanted this relationship to work out. He was trying to heal the wound as well. He had the grace to acknowledge he'd made some wrong decisions. I had to acknowledge that things weren't black and white. We needed to grapple with issues of power and personality. It was important to deal with this conflict between us: if we didn't try to address it, we'd no business being involved in conflict transformation work elsewhere. I knew that Wilhelm wasn't an academic without first-hand experience of conflict. As Prime Minister, his grandfather had been instrumental in the establishment of the apartheid system in South Africa. Wilhelm had his own story to tell. We're very different people, but we've forged a friendship that means a great deal to me.

In 2005 I went with him on another trek in a semi-facilitation role. We took another group out in 2007, and in 2008.

One of the joys of the treks is being with the guides. One in particular influenced my journey. His name is Ian Reed. He's a massive, Grizzly Adams type of guy with long hair. If I'd met him in a bar, I wouldn't have messed with him! He wasn't sentimental or romantic about nature, but he had a sense of the preciousness of life, and an immense understanding of the natural world. In difficult situations he wasn't afraid to share his own pain. He represented everything tough and hard and strong in terms of how he looked, and how he could survive in the wilderness, and yet he was as gentle as could be. He taught me that being strong and effective isn't about muscles and aggression, but often about listening and patience. He showed me the connectedness of nature, and how to pass through the bush without leaving any trace of having been there.

I found the power of Ian's gentleness compelling. When I have to use other more aggressive forms of language now, I feel diminished by that, however necessary it might be. In Northern Ireland I sometimes work with groups where the language of my teenage years is the norm. If I am going to get the group to work with me, I have to make it clear I'm a man who can hold his own in that context, and am familiar with it. That doesn't feel good. It's another example of complexity in my life. In my work I need to be gentle, sensitive and empathetic, but I also need to be analytical, and sometimes challenging.

By nature I don't think I have any difficulty being confrontational, if I think there's an issue that isn't being tackled and that needs to be brought into the open. I don't seek to avoid conflict. Conflict can be part of a creative process of breaking out and breaking free. If it's left simmering below the surface in a group, it can sabotage the process.

Honesty is very important to me, but honesty is difficult in the context of conflict. Honesty isn't about telling everything, because that might put you or someone else in danger. It's about saying where you are at any given moment without damaging your health or safety. Honesty has implications for self, family and community. At our storytelling workshops we encourage participants not to say anything they're unsure about. There'll always be another occasion. Trust takes time to build. When you come into a room of people who have been perpetrators and/or victims, you may not feel safe enough to share everything, and that's fine. My task as a facilitator isn't to make people say more than they're ready to say, but to make sure they don't use their words for point-scoring, or to avoid difficult issues, or as a weapon to hurt others.

Over the years my way of facilitation has become more participatory. Some facilitators will say that if two parties are in conflict about a particular issue, the facilitator must simply enable that debate, even if it isn't the real issue lying behind the words. I know I might well stir up a hornet's nest, but I won't be helping the group effectively if I don't enable them to see and tackle the real issue. I work very intuitively, listening carefully to everything that is said, to what is left unsaid, and to all the non-verbal ways in which people communicate. When I challenge a group, it is always on the basis of what I've picked up from them, and is rooted in my relationship with them.

I might say, 'I'm not happy with what's just taken place in the group.'

'What do you mean?'

'Well, this is what's just been said … and it provoked this discussion … but I wonder if we're avoiding something important here.'

'What do you mean?'

'I can understand if you see the real issue here and don't want to explore it because it's too painful. I can accept that, but as I've listened, this is what seems to be going on. *[I then go over what has been said, the issues they've raised, and what these might point to.]* We can keep discussing the subject you've raised, but on the basis of what you've all been saying, that doesn't seem to me to be the real issue. We'll take a break now and then when you come back, you can tell me whether we'll carry on as we were, or whether you want to do the deeper work that needs to be done.'

When the group I spoke to in this way came back, they said they wanted to explore the underlying difficulty, so we went with that, and I asked what a particular person had really meant by what they'd said. This opened up the understanding in the group and they were able to go forward to the next part of the journey.

As a facilitator I have power which I can use for good or ill. Power can be a helpful and useful tool. What's important is that I don't impose my agenda on the group but enable them to see what's present in the group.

Someone who says in a workshop, 'There's a war, people die, move on,' needs help to tease that out, and to see the impact that statement has on those who've been bereaved through the conflict.

'Are you saying that all those deaths don't mean anything, or that people shouldn't struggle because they've lost someone, or are you trying to avoid taking personal responsibility for what you've done?'

If a victim refuses to go into a room where there's a perpetrator, it's not my task to force a meeting, but I wouldn't be doing my job properly if I didn't help them tease out their feelings and explore their responses in a safe, non-judgemental space.

'I understand it's important for you not to go into the room with X, but I wonder if you could help me understand your reason behind that position, because people have different reasons about this and I don't want to make assumptions about what yours might be. Are there things you can talk about?'

Often these sorts of questions help someone who's finding it difficult to articulate their feelings to explore them a little more. As I've worked on my approach, I've made many mistakes along the way. There are things I haven't handled properly, or I've become defensive. Perhaps I've spent more time with one person than another. Reflecting on that afterwards, I've realised I warmed to one person more than another, but it's unprofessional if I allow that preference to impinge on how I work with a group. Nowadays, even if I feel a strong dislike towards a person, I make sure I spend with them the time they need. No facilitator can be entirely objective. We all carry our own baggage. If we're aware of that we can prevent it causing damage. Contrary to one line of thought, self can't be left outside the door, and shouldn't be. That self is as responsible for the work that goes well, as it is when things go wrong. What makes the difference is our level of awareness. I constantly analyse how I've facilitated a session, so that if I've made mistakes I don't repeat them. It's also helpful working with co-facilitators who I know will see and pick up on things I miss, or will draw my attention to a particular issue when we're debriefing.

When a victim speaks out about his painful reaction to having a gun thrust down his throat – something I did to others in my youth – I don't let that influence my response at the time, because I'm focusing on their story and their reactions to it. Afterwards I will think about the impact of those words on me.

Not being afraid to address difficult issues has stood me in good stead as I've worked with groups around the world. It doesn't always make me popular but it does enable work in extreme contexts to get done in a safe and therapeutic way.

Following my time in Stanford University, I was invited to the Philippines with Martin Snodden to take part in an international conference on 'Interrogating Reconciliation'. On the flight over, I met a girl from the Nationalist community in Derry. We talked throughout the flight. When we got off, she gave us a bag of goodies to keep us going. Such unexpected kindness always moves me.

In the Philippines I was struck by the poverty around us. Travelling abroad makes me aware of just how lucky I am living where I do. This is a novel thought, since I've often felt how terrible it was to grow up in Northern Ireland during the conflict. During the conference I experienced monsoon rain for the first time. It was fabulous. I met some amazing people. There were aborigines who taught me a great deal about community, respect for the land, and being disenfranchised. Among those we met there was no sense of bitterness. Those aborigines who had gained their PhDs hadn't lost touch with their roots. Their qualifications hadn't come through privilege but through sheer determination, and a refusal to accept the position others had forced upon them.

At dinner I sat next to Cory Aquino, the President of the Philippines. I have the photo still. Everyone dressed smartly, and me in my trademark jeans and T-shirt.

The conference was looking at social cycles and the way they relate to conflict. For me that meant talking about what was happening on the ground in Northern Ireland from a psychological perspective. I was the first person to address the audience. I felt very nervous. All the people were experts with PhDs. Those of us who were speaking from experience went first. There were two of us from Northern Ireland, one person from Stanford, and two from Eritrea. Our talks provoked an interesting response, relayed to me by the co-ordinator of the conference:

'You wouldn't believe the number of papers I've been asked to return to academics because of the input you five gave today. You set the tone, and now they're panicking. They seem to fear that what they've prepared doesn't fit with your experiences.'

Some were up reworking their papers until two in the morning. When one of the younger academics got up to give his presentation, he said that he'd been up all night worrying that his research wouldn't match up to the very powerful human stories he'd heard on the first day.

'I was going to change what I'd written, but I decided that wouldn't be right,' he said. 'I'm going to give the paper I prepared and then you can respond as you see fit.'

I warmed to him for his honesty and integrity.

Martin spoke on the last day. You could hear a pin drop. Martin had been a Loyalist gunman and bomber in the 1970s. One of his unit was killed, together with a woman in the pub they were bombing, when the bomb went off prematurely. Martin was blown up but survived. I was sitting alone in the upstairs gallery when he began to talk at the conference. He spoke about a young boy growing up, kicking a ball against a wall, and about his hopes and dreams. He was that boy, like any young boy around the world. The only difference was that he was living in a place of conflict. He then went on to say how he became involved in the violence. It was all stuff I could relate to, and it had me in floods of tears. I had to leave the hall. One of the women I knew saw me go out. She followed me. We walked around for about an hour before we went back in. We connected with one another because her father had killed himself in an upstairs room while she was sitting downstairs. She'd always wondered what was so bad that he couldn't come those few feet downstairs to speak to her. She too could relate to the pain Martin spoke about.

After the conference Martin and I stayed on a few days, experiencing the culture and its extremes, the poverty and the wealth. We loved the markets with their noise and colour. Walking into an eating-house out in the country, we wondered why the tables all had holes in them. Above us we noticed monkeys chained to the rafters. A local delicacy, it seemed, was to present a monkey's head with the top sliced off and the brains cooked. It was placed in the hole, and fixed with hooks under the table.

After the Philippines I went to Kosovo on a five-day residential, working with Serbians and Albanians, enabling them to share their stories and explore reconciliation. The third Balkan war had ended in 2001. The people of Pristina were in the early stages of struggling to come to terms with the legacy of that conflict. The participants found it challenging to see me and a Republican working together. At that point they couldn't contemplate ever working with each other. How, they wondered, could I work with someone who, a few years earlier, I'd have wanted to kill and who would've wanted to kill me? Our relationship couldn't be real, they felt.

We spent part of our time in the Muslim area of Pristina, home to the Albanian participants. To get into the Serb area, we had to cross a bridge. French soldiers belonging to the international force, K4, controlled the bridge. Our Albanian hosts could only take us half-way across, where we were met by our Serbian hosts. Around us were men in long black coats. Those of us from the Province recognised them as 'the boys' we were familiar with back home. They were checking who we were. They had the same mannerisms, body language and protocols as any similar group in any other conflict zone. They saw themselves as the ones with power. *It's up to us if you get let through or not.* I remembered my younger self manning the barricades we set up during the Workers' Strike. It was at this grassroots level, rather than the political realm, that I preferred to operate.

Returning one night to our hotel, we heard a song called 'The Billy Boys' being sung in a bar close by. It was a Loyalist song. We went and looked in and were astonished to see it was full of RUC men. They were dealing with security in the area. They were flabbergasted to meet us. We ended up in a confrontation with them because we wouldn't tell them why we were there. We didn't want to cause any problems for our participants. One of the officers became verbally unpleasant, and we responded in kind. Here we were in another conflict zone, finding our own police force and being confronted with all the mixed feelings we had about them. The Republican I was with was amazed by our reactions. He thought it was only Republicans who hated the RUC and had suffered under them. What we shared with him of our own experience challenged some of his long-held truths.

During the second workshop all the Serbian participants left the room at one point because they were offended by what had been said by the Albanians. They felt their experiences weren't being accepted and validated. I spoke to them about the issue, and what would enable them to come back into the room. I said we would explain to the Albanians what the problem was and that the Serbians would come back if they were assured that they could tell their stories without interruption. Of course, that would mean that they would extend the same courtesy back to the Albanians. For both groups, having their stories heard was what really mattered, so they all agreed. After that we were able to continue at a much more human level.

During another exercise we asked everyone to take a piece of paper and describe the most far-away place they'd been in their life. When everyone came back into the group and were discussing what they'd written, it was clear that many hadn't travelled beyond Serbia. Then we came to a young girl who, when asked for her answer, said, 'My imagination'.

I was blown away by that. She was the only person not to talk about a geographical place. She spoke about what she'd imagined as a young girl, what she wanted to do, where she wanted to go, and what it was like in her imagination. Her words crossed all the barriers in the room because everyone could identify with what she was sharing at a human level.

During that same meeting we had an American guy in the group who was representing the sponsoring organisation. He kept moving between the small groups until I told him to stay in one because he was distracting everyone. He chose mine. In this workshop there was a working agreement that we all speak in English so that everyone could understand what was said. In my small group one of the girls broke down completely while she was sharing her story. This was a big step for her because when she'd told it on other occasions, she'd never engaged with it emotionally. While she was crying she was comforted by a friend who spoke in their native language.

The American stopped them, saying, 'I'd like to remind you that we have a working agreement to speak in English.'

At that point I called a break and took him aside. 'Don't you ever do that again,' I said. 'One, you're here as an observer, not a facilitator, and two, this person is emotionally distressed. In that state she needs to speak in her own language. Otherwise it would be like me asking you, in a time of distress, to express yourself in German. You can't do it. It's not real. Speaking in English is about the sessions. This is different.'

The same man had introduced himself as coming from a country that wasn't involved in conflict – America. In the light of that extraordinarily inaccurate perception, perhaps I shouldn't have been surprised when he went on to act throughout the workshop with so little awareness!

During this workshop I was greatly helped by Phil, a Protestant from Portadown. We had come with a mixed group taken from all sections of society in the Province. It can be helpful for communities emerging from civil war, who can't imagine ever again being able to meet their enemy neighbour, to share experiences with men and women from other conflict zones who understand that perception from the inside, but who are further along in that journey. Phil worked really well in the group. He had a good sense of what I was trying to do, and was very supportive. We have become good friends. I think that the depth of our friendship would not be as it is, had our contact only taken place within the Province. Often I've found that being away from Northern Ireland has enabled friendships that otherwise wouldn't have been able to develop in my home context.

Part of my brief in Kosovo was to train facilitators from the group to run the workshops. I constantly developed the programme as I heard their stories and what they'd battled with. Among us were people who'd been raped, tortured and had members of their families, sometimes the whole of their family, murdered. I heard stories of men who'd been forced to have sex with their daughter in front of the captors, because if they didn't the daughter would be killed. Helping people deal with that kind of unimaginable trauma at the human level of the heart was my focus. I left the political dimension to others. Room had to be made for these experiences.

If you try to brush over the past, or rush on too quickly, it doesn't help. That's why I have questions about the Truth and Reconciliation Commission (TRC) in South Africa. Outsiders thought it a wonderful process that laid to rest the legacy of apartheid. Perhaps it did for some people, but on all my visits to South Africa, people from the poverty of the townships to those in luxurious homes, told me how they felt cheated by or excluded from the TRC. They didn't have their stories heard, and felt the unilateral pronouncements of forgiveness happened before they were at a point where forgiveness was possible for them. They felt the

TRC caused a whole lot of pain to be brushed under the carpet.

Time is a crucial element in conflict transformation, and mostly we don't allow enough time for change to happen. I notice in workshops how, when a participant gets into feelings that are hard to express or hold, others in the group often leap to their rescue, wanting to make things easier for the person speaking and for themselves as the listener, but such action, though well meant, is unhelpful. The rescuer in effect becomes a perpetrator, making people dependent and making decisions for them, with the result that they disempower the person, simply because they don't allow the necessary time and space for that person to do the work they need to do.

While we were in Serbia we worked with nature as part of the pro-gramme. Having found the natural world a very healing place myself, I wanted to develop therapeutic ways of using it in workshops, not just on wilderness treks. We were in a forest whose name means 'Golden Pines'. Two of the group were having great difficulty with the exercise. They explained that nature and the woods weren't places that held beauty for them because it was where their family had been murdered, and where they'd found them.

In another workshop one young woman spoke of discovering her grandparents and half the village where her childhood memories were rooted, lying dead in the local river. While I had a love of the ocean, water meant only pain and anguish for her. Hearing these stories came as a powerful reminder that what I find to be therapeutic and healing, may not be for others, and that I can't make assumptions. Some human beings have had their sense of beauty and wonder taken from them, because of what they've experienced.

When we left Kosovo we were stopped at a checkpoint and one of our group, a girl from Kosovo, had to get off because her papers weren't in order. I wanted everyone to get off and stay with her in protest, but it wouldn't have helped and we were ordered to drive on. We were assured that she'd get home safely. It took her a day.

On that trip to the Balkans I was accompanied by my partner, Louise. We'd met while I was working for EPIC. Louise was writing a book about the impact of the conflict, and its effects on children whose parents were sent to prison. She knew the experience first-hand. Her grandfather was Gusty Spence and many of the men in her family were involved with the UVF and Red Hand Commando. Louise had left Belfast to go to univer-sity in England where she'd studied psychology. On her return she became involved in community work. When we met she had very black-and-white views. That wasn't where I was at any more, but Louise had a knack of coming up with a very valid position through the clarity of her thinking. She cut through the bullshit and told things like they were. She was opinionated. That was helpful for me, as well as producing some really interesting conversations. We built our relationship around those. Louise had experience of losing people close to her, but she didn't have the hatred and bitterness that I'd grown up with. She was from a younger generation. She had Protestant and Catholic friends. She'd lived with violence as part of her life, but it hadn't eaten away at her goodness. She was beautiful and funny, and really great at her job.

I have reservations about working with a partner. It can add a dynamic that isn't always helpful, and it can be hard for participants to have a couple running the group, when they've had to leave their own spouses in order to come to the workshop. It can also make things difficult for other facilitators. Louise and I made a point of sleeping in separate rooms.

We married in 2004. It was a big step for me. I'd had important relationships after Valerie and I split up, but commitment was scary. The more I'd loved a person, the more I'd hold them at a distance at times, because I was afraid of things going wrong and losing them. The idea of marriage was terrifying, but somehow with Louise I wanted to make that commitment. We've rarely worked together since getting married, even though we're both involved in peace-building and conflict-transformation work.

After Kosovo, I returned to the Balkans to work in Croatia and Bosnia with groups of 20. I was teaching two modules on group-work dynamics and conflict transformation. We worked for ten hours every day. We had five trips to the Balkans, staying in Kosovo, Croatia, Bosnia Herzegovina, Macedonia and Montenegro. I went on my first visit to Bosnia and Croatia with a colleague, Grainne. We had to fly to Italy and find a place to stay overnight before catching a bus to Croatia. Neither of us spoke Italian. The course organisers had sent us money to get there, but had not included instructions. Eventually we found a run-down hotel to sleep in. I couldn't stand upright in the bathroom to pee. The bus journey the next morning was over eight hours long. Such uncertainty around the travelling was very frightening to me, and made me wonder if I was really up to doing this kind of thing.

When we started the course, I received a hostile reception from some of the Serbian participants because I was British. They were fine while they thought I was Irish, but when I said I was British, all their reactions to the British bombing of the Serbs became focused on me. I made them explore that. They realised that they were projecting onto me something I didn't deserve, and this was exactly what they were complaining that the outside world had done to them. So we worked with that. There were Bosnian Muslims present who I thought were coming to my defence, but they simply wanted to say they were glad the UN had intervened because of what that had meant for their lives. That took the focus off me and into the group.

There were a couple of disruptive, aggressive people in that particular group – one Serb and one Bosnian. They kept breaking the working agreement everyone had put together at the beginning of the workshop. Grainne and I had to challenge their aggression. They were trying to influence other people not to take part in certain activities in the group. This silenced a number of participants. We brought that out.

'There's a negative confluence in the group that I'm not happy about,' I said. 'Why did you come? To be controlled by other people? You have a voice here and you have valid thoughts and experiences to share, but you're allowing others to stop you expressing them. What does that say about you?'

They were annoyed by these words. What did they mean?

'Well, I've noticed in the last day that there are people sitting here silently who were talkative on the first day. I'd like to understand why that is. Has something been said that's annoyed them? Are they afraid of someone in the group? Are they being controlled? You tell me.'

The two disruptive men became aggressive. Grainne stepped in:

'That's not appropriate. We're not here to listen to that. We're not talking to you like that. If you don't like what's happening, leave the room now. Leave the group. That's your decision, but we came here to work with people who want to address the issues.'

This was one of those situations where quiet but firm talking didn't stop the aggressive language of the men concerned, so I began to respond to them with similar language. It brought them up short. As they started to react, I became quiet and measured again.

'Why are you getting upset about the way I'm talking to you?' I asked. 'That's the way you've been talking to me. Does that mean it's OK for you to talk like that, but not me? That's how a bully behaves. I want to understand what you're trying to do in this. Are you trying to bully people? Are you trying to intimidate me? It's not working. What's that about? I can tell you now, it's not going to get us anywhere. We're not going to learn from one another, and I want to learn from you because you obviously have a story to tell that's valid. You're not letting me hear it because you're caught up in this aggression.'

So they went away to think about what we'd said, and others in the group began to respond more. Our approach was a risky one, but sometimes without risk, nothing worthwhile happens. The risk may lead to someone leaving the group, but that may be necessary if they can't abide by the rules that everyone has agreed to, including themselves. As it turned out, the two men were put off the course a couple of weeks later because of the ongoing aggression. Those running the course at that point challenged the men as we had done. They were given the choice of leaving or being expelled, so they left. Later the Bosnian man wrote to me to say that leaving was the worst thing he'd ever done, and that he'd allowed himself to be influenced by the other man. He felt he'd lost out. It was a painful and important lesson for him to learn.

I was glad on that occasion of having Grainne as my co-facilitator. She was tough with those who weren't prepared to do the work that the course was there to accomplish. It was really insightful and helpful having her with me. Such exchanges are exhausting but necessary if any real understanding is to emerge. Conflict transformation is tough work. It's not about sitting around being nice and never addressing the issues that have brought people into conflict.

There was no time to deal with the weariness because we had to review the programme constantly in the light of what we were learning about the group, and adapt it to their needs. The course was five days long. At the end of it we had just a few hours' break before the next group came in.

In between my trips abroad, I continued speaking at conferences and in schools. Linda Britton and I ran numerous storytelling workshops, as we continue to do today. Often our third facilitator is Kate, the Director of An Teach Ban, the Peace Centre in County Donegal, where we hold many of the workshops. The Centre is in the village of Downings, and stands a little way up the hill overlooking a sandy bay and the Atlantic Ocean. It's a wild and windswept area, a breath of fresh air for many of the people coming from urban environments. I've also had the opportunity to develop the workshop in the prison context in England. This work came about through The Forgiveness Project.

I was contacted by Marina Cantacuzino, the Director of The Forgiveness Project (TFP). She's a journalist who was given funding to gather the stories of men and women from different situations of conflict, who'd been the victims and/or perpetrators of violence, and who'd chosen not to repeat cycles of revenge. She rang me to say she was putting the stories together in an exhibition about forgiveness. She was coming over to Belfast and wondered if she might discuss the project with me. When we talked further, I said I wouldn't be interested in being involved with an exhibition *promoting* forgiveness, because I felt that was problematic.

People define forgiveness in so many different ways. For some it's about breaking the psychological relationship a perpetrator has forced upon them. For others it's about making contact with the perpetrator and listening to their story, even making friends with them. I had experience of families in Northern Ireland where one member dealt with the pain of bereavement by engaging with the enemy community, and other family members saw that path of 'forgiveness' as the betrayal of the one who'd been killed. As a perpetrator, I would never ask the forgiveness of the family of the man I shot dead. They have suffered enough without having to respond to that kind of request from me. Forgiveness is a complex issue, and depending on how you define it, it may not always be a good thing.

The exhibition that Marina put together – entitled *The 'F' Word* – took note of this complexity. It explores the very different ways in which people understand, live out or stand back from forgiveness. Each story is accompanied by a photo of the person concerned. My story was part of the first collection. I was invited to the launch of the exhibition in the OXO Tower in London in 2004, and spoke to the gathered assembly of funders, celebrities, journalists and other interested parties. The exhibition then went on release around the country in churches and schools, in prisons and in any other venue to which we were invited. Those of us whose stories made up the exhibition would often go and speak where it was on show. I travelled back and forth to England, staying with Marina and her family. During one conversation I suggested to Marina that we shouldn't only show the exhibition in prisons but should arrange to have a speakers' panel made up of herself and some of those whose stories were told. Any prisoner could come to that, and then, if they were interested in exploring their own stories through the workshop I'd developed with Linda, they could speak with us, and we'd arrange with the prison staff for it to happen. We were able to do this work, receiving particular support from John Podmore, the then Governor of Brixton Prison, and Kate Quigley, the prison's Programmes Manager. On the evening we ran the first Speakers' Panel in Brixton, introducing the exhibition and the opportunity to take part in the workshop, I was given a verbal lashing by one of the prisoners who was from Northern Ireland. He attacked me during my presentation about my background.

'I can't look at you, or speak to you! You're a scumbag.'

As I spoke he whispered constantly to the big man sitting beside him.

I said, 'Look, I'm pleased that you feel able to express what you've just said, and I understand that what you're saying is coming from experience.'

At the same time I felt concerned because I had a sense that the big guy was an influential prisoner, and if he didn't buy into the process, then we wouldn't be able to get it off the ground. Thankfully, the big man, Mick, was interested. He went on the first workshop and found it deeply challenging and utterly transforming. He felt it opened up a whole lot of issues for him. People didn't mess with Mick because of the reputation he had. If such a man decides that he wants to live his life differently, that takes immense courage. The process of change can be very painful. I admire Mick greatly for how he engaged with that work.

During the follow-up meetings, I realised that Mick had the potential to be a great facilitator. He became our key man inside, selecting men to go on further workshops that we ran, and leading the self-help meetings that each group had after the workshop. He was the backbone of that work.

There were many teething problems. The prison system can be unpredictable. If there was trouble and a lock-down was initiated, the men couldn't be moved to other parts of the prison, including the education block where we ran the workshop. Some might be called out on court visits at times when we were working with them. Counselling follow-up had been set in place for those who needed it, but it wasn't always forthcoming. John and Kate did everything in their power to make sure these things didn't prevent the men from following through with the process. They could see the difference it made to those who attended. For some of them it was the first time they'd had the opportunity to reflect on their stories. The process was often charged with emotion, anger and tears, as men wrestled with the complexity of their experiences. Each participant forged a strong bond with the others in his group, because of the depth of sharing that went on.

With Marina, I went and spoke in other prisons. Because of the success of the work in Brixton, the trustees of The Forgiveness Project wanted us to develop it quickly in other prisons. My own plan, based on experience, was to have the workshops running well in Brixton for a period of time, so that we could make some assessment of the impact of them. We needed to follow through with the men who'd taken part, so that they weren't left high and dry. It's hard for people to sustain change in their lives without the right support to do that. My purpose wasn't to be able to tick boxes about how many prisons we were working in, or how many facilitators we trained up, or how many men had participated. We had a waiting list in Brixton and, when funding became available, I wanted us to develop the work there.

There's an issue here that I suspect is familiar to many charities. It concerns funders. Charities rely on funding to do their work. The competition for support is great. Funders, understandably, want to know that any money they donate is used well. They want to see results. In my line of work results are never instant, and how do you measure change in a person? It takes time to establish a firm foundation, to find and train facilitators who will be good at what they do, and to make sure that a process is developed that will provide participants with the care they need before, during and after the storytelling workshop. The danger for charities is that what they do becomes determined by funders, or the need for funding, rather than the needs of the people they seek to help. Where trustees are not experienced in the field focused on by the charity, there can be real tensions between those trying to do the work, and trustees whose task is to find and impress funders, and secure their financial support.

As we wrestled with this issue within TFP, prison officers at Brixton also needed to be persuaded that this kind of restorative justice work was worthwhile. Some of Kate's colleagues were supportive, but others thought we were wasting our time with hardened criminals. They didn't see them as being capable of change. My story contradicted that assumption. For that reason my personal experience was important to the prisoners who participated in the workshops. If a man with my history could turn his life round, perhaps they could too. They listened to what I said because they knew I understood their prison experience from the inside. That also made them open to the facilitators I brought in to work with me who didn't have the experience of imprisonment.

Mick should have been moved to another prison, but John Podmore recognised how key he was to our work, and how much difference it made to him, so he kept him at Brixton. Mick was with me when HRH Princess Anne came to the prison to meet people involved with different programmes being run there. I had to receive security clearance because of my background. She came over and spoke with us about the work.

I would love for it to have continued, but when I parted company with TFP, I ceased to be part of a registered charity, so the funding that had been given specifically for my work was no longer accessible. This was very painful, but the issue of safety for the people I work with means that I'm not prepared to make compromises that put vulnerable people at risk. That's why I work freelance with colleagues I trust. Often this has meant that I haven't been paid, or I'm paid a minimal amount for my work. I would rather it was that way round than being properly funded but causing participants harm through compromised practice.

What gives me pleasure as I think about the years I was involved with TFP, apart from meeting and working with men like Mick, is that what we were doing was valued by men like John Podmore to the extent that he was prepared to put me through training with prisoner officers, in order for me to be given the keys of the prison. That would enable me to come and go, without needing an escort every time I came to the prison. In order for this to happen, he had to apply to the Home Office for permission to do this. When it was granted, I was struck by how much my life had changed. An ex-terrorist and 'lifer' being given the keys to one of Her Majesty's prisons. Unheard of!

Chapter 15

Real education [i.e. learning] consists in drawing the best out of yourself. What better book can there be than the book of humanity.

Mohandas K. Gandhi

Feeling anxiety knotting up my stomach, I read the article in the *News Letter*, a Belfast newspaper:

Nesbitt takes role in drama on Troubles

A major new TV drama about the Troubles starring James Nesbitt will begin filming in Belfast later this month.

The BBC-commissioned drama will be directed by Oliver Hirschbiegel, whose groundbreaking film, *Downfall* – the first German-made film to cast a German in the role of Hitler – was nominated for an Oscar.

Five Minutes of Heaven, a fictional drama partly based on real events, will see 43-year-old Ballymena-born actor Nesbitt play the brother of a murdered Catholic teenager. It is thought Oscar-nominated actor Liam Neeson, also from Ballymena, may sign up to star in the drama, which will be broadcast on BBC Two.

The film will dramatise events from 1975 when 17-year-old UVF gunman Alistair Little murdered 19-year-old Jim Griffin [sic] in Lurgan.

Little was arrested two weeks later along with three others involved in the shooting and served 12-and-half years in prison.

Jim's murder was witnessed by his 11-year-old brother, Joe, and the drama will explore the impact of the murder on his family.

'The opening of the film is essentially an accurate, dramatised reconstruction of the events leading to the murder in 1975,' writer Guy Hibbert said.

'The action of the remainder of the film, set in the present day, is fiction based on their emotional response to the fictional situations their characters have been placed in, following close liaison with both men (Little and Mr Griffin).

'The impact of the drama is stronger still, as the story is about two real people who stand up and say it the way it is.

'It was important to get their full permission and cooperation. I have created this drama in their image, using their words and reactions.

'Working separately with both Alistair and Joe on the fictional areas provided a unique way of telling this story, and revealed there were no easy answers.'

Patrick Spence, BBC Northern Ireland head of drama, said it wanted to create a film which explores Northern Ireland's emergence from decades of violence in a responsible way.

'We have done this by recording powerful testimonies of the two individuals whose lives have been determined by the Troubles,' he said.

And BBC producer Stephen Wright added: 'This film is not about finding a resolution or a happy ending. What we are attempting to achieve, in a balanced way, is to create a place where both men can tell their individual stories.'

Sam McBride, *News Letter*, Friday, 9 May 2008

It's OK, I think. I feel the risk involved in peace-building more now than ever before. I've been consulted about this project on and off for the last two years. Filming is about to begin. Finally the BBC has released news about it. Not before time. The other day a friend connected to the UVF rang to ask me about what was happening. He seemed to know lots of details, despite the fact that it should still have been under wraps. This was what I'd feared all along. I rang Stephen at the BBC.

'I've just been talking to a friend who knows all about the film,' I said.

Stephen shares my concern. He's no idea about the source of the leak. He'll investigate and get back to me.

Later he calls to tell me the locations team had been out and about finding suitable places to shoot the drama. They'd said more than they realised was in the public domain. He deals with the situation as quickly as he can. He knows the risk I'm taking by following through with this project. When communities are emerging from a time of conflict, there has to be great care about the way in which communication happens. It's all too easy for one group to blame another for the ills of the community. Paramilitary groups are very sensitive to this because of the way they are frequently portrayed as the source of all the evils in the Province. Using them as scapegoats prevents religious, political or educational institutions, for example, from owning their own part in the conflict.

Hindsight can also distort the way in which people describe their earlier experiences. Some men who became involved in paramilitary activity claim they were forced into it by older UVF men who led them astray. In reality my personal experience as a teenager suggests that many young lads couldn't wait to join the fight.

Paramilitary groups have to hold the tension between recognising and taking responsibility for the devastating consequences their actions had on individuals, families and communities, and not being blamed for aspects of the conflict for which other institutions and individuals are culpable.

Peace-building involves negotiating a minefield of blame and guilt, vulnerability and bitterness, pain and grief. People and organisations at the heart of the conflict are understandably wary of media portrayals that fail to reflect complexity or are unfairly biased. I knew some groups would want to know exactly what the film was about, and whether it represented them as they thought appropriate. Because definitions of what constitutes 'appropriate' are diverse, I knew that what I was doing would not be easy.

The press may try to stir things up a bit, playing on the raw feelings of victims. Writing about a documentary telling my story some years earlier, one or two headlines had referred to me simply as 'Killer …' It caught the attention of the reader, I guess, but it wasn't very helpful. Journalists can either feed prejudice or foster understanding. It's a responsibility I'm not sure they always take seriously.

I'm expecting to be labelled by them in a similar way now. I know there'll be people critical of me because they think I'm profiting from my offences. Others will be jealous of me: isn't theirs just as powerful a story? I'm aware of men who sit in the wings and never step forward to do interviews because of the risk and personal cost of that. If I do a good job, they say 'Well done.' If I don't, they condemn me. They want to experience the positive things without the pain that is part of speaking publicly.

I've lost count of the number of times I've gone over in my mind my motives for working on this project. Every time I come back to the same thing. There are issues around victims/survivors, perpetrators and conflict transformation that need to be explored, not just by those who have first-hand experience, but also by the wider public. Unless we can tackle the legacy of the conflict as a Province, we'll run the risk of violence erupting again. My story and Joe's story will echo the experiences of victims and perpetrators in conflicts all over the world. Guy, the playwright, has gone to great lengths to understand the issues and convey them through the drama. I couldn't expose myself to the potential condemnation I might receive for any other reason than the hope that it'll help more people understand the dynamics of conflict, and how men and women live with the legacy of violence.

I've been deeply conscious that it won't just be me who might be affected by responses to the film. I've wrestled long and hard about the impact this could have on my family. Louise is with me all the way on it, but I know it will cause anxiety for my Mum and sister. I've thought a lot about how Amy will feel about it. She's 13 now. I don't want to do anything that makes life more difficult for her, or that damages our relationship. She's very much part of my life. After Valerie and I split up I saw Amy at weekends at my sister's home. Amy continued to go there every week. She came to my flat as well. Today she comes to stay for some weekends with Louise and me. Throughout her life I've tried to be aware of when the right time might be to tell her about my past. I haven't wanted her to learn about it from other people, but neither have I wanted to give her information she's not ready to hear. It's been difficult because the film isn't the first piece of work I've done involving the media, and my face and story are known by many people in Amy's neighbourhood.

The first invitations came from journalists wanting to write articles about my move from violence to non-violence, and working with victims. They'd heard me speaking at conferences on victims' issues. Around the same time, EPIC put on an exhibition about the history of the conflict, the UVF's involvement in it and the experiences of UVF men in prison. A play called *Yo, Mister!* was performed as part of that project. It was a monologue written by an ex-prisoner, W. M., and was about a prisoner waiting for a visit. I played the prisoner. I wrote an article about it for a local paper, and they ran a review of the play and the exhibition. After that I was invited to speak a couple of times on *Talk Back*, a BBC current affairs programme. One thing led to another. When journalists wanted comments in relation to relevant news events in the Province, they'd contact EPIC. I was one of the people EPIC referred them on to. I built up a reputation for having a good way of doing that sort of thing. I wouldn't be pressured into saying anything I didn't want to say, and I was also keen on building bridges rather than fuelling controversy. I was clear about what I'd tackle, and what I'd leave unaddressed because the time wasn't right.

One interview I did for the BBC flagship current-affairs programme,

Hard Talk, was broadcast in different parts of the world. It went out on the anniversary of 9/11. We were discussing the psychology of young men in relation to violence, and why they get involved in it. I received a lot of positive feedback about that, including phone calls from people I'd worked with in Kosovo, the US and Belgium. (I'd been to speak in Belgium at an international conference on child soldiers.)

Then Channel 5 asked me if I'd read and review Albert Camus' book, *The Outsider*. While I was talking about my response to it, relating it to my experience, the programme-maker stopped me. On the basis of what I'd said, he'd decided he wanted instead to make a documentary for the series *Witness* about me and a woman whose husband had been killed by the IRA. It was called 'Life after Death' and was directed by Carlo Gebler.

My words have also appeared in chapters of numerous books relating to the conflict. The writers have come to interview me, and have written up the interviews in their work.

I've been filmed by Scandinavian, German and Japanese documentary makers, and for American programmes. While I was doing work for TFP an American company saw the exhibition in the States and wanted to do some filming about the charity. While they were over in England I asked if they would be interested in the storytelling workshop we run alongside the Wilderness Treks. They decided they'd like to film one. The project has been fraught with difficulty because it's crucial to me that filming doesn't damage or manipulate the process. The men and women we ask to come on the Trek from different conflict zones around the world need to know that if they're filmed saying or doing something that might cause them difficulties or put them in danger at home, there'll be no question about those bits being edited out. I've been clear that the film crew must work around the participants, not the other way round. The film crew won't be allowed to interrupt the exercises and conversations we have, or ask for 'replays'. They're to be very much 'fly-on-the-wall'. Wilhelm has been working with me on this. It's been a tough process negotiating with the company what is and isn't acceptable, and making sure the contract reflects what we've agreed in conversations.

Early in 2008 Wilhelm and I flew to Israel to meet some potential participants and old friends. Through my work I'd met Chen who'd been an Israeli Major in a tank crew. He is now a member of Combatants for Peace. We became friends and I invited him to speak in Northern Ireland about his experience. At the same conference was a senior Palestinian fighter, Nour. He and Chen became friends. They have been on protests together. They've stayed in one another's homes. When we meet there's a real sense of kinship between us, perhaps because we are all living with the legacy of violence.

During our visit Wilhelm and I met with members of the Parents Circle. They are Palestinian and Israeli parents who've lost children in the conflict there. Hearing about the storytelling workshop, they invited us over to run the workshop for them. At present they're seeking funding for that. Our aim is to do the workshop and to train experienced people there to run it.

I like the way in which working on one project opens up conversations that lead to something else. Not that the outcomes are always as they should be.

In March 2006, BBC 2 launched a ground-breaking series called *Facing the Truth*. In the three programmes people from different sides of the conflict in Northern Ireland were filmed together at a country house in Ballywalter, near Newtownards. Archbishop Desmond Tutu was asked to facilitate the coming together of people like the UDA gunman Michael Stone and the widow and brother of a man he had murdered. There's a real tension here because it's important that the work of peace-building and conflict transformation is brought to the attention of the wider public as a means of building understanding. The difficulty is that there can be a clash between what is necessary to keep the process of conflict transformation safe, authentic and lasting, and what makes good television. The latter may demand compromises that put vulnerable participants at risk. Even the most experienced facilitators may find themselves caught in a difficult position as they work with programme-makers to bring the compelling nature of their work to a wider audience.

I'd been approached by the series-makers to see if I'd meet up with Joe Griffen. We both agreed to take part, but in the end both of us withdrew. I thought that was because Joe wasn't ready to meet me, certainly not in that setting, and I wasn't going to force an encounter. It was only later that I learned Joe was unsure why the meeting hadn't gone ahead. As I discovered more about how the programme would be done, my own reservations grew.

I'd told the researchers that it was crucial that if they used any photographs, they checked that anyone connected to the people in a photograph knew it was going to be used, and that they were OK about that. When the series came out, one victim I'd worked with suddenly found himself looking at a photograph of his family on the television. It was a terrible shock, revealing as it did details that he didn't know surrounding the murder of his father. Although the programme-makers had arranged counselling back-up for anyone who might need it, when my friend rang the number given for help, there was only an answer-phone.

I'd also expected the series to be a film about a group of people from different sides of the conflict brought together for a few days to do the kind of work we do in the storytelling workshops. I had many questions about filming a one-off meeting. Initially the programme-makers were going to call the facilitators of the meetings 'commissioners', which made it sound more like a mini Truth and Reconciliation Commission (TRC). I, among others, criticised that language. This was a programme about personal stories. It didn't take into account the wider religious, political and social structures behind the individual experiences shared. In this respect it could only be a partial perception of the truth of the conflict in Northern Ireland. I asked for a letter stating that it wouldn't be a TRC. I met with some of the senior people involved to talk through the safety issues. I suggested to them that they couldn't expect to have any long-term meaningful conversations by bringing people together for the first time in the presence of cameras.

Other people shared my concern and withdrew, as eventually I did. I felt the programme wasn't going to be safe. When it was clear that the meeting between Joe and I wasn't going to go ahead, I was asked if I'd sit across from a family who'd lost their son, but why would I do that? I'd no connection with them. Apart from listening empathetically to their story, I was no substitute for the person who'd murdered their son. The invitation to have that meeting struck me as an act motivated more by the need to get a programme made, than by the needs of those participating in it. It appeared to show little understanding of the dynamic between a victim and the perpetrator of their pain.

I was also uncomfortable about the encounters being filmed in a far more dramatic environment than the spaces we usually try to create – the helicopter flying in, the courtroom 'feel' to the place where they were filming, and the dark lighting. I felt some of the facilitation put emotional pressure on the victim to reach out to the perpetrator, without actually asking them directly to do that. I know that a number of the people taking part found the experience very helpful. I don't want to detract from what was meaningful for them. I know that meeting the 'other' might well have channelled some of their pain, but I also know that there are other, better ways of enabling that encounter and healing. I know, too, that the programmes caused others a great deal of heartache.

What struck me as I listened to reactions after the series went out was the difference between the responses of those who watched it without any experience of living in a conflict zone or extreme trauma, and those who knew first-hand the legacy of violence. Many viewers in the former category loved the programmes. The series restored their faith in human nature. Others, like me, and the people with whom I work, knew that reality is far more complex, and that lasting change relies on much more than one brief encounter.

Experiences like this make me very wary about becoming involved with broadcasters. That's why I was cautious in my response to Guy Hibbert, a programme-maker who contacted me in 2006. He'd seen footage of my meeting with the Dalai Lama in Belfast City Hall. He wondered if I'd be prepared to take part in a docu-drama based around my story and the issues around conflict and conflict-transformation, re-conciliation, and the journey from violence to non-violence. As we talked further, I told him about the murder, and that I'd shot James Griffen while his 11-year-old brother, Joe, was standing in the doorway of the next house. He asked me if I'd mind if they got in touch with Joe to see if he'd allow his story to be part of the drama. I said I didn't mind, so long as they made it clear to Joe that I hadn't instigated the contact. I didn't want him to feel any pressure from me.

When Joe confirmed that he was prepared to work with the writer on the script, we began a process that continued for about a year. We didn't meet at any point throughout that time. Guy would speak to each of us individually, then he'd work on the script and show us the result. I spoke regularly to Guy on the phone, and face-to-face. We went through the script at least seven times from start to finish, and then over parts of it on other occasions. We discussed it for two or three hours at a time. As Guy worked on the script, he relayed to Joe whatever my reactions and comments were, and vice-versa. The title of the drama, *Five Minutes of Heaven*, came from a comment Joe made describing how it would feel to face me and tell me exactly what he thought of me.

It's been a draining process. I've been able to do it partly because I like and trust Guy, the writer. He made every effort to understand where both Joe and I were coming from. He made it clear he wouldn't include any-thing that either of us felt uncomfortable about. He didn't go ahead with the project until those commissioning it guaranteed that it would be used. He didn't want to put us through the process if there was a chance the drama wouldn't make it onto the television. Both he and Stephen, from BBC Drama in Northern Ireland, were very sensitive in their dealings with Joe and me. They took seriously everything we said.

As I talked with Guy about violence, death and the killing of another person, I struggled. I'm used to exploring these things in my work, and being with people who, like me, know them first-hand, but this was different. For the first time I was hearing, via Guy, the impact of the murder I'd committed upon my victim's family. I listened to how it had destroyed their relationships, and what the 11-year-old Joe had been through as a result of my actions. I was confronted by the anger, pain and loss he carried. I had some understanding of that from my own experience, but I don't know exactly what Joe went through. Because I was responsible for his pain, and that of every member of his family, what I heard pierced my heart. I found it hard to talk about the time I was involved in violence, and about the actual shooting. I tried to think about the boy I was then, and found myself wondering yet again, how I could have done what I did. Then again, I had to acknowledge that I, like any other human being in certain circumstances, had the capacity to kill.

I took very seriously the fact that in being involved in this project, I was in a way entering into Joe's life, and had to be committed to the project. Unless Joe wanted to withdraw from it, I felt I had no right to walk away. I didn't want to cause him any further pain. I had to see this through.

For me the process has been risky and frightening. Risky, because I don't know how it will eventually be put together or received, and frightening because it may fail to do what I hope. I'm excited about the potential for it to raise debate and deal more deeply with the issues.

I felt immense responsibility each time I read through Guy's script. That responsibility wasn't only about making sure my own experience was accurately portrayed, but that the experiences of all the victims and perpetrators I'd met over the years weren't betrayed by the drama. I needed to be sure that the language used wasn't misleading, and that it didn't shift responsibility for what I'd done onto other people. At one point, Guy talked about me 'being blooded'. They were his words, not mine or Joe's. I felt this hunting phrase about animals fed the stereotype that people had about men like me not being human. It suggested that others were normal, and we weren't. I'd never heard it used by any of the boys I ran around with in my UVF days. Many of those men are my friends. They're loving fathers, sons, brothers and husbands, not feral animals.

Guy also had my character using 'Jesus Christ' as a swear-word. That wouldn't have happened. It was anathema to me. I'd grown up in a Brethren household where to use such words was blasphemy. With my mates I'd have said 'Fuck!' and 'Bastard!' frequently, but as a child I only ever heard Catholics saying 'Jesus Christ' and 'Holy Mary, Mother of God' in exclamation.

The drama won't tell our stories exactly as they've happened. Guy wanted to capture the experience of victims and perpetrators beyond Joe and me. He asked us to imagine ourselves in certain situations that we hadn't experienced, one of which was of us meeting each other. This was an interesting and disturbing process. I hadn't thought too much about it before. I said to him that if I ever met Joe, I wouldn't allow myself to be walked all over simply because I was the perpetrator. If Joe became aggressive and abusive, I'd stand up for myself.

When, a little later, Stephen Wright, Guy and I got together, we got into a more general discussion about violence between perpetrators and victims. I knew through my own work that by the time victims agree to meet with those who have caused their pain, they aren't usually looking for revenge but for justice, answers and greater understanding. When I have this sort of discussion with others who haven't perpetrated great violence, I notice that they often feel comfortable with the idea of the victim hitting out and wounding the perpetrator at such a meeting, but not the perpetrator fighting back. That seems to be because the victim is seen as the innocent party, the good guy, and the perpetrator is the guilty one who deserves all he gets. In reality it might well be that the victim has also been a perpetrator, and the perpetrator a victim. Even if that's not the case, it still suggests that they think some human beings are of less worth than others and can therefore be treated badly. If they felt able to justify an act of inhumanity against me, for example, because I was a perpetrator, what did that say about them? It was a helpful discussion because it highlighted how quickly people can unintentionally fall into double standards in the way they think others should be treated, but it was also exhausting stuff.

As always, Louise was completely supportive through all this. I don't know how or why Louise copes with me as I am. I'm not easy to live with, but she seems to understand when I get into dark places. She knows when to leave me alone, and doesn't make demands. She takes on board the stress and the difficulty and the problems and carries them. She chooses to do that for me. Louise holds a lot, keeps a lot within her. She doesn't say what others might say. It's helpful for me, and also hard to understand. She demonstrates more love and compassion in those situations than I think I'd be capable of, if our roles were reversed. I feel guilty about that. Knowing myself in all my complexity, I wonder how she can love me, and sometimes I doubt it when she says she does. I know how much I struggle with myself, so how can I be lovable? Reading around other conflicts, I see that my experience isn't unique. That's comforting.

Amy's response when she became more aware of the situation was also great. Valerie had talked with her. She didn't seem to want to talk much about it with me, but she simply said, 'Daddy, it doesn't change anything. I still love you. Will you be all right?'

I don't know exactly what's going on in her head. I guess that will come out over time. I know that at school they still talk about 'the boys' – the UVF and the UDA. It's still a live issue with them. Some have family members who were in prison. At least these days they're doing studies about the conflict at school, and addressing the issues in a way that never happened during my education.

While the film project has been going on, other work has continued to develop. I've been asked to do some training input at the Institute for Healing Memories in Cape Town around preparation for storytelling workshops. In 2004 I was a facilitator with Michael Lapsley at an international conference on Robben Island, where Nelson Mandela had been imprisoned, and I returned again in 2007 for the international gathering of facilitators connected with the Institute. I had the opportunity to share the process I'd developed in the Northern Island context.

With colleagues in England I'm using the storytelling workshop for men and women who've been stigmatised as a result of being HIV positive. This came about through my friend, Ruth Scott. Ruth had become a trustee of the Forgiveness Project when I was working with Marina. She became involved with the prison side of the work, and was supportive during the difficult discussions about how that might be developed. When I stopped working with TFP, Ruth and I continued meeting up and exploring how we might work together. She joined me in Northern Ireland and at Glencree as a participant in various workshops. She trained as a facilitator with me and with the Institute for Healing Memories. As an Anglican priest, her religious perspective is different from my own. Staying frequently with her and her priest husband, Chris, and their family, we discussed many aspects of religion and ethics. With them I experienced people and places that were not part of my own world. I remember feeling deeply uncomfortable at a midday Eucharist at a Franciscan Friary that Chris and I visited one day. It produced a lot of humorous teasing about 'heretics', as well as thought-provoking conversations.

It was through Ruth that the work developed with those living with HIV/AIDS. A priest colleague of hers, Rachel, who operates in this field internationally, asked us to run the workshop for some of the people she served. Some participants were also asylum seekers, so they were dealing with a double stigma. To help my own understanding about AIDS, Rachel enabled us to visit a hospital caring solely for men and women living with HIV/AIDS, and to speak with the staff and patients. She gave us material to read, and we talked about the special needs the participants might have relating to their illness. All these things challenged and expanded my own understanding. In the workshops I was deeply moved by the stories and stature of those participating. At some point, when the time is right, the aim is to bring together those who've been stigmatised with those responsible for the stigmatising.

As a result of the Wilderness Treks, Wilhelm and I have connected with other groups who run wilderness experiences in the UK. We've now run weekends for men and women from the Northern Ireland context, where they've kayaked around the islands off the west coast of Scotland, and camped in the highlands. It's become one of the steps that people take before doing the South African Trek. We do team-building exercises and begin to open up the storytelling process through that experience in the natural world.

At home in Northern Ireland, I'm sometimes called in as a facilitator when conflict erupts at a grassroots level. While organisations are committed to the peace process, individuals for a variety of reasons may kick against it, and there are always personality clashes and conflicts about power. Walking around Belfast City centre, you could be in any city anywhere in the UK, but up on the Shankill Road, or out in Andersonstown, or in any other socially deprived area in the Province, tensions still run high, and sectarian hatred is deep-rooted. The 'peace' walls remain in interface areas where residents don't feel safe enough for them to be dismantled. The outside world thinks we're now at peace, but there's lots of work still to be done. It's a fragile peace. Perhaps that explains in part why Special Branch tried to recruit me recently as an informer.

In 2007 I was flying with Wilhelm to Israel, via Heathrow. We were going out to meet potential participants for the Wilderness Trek that the American company wanted to film. The El Al staff at Heathrow found a problem with Wilhelm's passport. Following security policy, they called in the police based at the airport to check out one or two details. The officers looked up Wilhelm on their computer and saw that he worked at Glencree, particularly with ex-combatants.

'You work with some very interesting people,' they said.

This connection prompted them to check me out. The information on my passport brought my prison record to their attention. I was taken aside into a special room where they went through all my belongings, emptied my wallet, took notes of anything they found, including my mobile phone details, and questioned me about my family, my work and my past. What organisation had I been part of – UVF or UDA? Who paid for my work now?

'You know who we are and why we're here,' the police officers said.

'Yes, you're Special Branch,' I replied.

I was questioned for almost two hours. Afterwards I was escorted to the boarding area. They said they could stop me travelling but they weren't going to. I was left sitting with them while everyone was moved out. They asked if I'd be interested in working for them.

I laughed. 'Why would I want to do that? I've no interest in that.'

'Ah well, maybe we'll check in on you when you come back.'

'There's no reason to do that.'

Eventually I was allowed to board the plane. When I returned to London I was waiting in the departure lounge for my connecting flight to Belfast when the same officers came over and asked me about my trip. They stood outside the plane to check I boarded it. When I arrived in Belfast I saw two plain-clothes officers waiting. Sure enough, they took my passport and asked me to follow them to a side room. We went over everything again. They made comments about my tattoos. After I'd come out of prison I'd had new tattoos put over my UVF ones to disguise them. Then they asked how I'd feel about working for them. I repeated that I wasn't interested.

'If I went back and my superiors asked how Mr Little would feel about receiving a phone call, what would I tell my superiors?'

'Tell them I'm not interested. Why would I be interested in a phone call?'

'So what you're saying is that you'd prefer not to have any contact at all?'

'Yes, absolutely!'

'Well, we're satisfied you're not involved in anything you shouldn't be, but we'll probably stop you from time to time.'

Then they gave me a car-park ticket for Louise, who'd been kept waiting all this time.

On a couple of subsequent trips to England I've been stopped by the same men and asked how my work's going. I wonder if my mobile phone, home phone and computer are being tapped. I feel angry about them trying to suck me back in. And I feel vulnerable. I'm still out of prison on licence. I could be taken back in at a moment's notice without any charge being made. No matter what I do to try to move on from my past, it's always with me. It isn't past, it's very present. Whether it's the police or the wider public, I can never be sure how people will react to my history, whatever worthwhile things I've done in more recent years.

The fear of judgement probably explains why I was apprehensive the day Louise and I went to the film set of *Five Minutes of Heaven*. Up until that day I'd avoided going anywhere they were filming. It didn't seem appropriate for me to be there. I was all too conscious of the people who'd never get an opportunity like this because they'd been murdered by the likes of me. Then, Guy and Stephen asked me and Louise to join them towards the end of the filming with Liam Neeson and James Nesbitt.

We met Guy, his wife and daughter, and Stephen in Belfast, and followed them as they drove the 40-odd miles to Glenarm where that day's filming was happening in a large country house. Louise described it as a 'Laura Ashley show house'. It was huge, with different themes in each room. There were crowds of people at work when we arrived. They were filming actors coming in and out of the house or talking on the staircase. Cameras and lighting had been set up. There were all kinds of monitors. Technicians wandered around adjusting equipment and altering scenery. The director was concentrating on each shot. There was a man with a clapperboard, and make-up artists touching up the faces of the actors on set. Outside there were luxury loos, catering buses and caravans for the use of the actors.

I was so glad Louise was with me. Stephen, Guy and Guy's family were really down to earth. That helped to relax me. At one point they were filming Jimmy Nesbitt-as-Joe arriving in a big limousine. They had to do it a number of times. In between takes the director, Oliver Hirschbiegel, came over.

'Hello, I'm pleased to meet you Alistair,' he said.

After exchanging greetings he told me about the filming they'd been doing the day before. In relation to that scene, he said words to the effect that I'd got what I deserved. He was laughing as he said it but Guy's daughter gave a sharp intake of breath. The rest of us were silent, looking from one to the other. I thought if he made another comment like that, I'd have to say something. I knew he was trying to be humorous, but I took it as a judgement, and being judged was definitely not what I wanted to experience that day. When Oliver went off to do another take, we talked about what had been said. Guy said Oliver was nervous about meeting me, and he wasn't tuned in to all the sensitivities around the conflict in Northern Ireland. I understood that, but I didn't find it easy. Then Jimmy Nesbitt came over. He shook hands and said he was pleased to meet me. He was welcoming and warm. There was no sense of ego about him. That felt good.

We watched different scenes being filmed throughout the day. At one stage voice recordings of Jimmy were played so that Liam could react to them. The words were those of Joe after he'd arrived for the encounter with me on the *Facing the Truth* programme. I was supposedly overhearing him in the next-door room.

'I'm not going to meet that man with the cameras there,' Jimmy-as-Joe was raging. The intensity of his voice, and the reactions of Liam-as-me, made the hairs on the back of my neck stand up. It was really disturbing.

'This is powerful stuff,' I whispered to Louise.

At lunch we ate with the cast and the film crew. Oliver talked with Louise. I felt shy.

Later, while we were drinking tea, Jimmy came and joined us with a glass of wine in his hand.

'How's it been?'

I explained my reactions, and how intense I'd found what I'd seen.

'It's been like that all the way through,' he responded. 'I love the script, and the professionalism of Liam and Oliver.'

We chatted for 20 minutes or more. He was so direct and normal with me.

While Guy and his wife went to book in at a local hotel, their daughter opted to stay and chat with us. She talked about her work. That was a great help to me because it took the focus off me, and I liked the fact that she'd chosen to be with us.

While we were watching more filming, Liam came on set. Stephen had warned me that Liam didn't talk to people while he was filming. His whole attention was focused on his character.

'Don't take his lack of contact personally,' said Stephen.

I could see how Liam was totally absorbed in his work. I had no expectation that we'd meet, but just as we were thinking of leaving, he asked someone, 'Where's Alistair?' and came over to talk.

'Well, Alistair, I'm pleased to meet you. What you're doing is brave.'

We chatted about him growing up around Belfast and Lurgan, and the boxing he did in our neighbourhood. He asked me about my work. We got on to talking about the situation between Israel and Palestine.

'What a mess it's in!' he said.

I told him about the Combatants for Peace (CP) group and the Parents' Circle. CP is made up of former Israeli soldiers and Palestinians who've fought for the liberation of their land. They seek the ending of violence and the creation of two states living peaceably side by side. I'd met them while visiting the Middle East, and exchanged stories with some of the group.

'Why don't we hear about these kind of people?' Liam wondered.

Like Jimmy, he was welcoming and pleasant. I felt he wanted to be there to talk with us, that he wasn't just doing it as part of his job. I felt reassured by the seriousness with which they all were taking the drama. Maybe it really would be all I hoped it'd be.

When it was time to go, Liam gave me a strong handshake. 'Keep up the good work!'

I left feeling more at ease about the project than I'd felt for months. I'd also been accepted and not judged by those I'd met. After his initial uncomfortable comment, Oliver had become much more relaxed. I guess knowing myself as I do, I forget that meeting a man with my history can be an unnerving prospect for others, at least until they've actually talked with me.

The filming provoked a lot of interest in the communities where it took place. A street in a staunchly Loyalist part of East Belfast was the location for another part of the film. I heard about it from a friend I'd known in my prison days. He rang Louise's uncle, laughing about what he'd seen.

'D'you ever see Skittle these days? Tell him I'll have it in for him if ever I see him. They're turning this place into a Republican area! We've got green, orange and white painted kerbstones, and Irish tricolours flying from every lamp-post!'

My teenage self would never have believed that at some point in his later life, he'd be the cause of a Loyalist area getting a Republican make-over, even if it was just for a film!

Chapter 16

... everything can be taken from a man but one thing: the last of human freedoms – to choose one's attitude in any given set of circumstances, to choose one's own way.

Viktor Frankl

It's the beginning of 2007. I'm sitting outside a block of flats in Andersonstown, a staunchly Republican area of Belfast. There are many gable-end murals on the streets round here depicting Republican victories and slogans, and the portraits of Republican heroes or the victims of Loyalist attacks. I'm feeling increasingly anxious. I'm waiting for Gerry to return to my car. We've spent the day together visiting a school and sharing our different stories with the pupils: me, the Loyalist ex-gunman, and Gerry, the Republican ex-bomber. Twenty years ago, if we'd met each other on the street we'd have tried to kill each another. Today we're both men on a journey seeking a way forward that isn't about violence and revenge.

We met almost three years ago at a group for ex-combatants at Glencree. Gerry was encouraged to attend by his organisation. He came along reluctantly. His first experience of the group confirmed his belief that this kind of talking-shop wasn't his cup of tea, but he kept coming. He spent a lot of our early time together venting his spleen at me. He says now that because I took the abuse without retaliating, he began to get bored hearing himself say the same things over and over again. I knew the score. I'd been there myself and, for all the heated words, I liked Gerry. I recognised in him a kindred spirit. He'd a real desire to be honest in the journey he was making. He was genuine. I've found sometimes that when ex-combatants meet, there are some who say what they think they should say. Their words aren't true to their experience or present perspective. Gerry wasn't like that. He talked straight. I valued that and, whatever our differences, we also made each other laugh. Slowly we began to share something of our experience with one another. This growing connection gradually led to us meeting up to share our stories with different groups, but the legacy of past experience makes trust difficult.

That's why, as I sit in the car waiting for Gerry, my anxiety is escalating. Normally after a day working together, I drop Gerry off in Belfast city centre, and he catches a taxi home. Today I've brought him all the way to the block of flats where he lives. I don't feel easy driving through Republican strongholds. I'm afraid of being recognised. The Peace Process may be well under way, but in many communities across the Province hatred of the 'other' is still alive and well. Sectarianism still rules and it doesn't take much to spark violence into life again.

It's been 15 minutes since Gerry got out my car to fetch his own car keys from his flat: having dropped him home, I need him to guide me back to a particular roundabout that will take me into more familiar territory, but there's no sign of him. I'm suddenly afraid this may be a set-up. It's dark. People walk by, and I wonder if they're sizing me up. Two men stop to talk to one another at the end of the car. Now I'm seriously rattled. I want to drive off at speed. I think Gerry is trustworthy, but what if I'm wrong? Even if he's OK, others here may not be. I know that in some ways I'm being paranoid, but I also know the ongoing hostility that exists in many places. My paranoia might be justified. Danger still exists. My heart is racing and I'm in a bit of a sweat. Then, finally, Gerry is there, getting into the car. He laughs off my question about what took him so long. I say nothing about the fear I felt.

A few weeks later we're once again in a school sharing our stories. One of the children comments on how well Gerry and I get on together. He wants to know if our friendship is as easy as it appears to be. I tell him that Gerry and I have a long way to go. There are difficult conversations still to be had. For men with our backgrounds trust isn't easy. As an example of this, I decide to tell the group about my reaction outside Gerry's flat. Hearing about it for the first time, Gerry bursts out laughing.

'What's so funny?' I ask.

He tells us that when he left me in the car to go and get his keys, he was scared about me knowing which flat was his, just in case I wasn't all I seemed to be. He didn't want to open his front door one day and find a Loyalist paramilitary pointing a gun in his face. So he didn't switch on the light when he went in. Because it was dark he couldn't see a thing. That's why he'd taken so long: he was fumbling around, often on all fours, trying to locate his car keys.

It makes me laugh just thinking about our reactions on that occasion.

Gerry and I have a long way to go, but a letter I received recently from him captures something of the journey we're on, a shared journey that makes my work worthwhile, and helps to keep me going when the going gets tough:

Hi A,

Hope all is well with you. You were sort of correct about the C.D. course. It is run by 'fluffy' people but the course itself might be worth while.

As for your last e-mail, it has given me a lot to think about. Openness is what I expect from you. I remember we were once asked about our relationship; and I answered that although we get on well and have talked a lot about ourselves, there are some things we have not discussed yet and will probably not for awhile, but that we don't let that get in the way of our work or relationship and will talk about deeper things when we feel that we can talk about them, or words to the effect. I know you see things in me that even I don't. I am not too sure what you see, but I do believe we do work well together and do good work.

As for the friendship? I understand what you said. We have difficulties because of where we have come from, probably less from each other, but people looking at us from our own backgrounds will see it as strange. I sometimes find myself defending my relationship with you. I fully understand why people find it odd. Sometimes I don't defend it, just agree with things that are said because I know they are not trying to find out more about what we do, but just [criticising me for] meeting Loyalists. Thankfully these people are fewer now than ever before. They are falling by the way side. But I do feel guilty when I don't defend you. It's just I feel I would be wasting my time with them.

I know you have moved miles from where you were. I suppose we both have. You have talked about some of the work you are doing; I don't fully understand what it is you are trying to do or where you are trying to go as a person. I can see why Billy thinks I am more into political activism. I am. I really enjoy political work where as you seem to be into people's human stories. But the work you have got me into has let me see a different world, one I would probably never have gotten to see without you. This has opened new thoughts and ideas in my head, some of them very difficult to come to terms with. I can look at your background and wonder why I want to work with you. If I looked at it too much, I would probably be more 'plastic' with you or in the work we do, which of course you would see and that would end the work we do together. Of course I know you, or Loyalists in general, could look at my background and have just the same problems that I have.

I suppose what I am trying to say is that our friendship is at a stage where I think it is going to move to a different level. You are thinking of getting me into more work with you, probably into a new environment for me. That means being together more often and in places where we will talk more, especially about human emotions and how people deal with trauma etc. That will probably also mean we will talk about some of the things we haven't as of yet. That's what I mean by a new level. I believe I can deal with this as I now see you as a friend first and not a Loyalist first. No one thing defines us as a person as you know, but once we describe ourselves as Loyalist/Republican ex-prisoners that's all people see. You are the person who showed me to look beyond the labels and to try and see the person. I can do that with you, yet not with others, in other words, why do I see your jokes as jokes without the jags, yet with [X.] I see the jags? Maybe I should try harder, but you once told me not to ignore my gut feelings, hence my difficulties with some of the people I meet.

Well that's probably enough for now before I give you a headache, Christ I have a headache myself ...

So till I see you again take care.

Gerry

Journeying as we are isn't only a 'headache' at times, but a source of great heartache as well. There's a long road still to be travelled in transforming our pasts.

Way back in that past I saw life in black-and-white terms. Now I wrestle with many shades of grey. My experience is full of contradictions.

Sometimes I miss the excitement, power and sense of purpose that came with teenage years caught up in the conflict. That ache scares me. It makes me wonder if I've really changed at all. When I'm working with people today, people with power who may be well-intentioned but understand little of what conflict transformation is about, I feel the same old anger welling up. Sometimes I want to shout, 'Fuck you!' and walk out. The language matters. It's synonymous with the violence of my past.

Coming away from meetings where violent words command respect

215

and enable some form of dialogue to follow, I always feel disturbed and overshadowed by the experience. There's a perverse relief in such moments because they remind me that I have changed and moved on, and that I want to use every means possible to avoid resorting to violence. When I speak of such reactions, some of those listening to me feel afraid, more so than if I was someone who owned up to violent feelings without ever having acted upon them. Once a perpetrator, they think, always a perpetrator.

On the other hand, there are those in my own community who think I've betrayed them. That's exactly how I'd feel if I still thought as I did when I first went to prison. I understand where they're coming from, but I'm not in that place any more.

Between these two groups I'm pushed between the labels of 'perpetrator' and 'betrayer'. I wonder if I'll ever again feel that I truly belong anywhere. Even in the relationships where I feel most at home, I have to work hard. Sometimes I have an intense need to spend time on my own. Darkness overwhelms me. When I'm in that place, talking doesn't help. That's hard on those close to me. The Hungarian psychoanalyst, Sandor Ferenczi, wrote:

> Confronted with unbearable aggression, a person might 'give up their soul', mentally 'dying', while physically surviving death.
>
> Afterwards the pre-traumatic personality structure will be partially re-established, but a part of the person will have ceased to exist, will go on being dead or lost in the agonies of fear.
>
> So when dealing with traumatised persons, we always confront a double reality, on one side there is a person that can talk about, think about, and even tell us about what happened to them. On the other side, we have a person lost in the experience of death and of terror, for whom there are no words to explain their experience.
>
> (Ferenczi, S. *Ohne Sympathie Keine Heilung*. Das Klinische Tagebuch von 1932. Frankfurt: S. Fischer Verlag, 1988.)

I know this 'soul death'.

People say, 'Leave the past behind', but for me the past is always with me. What I've learnt to do is not allow the past to paralyse me. What I was involved with in the past is very much part of who I am in the present, for good or ill. I can't set it down and forget it. Even if I could, should I? It shapes the work I do, and my care of suffering people.

I'm aware of the capacity for any human being to be destructive and to use violence. I'm conscious of the anger that lurks within us all. I know that any human being placed in certain situations and under certain circumstances can reveal a dark side. Alongside that I see the wonderful things of which we're all capable. Nothing moves me more than experiencing the loving compassion of people who have every reason to hate and reject me. They help me keep the faith.

Sometimes I wonder if I have the right to be doing this work. There are days when I'm working with a group and talking about peace, inclusivity and acceptance, of people's grief and pain, and of healing, but am going through a dark personal time that conflicts with what I'm saying and doing with them. Sometimes I feel angry, even enraged about something, and I think I haven't really changed at all; that it's just superficial and the dark side of my nature remains as potent as ever. Then it feels hypocritical to speak about peace, when I'm not feeling it, or to discuss healing, when the last thing I feel is healed. I have to remind myself that all these things are part of being human and that when we least experience peace and healing, perhaps that's the time we most need to be conscious of it, and to hold out for it.

Then again, at other times I know that what I'm doing is the right thing to do. I can see I make a positive difference in the lives of the people I work with, and those encounters constantly offer new challenges and insights. I have a sense of vocation about my work. I feel obligated to do it. This is the work I need to do.

The most important part of my work is to create a protected space which is as safe as it's humanly possible to make it. In that space there'll always be the vulnerability and unpredictable reactions of those working within it. I want to humanise even the worst aspects of our nature so that we gain understanding about them. It's easy to demonise a person, to see them as a monster and to keep them in a box with that label. When you attribute behaviours and actions to a human being, not a monster, it challenges your own sense of self. Most of the people caught up in the violence of Northern Ireland are normal people, just like those who haven't been caught up in conflict, but they've committed acts of violence that have devastated the lives of others. It's the worst aspect of human nature, but it's still *human* nature. It's not the sort of thing we want to acknowledge because it challenges us to action. It becomes the responsibility of us all to create the kind of society that doesn't force some of its members to live out the dark side of their nature. If we pretend we don't share that nature, then we project it onto others, and the cycles of misunderstanding, violence and revenge are perpetuated. What is so fantastic for me is when I see two paramilitaries who were sworn enemies discussing their differences in a respectful way. They may be confrontational with each other, but they're not using violence. That's because they've come to see the humanity of the other, and because they are conscious of their own flawed humanity.

Sometimes it's difficult to understand the young boy I was, and what I was involved in. Sometimes I'd like to speak to that young boy. The man I've become is one that my teenage self would want to kill. He would see the things I say now, the work I do, the people I meet, as betrayal. If I met him I'd want to talk to him about the path he's considering walking down and what it will do to his life, and to the lives of others. I'd want to talk him out of it, but there's no guarantee he'd listen. With the arrogance of youth he'd probably just tell me I don't know what I'm talking about and to 'fuck off'.

I'd like to know what happened that enabled him to do what he did. I still don't fully understand that. Intellectually I can find the words to make sense of it, but emotionally, psychologically and spiritually, I can't. I was brought up in a home where for most of my life I was steeped in the Christian faith. Hatred and bitterness weren't terms I heard in the house. My Dad had his own political views, but he never talked in terms of hatred even though he was totally opposed to what was happening and saw action as necessary to protect our community.

Sometimes I wonder what my life would have been if Dorothy had taken me to Australia. Would I have settled to a different way of life, or would it have been too late by then? Would I have found other destructive channels for the anger and fear I felt deep inside? What might I have been capable of with the right opportunities?

My desire was always to be in the Army, but now when I look at young people today, I think I'd like to have had the chance to go to university, and to see where that took me. Maybe that's simply the present me wanting to prove to myself and others, that I could do it. Some of my desire comes from the frustration of being a former paramilitary and prisoner, and the baggage that comes with that as far as wider society is concerned. I've been among people in positions of authority and power who are less intelligent than me and many of the guys I knew in prison, yet I've been looked down on by them. I know academics who lack common sense and emotional intelligence, and whose knowledge doesn't bear out the reality of life for people like me. Maybe I'd just like to be an academic so that I could prove that working-class people with my background can work in that domain, and then I'd walk away from it because whatever its advantages, I know its limitations. I don't know if that's a desire for revenge, or simply wanting to draw to the attention of others how people like me have been treated, and to challenge common perceptions about wisdom. Some of the wisest men I know are former prisoners with no letters after their name.

The typical understanding of leadership is of a person who's 'in charge', who is educated and holds power, even someone of whom others are afraid. There's a difference between being a leader and showing leadership. Many leaders don't show leadership. I can think of women in my community who've worked in this conflict for 35 years. They don't hold the position of leader, but through their work and example have shown tremendous leadership that's never been acknowledged. They've held things together when everything around them was falling apart, and they've helped others to do the same. Yet they could apply for a post in conflict transformation work and be passed over in favour of someone fresh from university with the 'right' qualification. How can that be? University can't teach what these women have learnt from the day-to-day reality of living with violence.

Sometimes all that feels too much and I want to get away from Northern Ireland. When I travel to other countries, I catch a glimpse of a different Alistair inside. I begin to connect with an as yet unknown part of me. Some of that's to do with spiritual stuff that can't come out in my home context. When I'm abroad, I feel lighter. It's like a weight being lifted off. My mind is clearer and sharper, as if a haze has evaporated. I start thinking about life beyond my experience in Northern Ireland. I start to see people differently. Then I have to come home and the need to shut down in preparation for that closes off these new perceptions. Yet alongside this wanting to connect with another Alistair inside me that hasn't been allowed to see the light of day, I have a homing instinct for anything relating to conflict. The people I meet with abroad tend to be connected to conflict. The books I read are about human development, conflict and the skills I need to help me deal with it. The places in the world I'm attracted to are places of conflict. Conflict dominates my life, perhaps because I have an overwhelming desire to try to understand it. Perhaps because I'm afraid that away from conflict, I will cease to exist. Being surrounded by conflict is very normal for me. I have no time for small talk, or the pettiness of life that many people accept and are absorbed by.

I remember at the conference in Belgium about child soldiers, I was invited to a party. At one point the people I was with were talking about their jobs and lives, and they were asking me a little about mine. Suddenly, out of nowhere I found myself asking them, 'How do you get through every day with nothing happening?'

'What do you mean?'

'Well, you get up in the morning, you go to work, and you meet friends, but there's nothing happening in your life. How do you get by?'

They were flabbergasted. When they heard about my own daily life they were really disturbed that I saw normal life as abnormal and boring. That connects with conversations I've had with other guys caught up in conflict. They say to me, 'I miss the war. I miss the conflict.' It's not that they all miss the killing, though some men do, but they long for the purpose it gave their lives. The journalist Anthony Loyd captured that experience in *My War Gone By, I Miss It So*, his book about his work in the Balkans during the war there. How do you change a whole way of being to fit completely different circumstances? When I was in prison I worked out a way to survive, but the pattern I developed didn't work outside prison. As a teenager caught up in the violence of the conflict, I learnt how to live through that. The patterns went deep. That's why the younger a person is when they get caught up in conflict, the harder it will be for them to learn a different pattern. For people steeped in conflict, peace can be much harder to live with. Your sense of identity and belonging disappears, and only emptiness remains. I sound so contradictory, wanting to move away from places and experiences of conflict, yet fearful of that. I well understand what Charles Caleb Colton meant when he wrote:

> To dare to live alone is the rarest courage; since there are many who had rather meet their bitterest enemy in the field, than their own hearts in their closet.

And yet I'd like to be funded to live for a year in a country cottage within walking distance of a village pub in a place of peace. I don't earn enough to make that possible any other way. I've spent years doing work for which I haven't been paid. I'd like to learn how to keep a few chickens and pigs, to grow vegetables, to walk in the country, and to have time to see what emerges in me. I'd like to have just enough to live on, and to have signed a contract that says I'll stay for a year, and if I bolt before the year ends, I'd pay back all I'd been given to live on in that time. My purpose would be to see if there's an Alistair that can live outside the context of extreme conflict, and to discover what he thinks and feels. I imagine it'd be really tough. The thought of it scares me, but I have a deep desire for it. Is it possible to live away from conflict and find a way of being and working that challenges and stimulates me as much as my present work? Would I find another identity? I feel trapped where I am now because I sense this other self, perhaps the part of me that got lost in my youth.

I'm still on a long journey. I don't know if Joe and I will ever meet. It's said that those who most need forgiveness are those who have least right to it, but I don't think it's for me to seek it out. I must live with the consequences of my actions, and not impose those upon anyone else, least of all those most wounded by my violence.

I understand why others believe I've no right to any positive quality of life, but I know too that through my struggles to understand my own history, I've learnt so much. The skills and insights I've acquired through that journey have been and remain a source of healing for many men and women, both victims and perpetrators. As I continue in this work, maybe those who hear my story will not begrudge me experiences of grace.

I hope it's not too much to ask that every so often I may stand on the fells above Grasmere, or in any other heart-lifting landscape, to feel the freedom of insignificance and the connectedness of all things, and, for a short time, to be steeped in beauty.

Bibliography

The following books helped Alistair and I to pin down chronologically the memories he had, and to make connections between what he remembered and what was going on at the time. They enabled me to begin to get some idea about the context of Alistair's story, and the complexity of the conflict in Northern Ireland.

Ruth Scott

Jim Cusack and Henry McDonald, *UVF* (Dublin, Poolbeg, 1997).

Richard Deutsch and Vivien Magowan, *Northern Ireland 1968–73: A Chronology of Events, Volume 2: 1972–73* (Belfast, Blackstaff Press, 1974).

Martin Dillon, *The Dirty War* (London, Arrow Books, 1990).

Martin Dillon and Denis Lehane, *Political Murder in Northern Ireland* (Harmondsworth, Penguin, 1973).

Roy Garland, *Gusty Spence* (Belfast, Blackstaff Press, 2001).

David McKittrick, Seamus Kelters, Brian Feeney, Chris Thornton and David McVea, *Lost Lives: The stories of the men, women and children who died as a result of the Northern Ireland troubles* (Edinburgh, Mainstream Publishing, 1999).

Peter Taylor, *Loyalists* (London, Bloomsbury, 1999).